The Myths of Fiction

The Myths of Fiction

Studies in the
Canonical Greek Novels

Edmund P. Cueva

THE UNIVERSITY OF MICHIGAN PRESS
Ann Arbor

Copyright © by the University of Michigan 2004
All rights reserved
Published in the United States of America by
The University of Michigan Press
Manufactured in the United States of America
⊗ Printed on acid-free paper

2007   2006   2005   2004   4   3   2   1

A CIP catalog record for this book is available from the British Library.

Library of Congress Cataloging-in-Publication Data

Cueva, Edmund P., 1964–
      The myths of fiction : studies in the canonical Greek novels / Edmund P. Cueva.
        p. cm.
      Includes bibliographical references (p.) and index.
      ISBN 0-472-11427-1 (cloth : alk. paper)
        1. Greek fiction—History and criticism.   2. Mythology, Greek, in literature.   3. Canon
(Literature)   I. Title

   PA3267.C84   2004
   883'.0109—dc22   2004053664

For Shannon

Acknowledgments

I wish to thank Jean Alvares, Chris Collins, Colin Day, Margaret Edsall, Collin Ganio, Mary Hashman, Paula James, Brian Lavelle, Edwin Menes, John Makowksi, Anthony G. McCosham, John Murphy, Robert Murray, Perry Pearson, John Rettig, Gerald Sandy, Gareth and Karen Schmeling, David Scourfield, and Erin Snoddy for all of their confidence and invaluable advice on the writing of this manuscript. My greatest debt is to my wife, Shannon, for encouraging, advising, and inspiring me through a long and arduous endeavor. Finally, I would like to thank the following editors for allowing me to reprint (as originally published or with changes or deletions) some essays in this study of the novel: Robert E. Bennett, the editor of *Humanitas*, for "Longus as νυμφαγέτης: The myth of Chloe," *Humanitas* 21.2 (fall 1997): 3–16; Barbara K. Gold, the editor of the *American Journal of Philology*, and Heather Lengyel, the rights and contracts manager for the *American Journal of Philology*, for "Plutarch's Ariadne in Chariton's *Chaereas and Callirhoe*," *American Journal of Philology* 117 (1996): 473–84; Peter Green, the editor of *Syllecta Classica*, for "The Analogue of the Hero of Heliodorus' *Aethiopica*" *Syllecta Classica* 9 (1998): 103–13; Kent J. Rigsby, the editor of *Greek, Roman, and Byzantine Studies*, for "*Anth. Pal.* 14.34 and Achilles Tatius 2.14," *Greek, Roman, and Byzantine Studies* 35.3: (1994): 281–88, and "Longus and Thucydides: A New Interpretation," *Greek, Roman and Byzantine Studies* 39 (1998): 429–40.

Contents

Introduction

Time has not been kind to the ancient Greek novel. Indeed only five examples of this genre have survived in their entirety: *Chaereas and Callirhoe* by Chariton, *Ephesiaca* by Xenophon,[1] *Leucippe and Clitophon* by Achilles Tatius, *Daphnis and Chloe* by Longus, and *Aethiopica* by Heliodorus.[2] This present book is an exploration into one aspect of this selection on the fringe of the literary canon, namely, the interrelation of the function of myth and fictional literature, and the development of this relationship (cf. Bowie and Harrison 1993). This study will demonstrate that the utilization of myth increased as the sophistication of the novel evolved.[3]

This book does not touch upon all the facets of myth, but only on the novelists' literary use of it. Consequently, literary antecedents of a particular story are taken into account only when the novelist reflects these in his own text.[4] The novelists use or borrow myths found in other literary works. No new myths are created or mentioned, with the possible exception of the reference to the Heleioi in *Daphnis and Chloe* (3.23). This methodology of the novelists is similar both to that of the ancients who borrowed whole myths, lines, or passages from Homer as a source for their own stories and to that of modern authors who see the Old Testament as a fertile source for stories and quotations. These later authors do not necessarily incorporate any religious feeling in their works even though the religious quality of their source is apparent.

The question of the importance of myth for the novel appears to some scholars to be implicated in the origins of the genre. They argue that the roots of the ancient novel are found in religious texts associated with the worship of such deities as Isis and that the texts, which were used for purposes of instructing and edifying initiates and worshipers, contained myths that pertained to cult and ritual (cf. Merkelbach 1960, 1962, 1988; Kerényi 1927). From them, they contend, sprang the secular genre of novel, which retained the components of its religious progenitor (as Attic tragedy retains significant elements of Dionysus-worship). Many scholars have aligned themselves on one side or the other of this controversy; some have simply avoided the issue.

The premise of this book finds its impetus in work by Grundy Steiner (1969), who is among the first to set aside the debate on novels as *Mysterientexte* in favor of determining the function of myth in the novels. He suggests that specific mythological stories were used by the novelists as exemplars for all types of plot situations in which the characters found themselves, as moral patterns to be imitated, as evidence for what may happen to anyone under similar circumstances, and as illustration and graphic analogue. Myths were used selectively as analogues in certain places to support, explain, or enhance meaning. He stops short, however, of a thorough analysis of myth's function in the Greek novel and leaves many questions unasked or unanswered.

Although there has in fact been no comprehensive study on myth and the ancient Greek novel, no shortage of opinions exists. Myth has been seen as catalyst for the plot or as filler, and therefore of no essential purpose (Deligiorgis 1974). The novelists perhaps employed these stories to illustrate a moral or religious principle, but this suggestion resurrects the issue of novels as *Mysterientexte* and fails to consider the possible literary function of myth (Hägg 1983). Another popular view is that myth is essential for the completion of ring-composition and thus is structurally vital (MacQueen 1985). The research has not resulted in consensus, and a fresh look and evaluation is certainly justified.

This book focuses on the transition in the ancient Greek novel from the historical to the romantic and mythological, and on the increasing role of myth in enabling the change, but especially upon the nature of the various literary functions of myth introduced into the novel as that genre developed. Myth served as a central part of the later novel, which relied on earlier literary myths for structure, and as a source of stories familiar to both author and audience. These results should provide a clearer understanding of the use of myth in the ancient novel. This book, however, in no way attempts to supply a new theory on the origins of the ancient Greek novel; rather it illustrates how one element of the novel, the mythological, became the main ingredient of the fully developed genre.

THE ANCIENT GREEK NOVEL

The Novel as a Genre

The ancient Greek novel could not have come about without relying on or sharing elements with other, preexisting genres.[5] Although nineteenth- and twentieth-century theories acknowledge this, they do not take into account the resultant combination of the preexisting genres with myth. In any case a list of preexisting literary materials does not explain how the novel came about (Pervo 1987, 102). For certainly the novel transformed these genres and myth into something unprecedented.

J. R. Morgan describes the novel as "extended non-factual narration in prose" (1993, 175) and relates that there is little ancient literary theory about the novel as a genre perhaps because this genre was problematic due to the "narrative mode it shared with history, and the use of prose for fiction" (1993, 178), and because "it was within historiography itself that the contract of fictional complicity was first extended to narrative prose, thus allowing fiction, recognized and generally, if reluctantly, licensed elsewhere, to enter a new form and generate a new and more equivocal literature of pleasure in prose: fiction in the form of history" (1993, 187). In a later work Morgan adds to this definition by including that the ancient novel was a "free invention by a specific author; it must be acknowledged as fiction by both writer and reader; it must be of a certain length and complexity; and it must be literary" (1995, 130).[6] The connection between the novel, history, and fiction, moreover, according to David Konstan, "is not accidental: rather, there is a sense in which novels are fictional, whereas history, lyric poetry and tragedy are not" (1998, 3), and history differs from fiction "in that it is *about* what really happens or has happened, even if at times, or perhaps in the main, it gets things wrong" (1998, 5).

I would suggest that the novel is a lengthy prose piece, possessing a rather complex plot involving human beings, their feelings, thoughts, and emotions. This complexity is produced by intertwining aristocratic with bourgeois characters, ethical moral codes with reprehensible behavior, the past with the present and future, well-known stories (myths) with obscure tales, love with hate, rarities with everyday incidents. Pirates, kidnapping, deaths, burials, treasures, human sacrifice, recognition scenes, lively description, battles, and sex all conjoin, most importantly, to effect a suspension of disbelief.[7] There is no historical, literary, or archaeological evidence that can help to identify accurately the audience for whom this suspension of disbelief would have been pleasing. Analyses of papyrological data cannot tell us who read the ancient novels but do reveal, by a comparison of the number of novel fragments with those of other genres, that ancient readers possessed fewer novels than other literary forms (Stephens 1994, 405–18).[8]

Historiography, Contemporary History, the Epic, and the Novel

Of the many genres capable of influencing the development of the novel, the most significant, in an unusual way, was history.[9] The authors (e.g., Longus) chose to place their novels either in a time in which Rome had not yet become the ruler of the Greek world or in an idyllic, unreal setting.[10] The Greek view of Rome at the time of the development of the novel was itself very problematic and at the same time very simplistic. Some historical background is needed here; Albrecht Dihle (1994, 52–53) sums up nicely the situation in the Greek world under Roman rule.

> When Roman politics began to affect Greece directly at the beginning of the second century B.C., this led to the dissolution of the system of Hellenistic states and their piecemeal absorption into the Roman Empire, a process which was completed by the incorporation of Egypt after the Battle of Actium in 31 B.C.. The transition was accompanied by bloody wars and a steady decline in an economic as well as in a cultural sense. The Greek world, which had still produced numerous achievements of the highest order in many fields of intellectual life during the third and even the second century B.C., now had almost nothing to show, with the exception of philosophy. The people in the countries surrounding the eastern Mediterranean had become deeply depressed, mainly because of economic exploitation by the victorious Romans. Quite understandably, relief and

enthusiastic approval were the Eastern reactions to Augustus' final victory, and to the establishment of a global monarchy with a well-ordered administration.

The dawning of the Augustan age was perceived throughout the East as the beginning of an entirely different, better era. But because of this, the period also saw an astonishing degree of reanimation and intensification of the Classicist tendencies in Hellenistic civilisation. The good new times were to be like the good old times, and those good old times were those of the glorious ancestors who had defended Greece against the overwhelming might of the Persian Empire; who had created a political community of free citizens in Athens; and who had been the contemporaries of the great names in the literary tradition, of Sophocles, Plato, or Demosthenes. The uncontested greatness of literary achievements in Athens in the fifth and fourth centuries B.C. was, more often than before, seen in connection with Athens' political distinction, and its moral force. Thus a moral dimension was added to the literary-linguistic imitation which was firmly established as a method of higher education.

The movement which brought a more categorical affirmation of the ancient authors' authority than ever before bore the name of Atticism.

A. H. M. Jones writes that although Rome's "political wisdom" and "military power" might have impressed the Greeks, they never ceased to regard the Romans as "barbarians." In fact, the Greeks "were supremely satisfied with their own language and literature, and, except for a few antiquarians like Plutarch, who were curious about Roman history and institutions, felt no call to learn the barbarous Latin tongue or read its uncouth and imitative literature" (1963, 3).[11] The authors of the novel were writing in a time in which the Greek cities were politically dead, but at the same time these cities "retained, and indeed enhanced, their importance as centers of Hellenic culture" (Jones 1963, 8). This political extinction of the Greek city was most forcefully felt at the same time that there occurred a "consolidation of Greek culture" (Jones 1963, 19) that some scholars refer to as the Second Sophistic.[12] This is not to say that some Greeks did not attain political prominence in a world ruled by Romans: "Who would have dared to predict that, only four generations from the defeat of Antonius and the resonant victory of Italy and the West, the Greeks could have command of Roman legions, govern provinces, and accede to the highest honours in the state?" (Syme 1963, 14). Nevertheless, the Greeks were not all happy with Roman rule—especially the lower classes.[13] It must be stressed that Roman rule did not lead to a capitulation of culture or identity.[14]

This unhappiness and continuation of the indigenous culture had many consequences, one of which was a literary reaction (Bowersock 1965, 108).[15] The writers of the Second Sophistic employed as chief characteristics of the literature of the second and third centuries a "predilection for antiquity and archaism" (Bowersock 1969, 16) and an "atticistic fanaticism" that expressed itself not only in "language and style" but also in content: "The motifs, the ways of thinking, the things for which they expect the reader's attention are not drawn from contemporary life, from the surrounding world with its pleasures and sorrows, but from a past which is to be found in books, in schools, and nowhere else" (Van Groningen 1965, 49).[16] This new approach in Greek literature had the past as its "principal bond of common experience" (Millar 1969, 13), which even up until Byzantine times was recognized as "fundamental" and "profound" (Millar, 1969, 29).

These authors on the whole were dissatisfied with the "political situation of the present" (Bowie 1974, 167) and favored themes that "harked back constantly to the classical period" (Bowie 1974, 170) that did not postdate "326 B.C." (Bowie 1974, 172).[17] This archaizing trend also appeared in epistolography, the novel, and historiography; in mythography, interestingly enough, Roman versions of Greek myths (for example, Apollodorus) were absent (Bowie 1974, 189–90). There was, in other words, an overall escape to the past; in order to "reassure themselves that Greece had a claim comparable to that of Rome, they began to dwell more and more, in their principal cultural activities, on the political greatness of the past" (Bowie 1974, 208–9). Sophists preferred "historical topics" in their forensic displays—definitely from the "golden age of classical Greece" or "Alexander's conquests" (Lightfoot 2000, 249).[18]

This looking-back to the past was meant to alleviate the demoralization caused by living in a society in which the polis had lost its autonomy and no real, meaningful public debate was allowed. This society, alienated from the present and dislocated from the past, resorted to strategies that "revolved around refashioning the relationship between Greek past and Roman present. The same past that provided Greeks with the resources to jockey for position and favour in the Roman world, is now revealed as a source of disquiet, promoting dissatisfaction with the present order of things and thereby inhibiting the assimilation of Greeks into it" (Woolf 1994, 125).[19] As Greg Woolf (1994, 131) points out, this retention of Greek culture did not occur without Roman consent:

> Greeks remained Greeks, at least in part, because Romans allowed them to. By valuing the Greek past and permitting the Greek language to operate as an official one throughout the early Empire, Romans made no assault on the central defining characteristics of Hellenism. The diversity on flexibility of Hellenism, on the other hand, allowed Greeks to accept (and often welcome) changes both in material culture and also in the political life of their cities without feeling any overwhelming threat to their identity. Such tensions as were created by the end of autonomy and by the invidious contrasts that might be drawn with the past, served only to reinforce a sense of collective cultural alienation and hence integrity.[20]

It should be pointed out that there were some Greek authors who were pro-Roman, but they had to explain why they were favorable to the Romans.[21]

The authors of the novel were not just appealing to a sense of nostalgia—they could work only with preexisting materials. By using a historical background the authors of the earlier novels showed that the narrative plot was at least plausible and realistic,[22] and thereby helped the reader suspend disbelief (Morgan 1982, 222).[23] This historical background is most evident in the earlier pre-sophistic novels and disappears as the genre develops.[24] Chariton in particular,[25] and to a lesser extent Xenophon, unquestionably fashions the plot "around situations or characters described by Greek historians of the Classic or Hellenistic era" (Dihle 1994, 132),[26] but in the later sophistic novels the authors include and devise "more fantastic events and adventures for their couples" and place the action in "more exotic settings" (Dihle 1994, 236).[27]

The novel clearly reflects the times in which it was written[28] by avoiding any contemporary reference.[29] The novels in fact center on what the authors believed was a superior Greek world—a world free of Rome and its influence and control (Bowersock 1994, 41 and 50). The novelists go so far as to create a "paratextual device" that elevates the genre by supplying a "(historiographic) authenticity to the fiction" that downplays contemporary historical times (Fusillo 1997, 212). Most recently Tim Whitmarsh (2001, 87) has consequently written that "the Greek novels are crucial test-sites for theories of acculturation, education, and identity; but the interwoven discourse of nature and culture are also deployed self-consciously in order to site these texts in a posterior relationship with the Classical World."

No writer, however, writes in a vacuum. Whereas in the Roman novels, Petronius's *Satyricon* and Apuleius's *Golden Ass*, there are myriad and constant references to the contemporary world of their authors (Millar 1981, 65–66, 74), this is not the case in the Greek novel. The geographical details are, for the most part, right and factual, though not necessarily accurate (Morgan 1993, 198ff.). The point of the inclusion of these geographic minutiae "is to enable the reader plausibly to locate the fiction within the real world or generally held perceptions of it" (Morgan 1993, 199). In other words, the "historical material is applied rather than organic to the plot" (Morgan 1993, 200). In the case of Chariton, for example, Douglas R. Edwards (1994) has established that although there was a massive Roman presence in Aphrodisias, what comes through in the novel is only the goddess Aphrodite. Chariton casts aside all allusions to Rome, Edwards (1994, 712) argues, not so much to minimize the Roman impact but to maintain the glorification of the chief deity of Chariton's homeland:

> Aphrodisias used the myths, symbols, and general popularity to define itself amidst the Roman world of the first centuries of the common era. Aphrodite's appearance throughout the *oikumene* in multiple forms (statues, coins) and the local iconographic displays in Aphrodisias illustrates local elites' presentation of the power, significance, and prestige of the city, its populace, and its goddess.
>
> Chariton reflects the concerns of those local elites in Asia Minor and the Greek East who sought to make sense of their relationship to Roman power through legitimate means. He identifies his civic affiliation with a Greek city in Asia Minor that was formerly independent but now owes its prosperity to an outside benevolent power. (712)

J. R. Morgan (1993, 229) accurately observes that the "problem with the Greek novels is that they depict not the world as it is, but the world as it ought to be." I believe that the world the novelists want is a world free of Romans.[30] The novelists want not only to go back to a time when the

Greeks lived as they wanted, but perhaps also to break away from the political and "cultural conformity introduced by Augustus" (Bowersock 1994, 31). It cannot be said often enough that the "novel . . . is a product for a fragmented and depoliticized readership" (Morgan 1995, 144) and that it is extremely important to remember that the "novels are mostly set in the glorious Hellenistic past, enabling the reader to recapture a sense of meaningful Greekness in a world of foreign rulers" (Morgan 1995, 145). It must be understood at the same time, however, that the novel does not have as its primary aim a return to the past; rather the novel should be viewed as one of many outlets "for the cultural ideals and formulas" of the Greek cities and "as another expression of their cultural hegemony" (Swain 1996, 109) that sets it plots in the Greek world of the past—a world without Rome.[31]

Asia Minor, in particular Caria, was a fertile ground for literary production. Ionia claimed Homer, the earliest author to be associated with epic.[32] The island of Chios, home of the Homeridae, and the city of Smyrna both have been cited as the possible birthplace of Homer, and it is in this general area that we first find epic. With its long narrative and its hero engaged in a quest, epic might employ myth, legend, history, and folktale. It recalls a past time, and by doing so it also recalls the culture of that period. Supernatural elements, such as gods, magic, oracles, and prophets, may also comprise a considerable portion of an epic. The novel shares some characteristics with epic, such as a long narrative involving a quest: in Homer the quest is for honor or home, while in the novels it usually is erotic in nature. The novels, at least the earlier novels, employ more history than myth, but as the genre develops, the historical in the novel gives way to the mythological. The supernatural also plays a very important part in the novel; it directs the plot by means of the gods, and myth shows up in dreams, omens, oracles, and prophecies. Certainly a major difference is epic's use of dactylic hexameter verse, while the novel employs prose.

Chariton, in fact, relies heavily upon epic. In *Chaereas and Callirhoe* he not only borrows lines from the *Iliad* and the *Odyssey*, but also uses the moment of the story in which these lines are found to lend plot structure to his own story. In the first book of the novel we find suitors planning to get back at Chaereas for marrying Callirhoe, whom they thought should have married one of them. The disaffected suitors and their plotting are reminiscent of the Helen-myth, as well as the first two books of the

Odyssey. This competition for Callirhoe also suggests the "Wooing of Agariste" in Herodotus (6.129–30), another writer from Asia Minor. Perhaps Chariton, too, incorporated this local motif because he predicted its favorable reception by an indigenous audience.

The genres of novel and history are similar in certain aspects: lengthy narratives in prose, third-person narration in the past tense, rhetoric, and exciting and moving plots (Morgan 1982, 223f.). In fact, it has been suggested that novels were "histories written to promote cultural survival" and to glorify "national heroes" (Hadas 1972, 127–28). Quasi-historical elements in the novels, however, are decorative and do not dictate the plot.[33]

The novelists employed what might be described as degenerate Hellenistic historiography in order to give their erotic writings a semblance of respectability. Although travel stories were written before the Hellenistic period, one of the most prolific genres of that period and of Classical was the *periegesis*. The travel dimension of *Chaereas and Callirhoe* may have its roots in travel stories such as those of Ctesias synthesized with such historical legends as those found in the *Iliad* and the *Odyssey* (Reardon 1991, 141ff.). As I show in the forthcoming chapters, notwithstanding the sources for the historical elements of the novel, it is undeniable that the earlier novels, *Chaereas and Callirhoe* and *Ephesiaca*, were more historical in nature than the later novels (cf. Reardon 1971, 315).

Chariton used more historiographical than mythological elements in his novel (see chap. 1). The historical parameters of his work, however, did not constrain his inventiveness, but rather supplied him with a framework within which he could develop his plot. In other words, Chariton uses history but is not bound to follow it: he conflates all his historical information. A suggested possible explanation for why Chariton employed a historical framework is that Chariton was a literary conservative who could draw from Xenophon, Ctesias, and even Cicero for authority to give prose fiction the appearance of history (Schmeling 1974, 55f.). Hence prose fiction resembling history would be more palatable to ancient readers than fiction written in prose rather than in verse. Precedents for Chariton's use of a historical background can be found in the *Ninus Romance* (ca. 100 B.C.) and in the *Parthenope Romance* (ca. second century A.D.).[34] There were, however, restrictions placed on the writing of prose fiction in the disguise of history. Verse was the "correct literary vehicle for expressing τὸ μυθῶδες, τὸ τερατῶδες, τὸ ψευδές," and literary critics did not particularly like "genres that lacked *utilitas*" (Scobie 1969, 16).

Traditional Literary Narratives or Myth

The difference between myth and history in the novel is often difficult to discern. Peter Munz (1956) notes that in general (he does not deal with the novel) "myth may arise through the telescoping of a historical narrative" (6) and when "history is telescoped into myth, the myth-maker always has the object of bringing out certain features deeply characteristic of human behaviour" (7). In this instance the characteristics are formed by the Greek view of Rome and the desire to go back to Greece's glorious past. A. E. Wardman (1960) notes that in Greek historiography, an important influence on the novel, "myth as a *method* had been ousted by personal enquiry, the practice of those historians whose subject was the history of their own times; such writers had to choose between tradition and enquiry, and rightly preferred the latter" (411). Jon van Seters (1986, 49) astutely quantifies the problems in differentiating between the two:

> Anyone who undertakes to speak or write about the relationship of myth and history in antiquity is asking for trouble, because he or she is immediately faced with the task of defining these difficult terms . . . myth is a traditional story about events in which the god or gods are the primary actors, and the action takes place outside historical time. In addition myth contains some structure of meaning that is concerned with "serious" subjects or reflections on deep problems of life or on collective and societal preoccupations. Under the category of history . . . I include the broad range of historical texts in which peoples and nations or their leaders maintain records of past events and the names of public figures that are of communal interest, within a chronological framework.

In the case of the ancients this differentiation was not so problematic: "The notion of the historical content of a myth presupposes a distinction between myth and history which is fundamental for us but anachronistic for the Greeks" (Brillante 1990, 91; see also 93 and 102).

Greg Woolf suggests that in the case of the Greek novels myth offered "both a way of relating gods and men and a cultural vocabulary shared by all Greeks" (1994, 129). In Classical times attempts were made to find the basic substances of the universe; in the Hellenistic period the foci of inquiry changed to humans, the pursuit of personal satisfaction, and purpose in life. During this time astrology and mystery religions filtered into the Hellenistic world from the East. More importantly for the study of the ancient novel, mystery cults and religions played greater roles in the lives of Hellenistic people (Hägg 1983, 86–87).

On the basis of the importance that mystery cults and religions had in the Hellenistic and post-Hellenistic world, it has been suggested, as mentioned above, that the novels have their origins in mystery religions and that the novels, except Chariton, could be read by anyone, but could be properly understood only by the initiates of the mystery religions.[35] The plots of the novel were to have reflected the adventures that Isis and Osiris, her brother-husband, had undergone: separation, death, wandering, and reunion or rebirth. This is an interesting theory, but this leads to every incident in the novels as having some sort of religious or mysterious significance.[36] What clear-cut religious interpretation can one give to the description of the suitor in *Chaereas and Callirhoe*, to the homoerotic story of Hippothous in the *Ephesiaca*, or to cicada hidden in Chloe's bosom in *Daphnis and Chloe?* This is not to say that the novels did not reflect the religious atmosphere of the Hellenistic and Roman world: due respect is given to Aphrodite in *Chaereas and Callirhoe*; Apollo, Isis, Apis, Helius, and Eros are properly revered in the *Ephesiaca* and the other ancient novels.

There can be no mistaking the fact that any literary work must, in one minimal way or another, reflect the times in which it was written. Elements such as religious sense, feeling, spirituality, and cult were components of the times in which the novels were written, and therefore some form of religion must find its way into the novel. The problem, although maybe not conscious, for the author is how to integrate religion, specifically divinities, into the work (Anderson 1984, 75–76). As I demonstrate in the coming chapters, the easiest way to integrate religion, whether or not the author was religious, into the novels was through the use of myth. The inclusion of myths, however, should not be taken to mean that the authors were intentionally trying to create religious documents.

At this point a definition of myth seems necessary. I do not mean by *myth* that "for the common man speaking in modern English the essence of *myth* is that it is false in direct contrast to *history* which is presumed to be true" (Leach 1982, 2). Nor do I mean that "the prevalent use of the word 'myth' among historians: an interpretation that is considered blatantly false" (Heehs 1994, 2). What I mean is, if I can borrow a line from M. I. Finley, "what is commonly meant, in ordinary usage, by 'myth' or 'legend,' and not the more metaphorical senses" (Finley 1965, 282). Myth is a literary form that an individual author uses to tell a traditional story that has a history (Conradie 1997, 56ff.),[37] but that is "a non-historical narrative" (Lightfoot 1999, 232).

Myths in this text are "literary texts which have been divorced from their original context of time and space" (Leach 1982, 4).[38] I concur and borrow from Glenn Most (1999, 44), who accurately delineates myth as "a transmitted body of stories, often poetic and individual, always at least in part freely invented and usually localizable in a particular historical context, or on the other hand as 'the *mythic*', a vanished numinous quality attributed to a lost people's religious sense, entirely unfree (since it was seen as the immediate expression of a whole people's identity, not just an individual's) and necessarily prehistoric (for otherwise it would inevitably seem locally conditioned and arbitrary)." The supernatural element in the novel does render the narrative a myth.[39]

Myth shares a similar development to the Greek view of the Roman world that the authors of the novels had. Jan Bremmer (1986, 5) contends that the "popularity of myth lasted well into the Roman Empire, but the *mythoi*, which once helped men to understand or order the world, now functioned primarily as a major part of a cultural tradition whose importance increased as Greek independence diminished." Gregor Nagy (1990) appears to concur with Bremmer's view in that myths not only are composed of special speech as opposed to everyday speech, but that they also "stand for an undifferentiated outer core consisting of local myths, where various versions from various locales may potentially contradict each other, while alētheia 'truth' stands for a differentiated inner core of exclusive Panhellenic myths that tend to avoid the conflicts of local versions" (1990, 66). When the *poleis* collapse as autonomous institutions, all that is left is the Panhellenic stratum (1990, 67). Kendall L. Walton sees a close relationship between myth and the novel: most novels that have narrators are fictions (1983, 83), and a work of fiction can be identified as "a prop in a game of make-believe of a certain sort, a game played by appreciators. Fiction-making is merely the activity of constructing such props." He continues by noting that we get a "sense of the action of fiction-making from the work produced, a sense of what decisions were made about how the fictional world was to be, about what fictional truths were to be generated, and how they were to be generated, and a sense of why the maker decided as he did" (1983, 87).[40]

In this book myth is defined and will be studied only as a traditional story, dealing with the supernatural or the marvelous, which has made its way into written form or whose literary origin can be identified. The literary component of myth allows me to approach my analysis of myth and the novel in an intertextual manner: this book focuses on how the ancient novelists incorporate myths into their writings through literary allusion.[41] Authors from Homer to the time of the Greek novels utilized myth in many different ways, perhaps as each found it best for his own purposes. In this study I do not enter into the controversies surrounding sociological or religious interpretations of myth; rather I treat myth as a literary construct: the change in context and literary effect caused by the inclusion of myth.[42]

Chariton, History, and Myth

Chariton's novel is the earliest novel and has been dated from as early as the first century B.C.[1] to as late as the second century A.D. The first century B.C. date has been justified by some scholars on account of the novel's lack of Atticism (Papanikolaou, 1973a). The latter dates are suggested on the basis of the novelist's inclusion of historiographical elements, language, and style (Perry 1967, 343–45). Papyrological evidence seems to support this date (Reardon 1971, 334 n. 55). *Chaereas and Callirhoe* had originally been dated to the fourth or fifth century A.D., but papyri demonstrates that the *terminus ante quem* of this novel must be the second century A.D.[2] The search for the exact time of composition has been further narrowed down to the first decades of the second century A.D. (Ruiz-Montero 1980, 63–69; 1989, 107–50) based on inscriptions found in Aphrodisias (*C.I.G.* 2782, 2783, 2846) and on references in the *Palatine Anthology* (11.180, 181, and 150) to a certain Athenagoras, very possibly the employer of Chariton, found in the poetry of Ammianus (A.D. 88–145).

It must be emphasized, however, that there is very little archaeological or historical evidence with which to date firmly any of the ancient novels. None of the authors, except perhaps Chariton, can be historically or archaeologically verified; there are in fact only two very thin historical threads that can be tied to Chariton. Firstly, Philostratus addressed a letter (66) to Chariton in which he wrote: Χαρίτωνι· Μεμνήσεσθαι τῶν σῶν λόγων οἴει τοὺς Ἕλληνας ἐπειδὰν τελευτήσῃς· οἱ δὲ μηδὲν ὄντες ὁπότε εἰσίν, τίνες ἂν εἶεν ὁπότε οὐκ εἰσίν;.[3] Secondly, inscriptions C.I.G. 2782, 2783, and 2846 may identify Chariton's employer, Athenagoras, as an official in Aphrodisias, Chariton's homeland, and Chariton as a physician. Neither of these two pieces of data supplies any conclusive information capable of accurately dating Chariton the novelist. Philostratus tells his reader that Chariton was a writer and nothing more; the inscriptions reveal that a certain Athenagoras was an official at Aphrodisias and that the physician Chariton had erected a funeral mound. The inscriptions do not mention that Chariton was a writer.

Chaereas and Callirhoe is not only the earliest extant Greek novel, but also the only one of its genre to use extensively historiographical features (Ruiz-Montero 1981, 237). Later novelists include such features but do not rely on them for background and structure as much as Chariton does. Accordingly, the reader of Chaereas and Callirhoe finds verifiable historical detail in the correctly assigned dates, accurately related events, and realistically depicted places and figures of the novel.[4]

The story, for example, takes place in the past, famous historical figures are included, and history has a tremendous effect on the behavior of the characters. In this way Chariton imitates the classical historians in technique, not for the purpose of masquerading as a professional historian, but rather, as Hägg (1987, 197) suggests, to create the "effect of openly mixing fictitious characters and events with historical ones."[5] This effect is partially created by the use of a historical source that deals with myth.[6]

The introduction of the two youths in the beginning of the novel exemplifies the primary function of myth in Chariton: throughout the text the novelist assigns his leading characters analogues in the form of mythical or legendary beings.[7] For example, Chaereas at different times becomes Achilles, Nireus, Hippolytus, and Alcibiades. Chariton assimilates Callirhoe to Aphrodite and Ariadne, and to a much lesser extent to Artemis, Helen, Medea, and the nymphs. Most often Chariton compares Callirhoe's loveliness to that of Aphrodite, as at the beginning of the novel: ἦν γὰρ . . . αὐτῆς Ἀφροδίτης Παρθένου (1.1.2).

Most importantly, Chariton likens Callirhoe to a sleeping Ariadne: πάντες εἴκαζον αὐτὴν Ἀριάδνῃ καθευδούσῃ (1.6.2). Homer (Od. 11.321–25) writes that Theseus took Ariadne from Crete to Athens but that he abandoned her on the Isle of Dia (Naxos), where she was killed by Artemis at the bidding of Dionysus. Hesiod (*Theog.* 947–49) relates that Dionysus took Ariadne as his wife and that Kronos made her immortal. Chariton's version in 1.6.2, therefore, loosely follows the narratives of Homer and Hesiod. The novelist introduces this myth after the heroine has been kicked into a coma by her husband, a fitting moment for the myth of Ariadne: she, like Callirhoe, suffered an injustice at the hands of someone she loved.[8]

In the third book of the novel Chaereas attributes the disappearance of his wife to some divinity, and likens her disappearance to Dionysus's theft of Ariadne from Theseus (3.3.5). Unlike the version of the Ariadne myth found in 1.6.2, this version is slightly different. It becomes obvious that there is a specific source Chariton is using to draw these different versions. I shall show that Chariton must have used Plutarch, or perhaps, though unlikely, Paeon, one of the imperial historian's sources. A narratological and verbal comparison of Plutarch's account of the adventures of Theseus and Ariadne, as found in Plutarch's *Theseus*, and the Ariadne-like adventures of Callirhoe makes it clear that the novelist drew upon Plutarch. This use of Plutarch, moreover, elucidates Chariton's attempt at historical veracity in dates, events, places, and figures.[9]

Plutarch in *Theseus* associates Aphrodite with Ariadne (just as Chariton does) and supplies various accounts of the adventures of Ariadne and Theseus. These accounts are found in the works of other authors whom Plutarch names (cf. Frost 1984), and it is mainly on these stories that Chariton models his version of the Ariadne myth found in 3.3.5 and in the rest of the novel.

The historian writes that Ariadne fell in love with Theseus when he arrived on the island of Crete. She gave him the clue that enabled Theseus, after killing the Minotaur, to exit the Labyrinth. The historian uses the accounts of Pherecydes (fl. ca. 550 B.C.), Demon (fl. ca. 300 B.C.), Philochorus (b. 340 B.C.), and Cleidemus (fl. ca. 350 B.C.), all of whom give differing versions of the escape of Theseus, of the death of the Minotaur, and of the love of Ariadne for Theseus. Cleidemus's account is of particular interest, because he describes the escape of Daedalus from Crete and points attention to the ship sent by Minos to pursue Daedalus, noting that only five men manned the ship because: ὅτι δόγμα κοινὸν ἦν Ἑλλήνων μηδεμίαν ἐκπλεῖν τριήρη μηδαμόθεν ἀνδρῶν πέντε πλείονας δεχομένην. (19.8).[10]

Plutarch then proceeds to relate more variants of the love story of

Ariadne and Theseus: Πολλοὶ δὲ λόγοι καὶ περὶ τούτων ἔτι λέγονται καὶ περὶ τῆς Ἀριάδνης, οὐδὲν ὁμολογούμενον ἔχοντες (20.1).[11] He supplies six versions:

1. Theseus deserted Ariadne on Naxos, and she then hanged herself.
2. Ariadne was taken prisoner by sailors to Naxos.
3. Theseus abandoned Ariadne because he was in love with someone else.
4. Ariadne bore to Theseus two sons, Oenopion and Staphylus.
5. The fifth story constitutes a peculiar, lengthy digression related by one Paeon of Amathus on the plight of Ariadne and Theseus.
6. The last version is supplied by Naxian writers, who record that there were two Minoses and two Ariadnes. One Ariadne bore Staphylus and Oenopion to Dionysus; the other was abducted and then deserted by Theseus.

Unlike the other sources cited by Plutarch, Paeon (variation #5) is undatable. In fact, we know about this author primarily from his appearance in *Theseus*, and all that Plutarch tells us is that Paeon was a Cypriot from Amathus. Jacoby (*FGrHist* 757) supplies the third century B.C. as a possible date for Paeon. Seel (*RE* 2403) is a bit more wary about a possible date: "P. aus Amathus ist ein Lokalmythograph der Zeit zwischen Alexander dem Großen und Plutarch (wobei man weder nach oben nach unten zu nahe an diese Grenzepunkte herangehen darf)." The only other reference to Paeon, which does not aid in the dating, is made by the lexicographer Hesychius in the fourth or fifth century A.D.: Ἀφρόδιτος· Θεόφραστος μὲν τὸν Ἑρμαφρόδιτόν φησιν, ὁ δὲ τὰ περὶ Ἀμαθοῦντα γεγραφὼς Παίων εἰς ἄνδρα τὴν θεὸν ἐσχηματίσθαι ἐν Κύπρωι λέγει. All one can glean from Hesychius is that Paeon wrote about Amathus, presumably the same Ariadne-Aphrodite story found in *Theseus*.

Paeon's story, however, is most significant to our understanding of Chariton's use of history and myth.

Now the more pleasing of these legends are common knowledge, one might say, but a very singular version of the story has been given us by Paeon, a native of the Cypriot town of Amathus. He says that Theseus was driven off his course by a storm to Cyprus, that Ariadne, who was pregnant and was suffering terribly from the motion of the ship, was put on shore by herself, and that Theseus, while trying to rescue the vessel, was swept out to sea again. The women of the island took care of Ariadne and tried to comfort her distress at being left alone by bringing her forged letters, supposed to have been written by Theseus. They nursed and tended her while she was in labour, and when she died before her child was born, they buried her. Paeon adds that Theseus returned later and was overcome with grief: he left money with the people of the island, charging them to offer sacrifices to Ariadne, and also had two statuettes set up in her honour, one of silver and one of bronze. Paeon further tells us that at the sacrifice in her memory, which is held on the second day of the month Gorpaieus, one of the young men lies on the ground and imitates the cries and movements of a woman in labour, and also that the people of Amathus call the grove, where they show the tomb, the grove of Ariadne Aphrodite. (20.3–5).[12]

The important parts of Paeon's account, and therefore very relevant to my argument, are as follows: women take care of Ariadne while her husband is away; correspondences are forged; Ariadne gives birth to Theseus's child; Ariadne dies; statuettes are set up in Ariadne's honor; and lastly, Paeon associates Ariadne and Aphrodite. As I will show, all these incidents or details find parallels (narratological and verbal) in the plot of Chariton's novel.

As Plutarch's narrative continues, Theseus stops at Delos, where he dedicates a statue of Aphrodite in the temple of Apollo. The statue, which was not previously mentioned by Plutarch, had been given to him by Ariadne. Theseus then causes the death of his father by forgetting to hoist the right sails on his approach to Attica.

As previously mentioned, Chariton frequently models his hero on divinities or heroes and Callirhoe is physically Aphrodite-like in many respects. It is the myth of Ariadne, however, which Chariton uses to direct many of the major portions of the plot of the novel: Callirhoe is the daughter of the general Hermocrates, who, like Minos, had made a name for himself at seafaring and like Minos had gone to war with Athens. She marries Chaereas, who unintentionally causes her apparent death (*Scheintod*) by kicking her in the stomach. Chariton then tells us that the dead Callirhoe resembled Ariadne sleeping on the shore of Naxos (1.6.2), thereby alluding to Plutarch's first and third versions of the myth: Theseus's desertion of Ariadne on Naxos.

The death-kick of Chaereas causes many things to occur. In particular the identity of Callirhoe is altered. She who once had been alive and free is now dead and entombed; even though she recovers from her *Scheintod*, she does not recover her former freedom. She is first sold as a slave by a Cretan pirate named Theron and then forced to commit bigamy by marrying a Milesian nobleman. That Callirhoe's second husband is named Dionysius fits in perfectly with Chariton's use of Plutarch: in the sixth account of Ariadne's adventures in *Theseus* Ariadne's new husband is identified as the god Dionysus.

When Chaereas visits his dead wife's tomb he discovers that it has been broken into and that the corpse has been stolen. He immediately stretches his hands to the heavens and delivers an emotional soliloquy.[13] In this impassioned outburst Chaereas relates some very interesting things: he compares Callirhoe to Ariadne; he says that Dionysus took Ariadne (Dionysius indeed has taken Callirhoe); and he vows that he will search for Callirhoe even in the heavens, which hints at the celestial metamorphosis of Ariadne.[14]

Theron's kidnapping of Callirhoe recalls version #2 in Plutarch, in which sailors take Ariadne to Naxos. At his trial Theron identifies himself as a Cretan and attempts to exculpate himself. He is eventually sentenced to crucifixion but not before relating the details of the kidnapping and sale of Callirhoe at Miletus. At Chariton's insistence, Hermocrates declares that only five men—two from the assembly, two from the council, and Chaereas—should be sent to look for Callirhoe: ἀρκοῦσι δὲ πρεσβευταὶ δύο μὲν ἀπὸ τοῦ δήμου, δύο δὲ ἀπὸ τῆς βουλῆς· πλεύσται δὲ Χαιρέας πέμπτος αὐτός (3.4.17).[15] This is in keeping with Cleidemus's account in *Theseus* (ὅτι δόγμα κοινὸν ἦν Ἑλλήνων μηδεμίαν ἐκπλεῖν τριήρη μηδαμόθεν ἀνδρῶν πέντε πλείονας δεχομένην).

Chaereas and his crew arrive in Miletus, where he and his best friend, Polycharmus, come upon a statue of Callirhoe in a temple of Aphrodite (3.6). This clearly recalls Plutarch's version #5, which is Paeon's narrative. Nowhere has it been mentioned that anyone has dedicated a statue in the semblance of Callirhoe to Aphrodite. This small detail, I suggest, has to have been taken from Plutarch's rendition of Paeon's version of the myth. In fact Chariton is recalling the Ariadne-Aphrodite grove of Paeon's version. A little later, but not much later in the narrative, Chariton further emphasizes the Ariadne-Callirhoe association by saying that Callirhoe's name is more famous than Ariadne's (4.1).

The forged-letter component of Paeon's story (γράμματα πλαστὰ προσφέρειν ὡς τοῦ Θησέως γράφοντος αὐτῇ)[16] is also included in

Chariton's novel: a certain Mithridates, who has fallen in love with Callirhoe, suggests to Chaereas that he may be able to recover his wife by writing a letter to her (4.5). This letter, however, is intercepted by Dionysius, who thinks that it is a forgery by Mithridates in an attempt to seduce his new wife. Dionysius appeals to the satrap Pharnaces, another love victim of Callirhoe, who in turn writes to Artaxerxes, a future love victim of Callirhoe. As can be seen the letter motif is heavily accentuated in this novel.

At the end of the novel, after Callirhoe has been recovered by Chaereas, she writes to Dionysius and bids him to take care of their son. The child, however, belongs not to Dionysius but to Chaereas. Before Chaereas caused the pseudo-death of Callirhoe he had made love to her. Callirhoe, therefore, was pregnant when she was sold as a slave and then married to Dionysius. She did not want her child to be brought up as a slave and so tricked Dionysius into thinking that it was his son (a pseudo-premature birth is involved).[17] Versions #4 and #6 in Plutarch are recalled: Callirhoe, like Ariadne, is pregnant in the story and, in a sense, gives birth to two sons. The child of Dionysius is also the son of Chaereas.

After the hero and heroine have experienced the many and varied adventures required of all lovers in the ancient novels, they sail back for Syracuse. Before Chaereas heads home, however, he returns to Artaxerxes the captives he had taken at Aradus, among whom is Statira, the Persian king's wife. In the account of the ship heading back to Artaxerxes, Chariton includes the next-to-last allusion to the Ariadne-Theseus myth: as the ship approaches Chios, the king and his forces do not recognize the vessel and think that it is an enemy ship. This erroneous notion is corrected when the ship hoists a friendly standard.

The last reference to the Ariadne myth is found in the fifth chapter of the last book (8.5), where, in keeping with Paeon's account, Dionysius, after having read Callirhoe's letter, returns to Miletus and sets up numerous statues in her likeness.

The many parallels between the versions of the Ariadne myth supplied by Plutarch, Paeon's version in particular, and the adventures of the Callirhoe character indicate that Chariton is using Plutarch as a source. There are, moreover, verbal echoes to Paeon's account.

(a) Chariton 3.5.5: ἀποθάνω· θάψον δέ με καὶ ἄπιθι. Ἡ δὲ μήτηρ

Plutarch 20.5: ἀποθανοῦσαν δὲ θάψαι μὴ τεκνοῦσαν

The first part of the passage from the novel is spoken by Chaereas's father when the hero is about to board the rescue ship. He begs his son not to abandon him in his old age, but rather to wait a few days so that he can die in his son's arms. Chaereas's mother then, in Homeric language, pleads with her son not to abandon her poor parents: Τάδ' αἴδεο καί μ' ἐλέησον / Αὐτήν, εἰ ποτέ τοι λαθικηδέα μαζὸν ἐπέσχον (Il. 22.82–83 in 3.5.6). The passage from Theseus relates the death of Ariadne: During a storm Theseus had boarded his ship in an attempt to secure it and consequently was blown out to sea. Distressed, Ariadne then dies while in travail. In both passages the hero of the story has boarded or will board a ship, and those left behind on land suffer because of the departure of the hero.

> (b) Chariton 4.1.4: ἐν ᾧ ποιήσει τὸν τάφον. Ἤρεσε δὲ αὐτῇ πλησίον τοῦ νεὼ τῆς Ἀφροδίτης
> Plutarch 20.4: ἐν ᾧ τὸν τάφον δεικνύουσιν, Ἀριάδνης Ἀφροδίτης
> Chariton 5.10.1: τάφον ἔχω; Δέσποινα Ἀφροδίτη

In the beginning of the fourth book Dionysius advises Callirhoe to look for a place to construct a tomb for her dead husband Chaereas. Callirhoe chooses a place near the temple of Aphrodite because the locale will allow posterity to remember the love shared by Callirhoe and Chaereas. After having constructed a lavish tomb, Callirhoe decides to have a mock funeral; better said, she decides to imitate a funeral: τότε ἤδη καὶ τὴν ἐκκομιδὴν ἐμιμήσατο τὴν ἐπ' αὐτῷ (4.1.6). In 5.10.1 Dionysius recalls the tomb of Chaereas built near the temple of Aphrodite. The thematic link that binds the passages from the novel with that of Paeon's account is imitation or mimicry. In the novel Callirhoe carries out an imitation of a funeral, while in Theseus we read about the young men of Cyprus imitating women in travail. In both narratives serious moments of life are imitated near a temple of Aphrodite.

> (c) Chariton 8.1.2: τὰς ἀλλοτρίας γυναῖκας ἀναλαβὼν ταῖς τριήρεσιν ἀπαγάγῃ, μόνην δὲ τὴν ἰδίαν ἐκεῖ καταλίπῃ οὐχ ὡς Ἀριάδνην
> Plutarch 20.5: Τὰς οὖν ἐγχωρίους γυναῖκας τὴν Ἀριάδνην ἀναλαβεῖν καὶ περιέπειν ἀθυμοῦσαν ἐπὶ τῇ μονώσει

In the last book of the novel Chaereas seizes Aradus and takes captive the wives of the Persian nobility. Among these women is Callirhoe, whom Chaereas is about to leave behind on the island (just as Theseus had abandoned Ariadne). Aphrodite, however, intervenes and causes Chaereas to reunite with his wife. In *Theseus* the women of the island take the abandoned Ariadne into their care and attempt to comfort her by bringing her some letters from Theseus. These letters, however, are forgeries. The novel passage is antithetical in structure to Paeon's account: Ariadne is rescued in the novel, while in the biography Ariadne dies abandoned on Cyprus. This reversal is fitting, since it is the last verbal echo of Paeon's narrative. Although he borrowed from the historical work, Chariton appears not to want to give a sad ending to his work, and he alerts the reader to his intent by adapting the lines from the biography in a reversed manner.

It may be suggested that perhaps Chariton read a source shared with Plutarch, rather than Plutarch's *Theseus*. In other words, perhaps the novelist read Paeon. This problem is easily settled: after Plutarch relates the versions supplied by Pherecydes, Demon, Philochorus, and Cleidemus, he writes that there are Πολλοὶ δὲ λόγοι καὶ περὶ τούτων ἔτι λέγονται καὶ περὶ τῆς Ἀριάδνης. Chariton, as I have shown, uses these πολλοὶ λόγοι in addition to the story of Paeon. If he had read only Paeon, he would not have likely included the other five variants listed by Plutarch. In particular Chariton would not have been able to parallel Cleidemus's observation on the number of crew members sent in search of Ariadne; Paeon does not include a description of a ship's complement.

It should also be noted that numerous imperial writers use Plutarch as a source. Ziegler (1951, 947–49) points out that authors such as Favorinus, Gellius, Galen, Apuleius, Arrian, and Pausanias employ or are familiar with Plutarch. Stadter (1965, 13–29) also shows that the Macedonian Polyaenus uses Plutarch in the composition of his *Strategemata*. One should likewise understand that *Theseus* is a tour de force in scholarly research and quotations. Frost (1984, 67) notes that in *Theseus* Plutarch cites twenty-five different authors in fifty-one places.

The conclusions are as follows: Callirhoe is likened to Ariadne, who, like Callirhoe, is likened to Aphrodite. Plutarch, using Paeon of Amathus as a source, unites Ariadne and Aphrodite in a peculiar account. Some of the plot involving Callirhoe seems to follow the outlines of Paeon's treatment as found in *Theseus*. Other elements, such as letters, the destinations of both characters as Cyprus, and the statuettes, may also be from Paeon.

Ariadne is separated from her lover, Theseus, by the sea, as is Callirhoe. Callirhoe and Ariadne are both pregnant when separated from their lovers. Lastly, the account of Paeon is romantic in nature and can be easily seen as a prototypical love story.[18]

The second approach to myth taken in this chapter is an analysis based on Kristeva's theory of intertextuality (1970; 1984); Kristeva suggests that in order to study the structure of a novel, or perhaps any literary work, one must understand that there is a literary dialogue occurring between many texts, and that consequently the lines or passages borrowed from one text and placed in another demand new interpretation in light of their new literary surroundings (1970, 66–68). On this textual dialogue Chariton constructed his work. This approach, therefore, is a study of the "sources" of the literary borrowings and, if possible, a "new articulation" or understanding of the transposed lines and passages (1984, 60).

The story begins with an introduction of the author by the author: Χαρίτων Ἀφροδισιεύς, Ἀθηναγόρου τοῦ ῥήτορος ὑπογραφεύς, πάθος ἐρωτικὸν ἐν Συρρακούσαις γενόμενον διηγήσομαι (1.1.1).[19] He then proceeds to the introduction of the two main characters of the story, Callirhoe and Chaereas. Before introducing the hero and heroine of the romance, however, Chariton points out that he hails from Aphrodisias; indeed, what better place to set a love story and to narrate a πάθος ἐρωτικὸν than in a city which is devoted to the goddess of love herself?[20] Straight away Chariton has set a romantic tone for a novel in which Aphrodite and her son will take very active roles.

As previously mentioned, the hero of the novel resembles mythological, legendary, and historical heroes: Achilles, Nireus, Hippolytus, and Alcibiades. These four men serve to illustrate the multifaceted persona of Chaereas. Achilles is said to be the handsomest man in the Greek host, with Nireus as second in handsomeness. By such a comparison Chariton is not attempting to depict Chaereas physically, but rather he is trying to manufacture an image similar to that of Achilles. This idea is supported by the author's comparison of Chaereas to Nireus, a man who might have been quite attractive but who could muster the following of only a few people (cf. *Il.* 2.671–75). Chariton perhaps is pointing to a dichotomy in Chaereas's character: on the outside Chaereas may be physically strong and handsome like Achilles, but inside he is less than perfect. This dichotomy is observable in the many scenes that the handsome Chaereas either cries or opts for suicide rather than facing his problems.

Hippolytus is the third character to whom Chaeraes is likened. In

Euripides' *Hippolytus* and in Seneca's *Phaedra* the general idea of Hippolytus's beauty is made clear, but not through actual description. Hippolytus's beauty is shown through the actions of Phaedra. In addition to the beauty of Hippolytus, Chariton evokes the conceit of Hippolytus: the son of Theseus rejected the worship of Aphrodite and had to be punished. Likewise, Chaereas commits an outrage against Aphrodite and, accordingly, must suffer the consequences.[21]

Lastly, Chariton compares Chaereas to Alcibiades, who was known for his handsomeness (cf. Plato *Symp.* 216d). The inclusion of Alcibiades in Chariton's list is perplexing, since Alcibiades is not a mythological being. It may be that although Achilles, Nireus, and Hippolytus are much better models than Alcibiades, Chariton, in keeping with the historical veneer of his work, includes Alcibiades, a historical figure, because of the background of his novel is historical rather than mythical.

The comparison to Achilles is positive, but the other three comparisons have negative qualities: Nireus was handsome but had trouble attracting loyalty, Hippolytus incurred the wrath of Aphrodite, and Alcibiades was a handsome, rakish youth who put his own interests ahead of those of Athens. Chariton delineates his character's qualities by likening him to legendary or mythological heroes who adumbrate a likeable but faulty character.

When Chariton compares Chaereas to Achilles, he sets the precedent for the use of numerous Homeric quotations.[22] It seems that Chariton wants to let the reader know right away that he will be relying on Homer and the myths included in his epics as the source for most of his mythological allusions.[23] When Callirhoe thought that she was being forced to marry someone she did not know, she fainted in Homeric style: τῆς δ' αὐτοῦ λύτο γούνατα καὶ φίλον ἦτορ.[24]

The Homeric line refers to the death of pitiable Lycaon, the son of Priam. Achilles had captured Lycaeon and sailed with his hostage to Lemnos, where he sold Lycaon to Euneüs, the king of Lemnos. From there the ransomed Lycaon traveled to Imbros, an island, and then to Arisbe, a coastal town. From Arisbe he made his way back to his father's home in Troy, where he lived for twelve days before dying in combat with Achilles, who was slaughtering Trojans and doing battle with the river Xanthos.

Before he died, Lycaon grabbed the son of Peleus by his knees and begged him not to kill him, but rather to take pity upon him as a master takes pity on a suppliant. He implored Achilles not to kill him because, although he was the brother of Hector, he was not born from the same womb. Achilles countered by stating that he lost all sense of pity the day Patroclos died and that since that day not one Trojan would escape death. At the end of his rejection of Lycaon's plea he tells him that better men than he have died, namely, Patroclos, at which time Lycaon's λύτο γούνατα καὶ φίλον ἦτορ.

One may attribute the inclusion of this line to a show of erudition,[25] but there seems to be more behind it. After all, this line refers to the murder of Lycaon by Achilles, which ranks second in vileness only to the shameful treatment of Hector's body. This easily recognized line foreshadows Chaereas's atrocious treatment of Callirhoe: she will be kicked to death (really a *Scheintod*). A closer examination of this line, in view of its new literary surroundings, may also hint at the adventures of Callirhoe: she will be captured, sold as a slave, and sail to islands and coastal cities. Even if Chariton does not intend the background of this line to prefigure the adventures of Callirhoe, the line itself, with its undertones of death, relentless vengeance, and cruelty, should alert the reader to its special qualities, in that it was associated with a time that should have been filled with immense joy for Callirhoe.

Another example of this Homeric structuring through myth occurs when the cabal led by the tyrant of Acragas convinces Chaereas that Callirhoe had been unfaithful. Chaereas, in keeping with the Nireus component of his persona since he could not muster the support of his fellow suitors, faints with Homeric flair: Ὣς φάτο· τὸν δ' ἄχεος νεφέλη ἐκάλυψε μέλαινα / Ἀμφοτέρῃσι δὲ χερσὶν ἑλὼν κόνιν αἰθαλόεσσαν / Χεύατο κὰκ κεφαλῆς, χαρίεν δ' ᾔσχυνε πρόσωπον (*Il.* 18.22–24 in 1.4.6).[26] The Homeric line refers to Achilles' fainting upon hearing that Patroclos had fallen in battle. In Chariton, the hero of the novel imitates the action of the Homeric hero: both lament in the dust for a considerable period of time. There are, however, some differences between these passages. Firstly, in the Homeric passage it was a trusted companion of Achilles who delivered the account of Patroclos's death and despoilment at the hands of Hector. In the novel Chaereas heard about Callirhoe's alleged adultery from the tyrant of Acragas, who wanted Callirhoe for himself. There is good reason why Chariton's tyrant is from Acragas: the legendary tyrant of Acragas was known for his cruelty, particularly his unusual manner of executing his prisoners in a bronze bull.[27] In no way can Chariton's tyrant be considered a trusted companion. Secondly, the news reported to Chaereas was not that someone he loved was dead, but rather news that forces the hero to seek Callirhoe out and to kick her to death (once again, a *Scheintod*).[28]

Chaereas wants to kill himself when he realizes what he has done, but Polycharmus, his best friend, prevents this. Chariton writes that Polycharmus was: φίλος ἐξαίρετος, τοιοῦτος οἷον Ὅμηρος ἐποίησε Πάτροκλον Ἀχιλλέως (I.5.2). With this reference to Homer, Patroclos, and Achilles, Chariton is closing the ring-composition he started when he quoted lines 18.22–24 of the *Iliad*. Patroclos had to appear in this passage because the cause of Achilles' swooning and lament was the death of his beloved Patroclos. In other words, Chariton is telling his reader that although it may seem odd that he is borrowing from Homer and even odder that he is sticking the lines into what seem to be incongruous places, there is nevertheless an explanation for this usage of Homer: the lines he borrowed deal with Patroclos and supply a closure to the Homeric structure by comparing Polycharmus with Patroclos.

Structuring of the plot after Homer is also found in book 2 in the dream of Callirhoe, who had gone to bed having decided to abort the child. Chaereas appears to her in a vivid dream: Μέγεθός τε καὶ ὄμματα κάλ᾽ ἐϊκυῖα / Καί φωνήν, καὶ τοῖα περὶ χροῒ εἵματα <ἕστο> (*Il.* 23.66–67 in 2.9.6).[29] In this dream Chaereas asks Callirhoe to take care of the child. The Homeric line refers to when Achilles had killed Hector and dragged him under the bier of Patroclos. After some mourning and weeping on the part of Achilles, he fell asleep and dreamed that Patroclos came and spoke to him. Patroclos then disappeared after telling Achilles that Achilles' ashes will lie in the same urn as his own ashes. Achilles reached out to embrace Patroclos, but like Callirhoe, awoke only to find out that it was all a dream. Callirhoe, after Chaereas told her to save the child and not destroy it, decided to rear the child.

The beginning of book 4 finds Callirhoe weeping over the death of her husband, which causes Dionysius to suggest to her that perhaps Chaereas, although dead, might be saying: Θάπτε με ὅττι τάχιστα, πύλας Ἀΐδαο περήσω (*Il.* 23.71 in 4.1.3).[30] Chariton is referring to Patroclos's appearance to a sleeping Achilles, whom Patroclos accused of being neglectful. Chariton places this appropriate line in an appropriate place. Callirhoe, however, was not forgetful; she did not want Dionysius to know the cause of her grief.

The young widow/bride takes her new husband's advice and looks for a place to set up a memorial tomb for Chaereas, choosing a spot near the temple of Aphrodite. Dionysius, however, wants this real estate for himself and suggests to Callirhoe that the tomb of Chaereas should rather be built at a lofty place: Ὥς κεν τηλεφανὴς ἐκ ποντόφιν ἀνδράσιν εἴη (*Od.* 24.83 in 4.1.5).³¹ This Homeric quotation closes off the Homeric frame begun when Dionysius told Callirhoe what Chaereas might be saying. In the previous Homeric passage Patroclos accused Achilles of being neglectful, and Patroclos had also mentioned in the same passage that his remains and Achilles' were to lie together in the same urn. The second Homeric reference recalls the fact that Achilles' remains came to be in the same urn with Patroclos's.

In book 5 a lessening of structuring through Homeric quotations parallels the diminution of characterization through myth. One rare example is when Chaereas learns that his wife is married to another man and contemplates suicide: Εἰ δὲ θανόντων περ καταλήθοντ᾽ εἰν ᾽Αΐδαο / Αὐτὰρ ἐγὼ καὶ κεῖθι φίλης μεμνήσομ᾽ ἑταίρου (*Il.* 22.389–90 in 5.10.9).³² He sees no other escape from the loss of his wife; it was not so bad if his wife had died, it was terrible that she was married to another man, but he could not endure the fact that Callirhoe had not embraced him when they had first seen each other after their long separation.

Εἰ δὲ θανόντων περ καταλήθοντ᾽ εἰν ᾽Αΐδαο / Αὐτὰρ ἐγὼ καὶ κεῖθι φίλης μεμνήσομ᾽ ἑταίρου are the words spoken by Achilles to the assembled Achaeans after he had finished mutilating Hector's body. The hero of the *Iliad* then went on to tell his men that they should take the dead Hector back to their ships. Before he finished speaking to the warriors, Achilles also told them that Patroclos would not go unremembered. Chaereas, on the other hand, spoke those words to Callirhoe, who was not present, and then proceeded to attempt to hang himself. Luckily, and in keeping with the context of the Homeric paraphrase. Polycharmus, Chaereas's Patroclos, was present to stop the suicide.

The decrease of the use of myth begun in the previous book continues in book 6. The trial had also affected King Artaxerxes, who, on the night before he was to give his verdict, did not sleep at all. Chariton says that the king: ἄλλοτ᾽ ἐπὶ πλευρᾶς κατακείμενος, <ἄλλοτε δ᾽ αὖτε / ὕπτιος,> ἄλλοτε δὲ πρηνής (*Il.* 24.10–11 in 6.1.8).³³ In the *Iliad* Homer goes on to tell how Apollo had kept the face of Hector from suffering disfigurement at the hands of Achilles. Chariton, in the novel, does not build on this Homeric line, but makes the king say that Callirhoe had been chosen by the sun as a gift for him and that only Eros can advise a lover.

Artaxerxes plans to take his mind off the matter at hand by going hunting; however, he cannot escape Love: the king cannot concentrate on the hunt; rather, he thinks only about Callirhoe. He sees Callirhoe as Artemis: Οἵη δ᾽ Ἄρτεμις εἶσι κατ᾽ οὔρεος ἰοχέαιρα / Ἢ κατὰ Τηΰγετον περιμήκετον ἢ Ἐρύμανθον / Τερπομένη κάπροισι καὶ ὠκείης ἐλάφοισι (*Od.* 6.102–4 in 6.4.6).[34] The king's plans for the seduction of Callirhoe, however, are interrupted when Egypt, one of the king's subject nations, rebels. Book 6 ends with the king and his royal entourage, which includes Callirhoe, setting off to crush the rebellion.

Book 6 ends with the stage set for a war and hints at the predominantly military and historical aspect of book 7. Chaereas had remained behind in Babylon, since he was a free man and therefore not subject to the king. He had hoped that Callirhoe also would have remained in Babylon, but when he found out that she had left, he fell into despair and even madness. Dionysius, who had left with the king, had left word for Chaereas that the king had adjudged Callirhoe to Dionysius because he was an ally of the king. Chaereas swore to get even with Artaxerxes and judged that the best way of doing so was to join the rebellious Egyptian forces.

Chaereas went to Egypt, where he met the Egyptian king and offered himself and Polycharmus as volunteers for the Egyptian cause. He, however, would fight only to make his personal enemy suffer and would not die before he revenged himself on Artaxerxes: Μὴ μὰν ἀσπουδί γε καὶ ἀκλειῶς ἀπολοίμην / Ἀλλὰ μέγα ῥέξας τι καὶ ἐσσομένοισι πυθέσθαι (*Il.* 22.304–5 in 7.2.4).[35] A bad Homeric choice of words, since it was Hector who spoke these words before he engaged in combat with Achilles. Chaereas is no Hector: he cries at the drop of a hat and attempts suicide only when there is someone nearby.

The Egyptian king agreed to Chaereas's request and put him in charge of a group of three hundred Greek mercenaries, but only after the hero had said: Νῶι δ᾽ ἐγὼ Πολύχαρμος τε μαχησόμεθα / Σὺν γὰρ θεῷ εἰλήλουθμεν (*Il.* 9.48–49 in 7.3.5).[36] Once again Chariton has made a strange choice of Homeric words. These lines are spoken by Diomedes when Agamemnon suggests that the Greek expedition against Troy should be discontinued because Zeus had turned against them. Diomedes rejects this suggestion and, at the advice of Nestor, an embassy is sent to Achilles in order to correct the mistake. It seems that Chariton is no longer attempting to fit the Homeric lines and the plot behind them with the plot and characters of the novel. In other words, the use of Homeric lines and the myth alluded to in those lines have become purely decorative.

Although the Egyptian king had placed Chaereas in charge of the mercenary force, nevertheless Chaereas elaborately refused the command and would accept it only if the soldiers thought it best. The soldiers made it quite clear that they wanted him as commander, and Chaereas, in turn, replied that they would not regret doing so, that they would become famous, rich, and celebrated for their courage, just as the men Othyrades and those of Leonidas are celebrated. It is at this point in the narrative, when Chaereas mentions Othyrades and Leonidas, that the few instances of mythological allusions and the use of the Homeric epics give way to an almost complete historical background. This is not to say that at any point in the narrative the mythological and Homeric elements overwhelmed the historical, but rather that the historical was always present and actually predominant.

Leonidas and his deeds are well known.[37] Othyrades[38] is mentioned in Herodotus (1.82) as having been the only Spartan survivor of an arranged battle, the "Battle of the Champions," between the Argives and Spartans over a place called Thyrea. Not all of the Argive and Spartan forces fought in this battle, but rather three hundred men, the same number as Chaereas's forces, were chosen from each side to fight. There were two Argive survivors, Alcanor and Chromius, and one Spartan, Othyrades. Since there were two Argive survivors, the Argives thought that they had won and therefore returned to Argos. Othyrades, on the other hand, stripped the bodies of the fallen Argives and carried their armor back to his camp. The two armies could not decide who had won, and consequently both armies entered again into battle. The Spartans won but Othyrades, on account of shame, did not return to Sparta and committed suicide.

Chaereas led his three hundred mercenaries against the city of Tyre that the Egyptians had not been able to capture. Chariton tells the reader that Chaereas led his men ἀσπὶς ἄρ' ἀσπίδ' ἔρειδε, κόρυς κόρυν, ἀνέρα δ' ἀνήρ. The two places in the Homeric texts in which this military formation is mentioned are Il. 13.131 and 16.215. In Il. 13.131 the description of the battle formation is in reference to Hector's assault against the Achaean ships, and Il. 16.215 refers to Achilles' encouragement of his troops as they entered battle with Patroclos as leader. These Homeric lines are decorative in function.[39]

Chaereas enters the fortress of Tyre, having convinced the Tyrians that they were Greeks who did not want to serve the Egyptian king, but rather did want to join the Tyrians in their struggle against the Egyptians. The Tyrians let the Greek mercenaries in, and once in, Chaereas went on a slaughter and τύπτε δὲ ἐπιστροφάδην· τῶν δὲ στόνος ὄρνυτ᾽ ἀεικής. Three places in which this line occurs are *Od.* 22.308 and 24.184 and *Il.* 10.483ff. *Od.* 22.308 and 24.184 deal with the suitors of Penelope. The first reference recalls the actual slaughter of the suitors by Odysseus, while the second occurs when the dead suitors recount their death to Agamemnon. The use of *Il.* 10.483ff. is especially suitable in the novel, because, like the *Iliad* passage, the novel passage continues with a simile in which Chaereas is likened to a lion falling upon a herd of unguarded cattle.

After Tyre falls, Chaereas refuses to partake of the victory celebration, because he does not have Callirhoe. Unbeknownst to Chaereas, Artaxerxes had left her, Statira, and other noble Persian women on the island of Aradus, which is sacred to Aphrodite. At the end of the book Chaereas takes the island and holds the Persian retinue as prisoners. Chaereas is unaware, however, that the Egyptian rebellion had been quashed on land. With his mercenaries, nevertheless, he retains naval supremacy.

Book 7 is a military book, and in it there are battles and war strategies that are of two types: actual land or sea battles and erotic struggles. The use of myth drops drastically; there are only vague references to myths, and, in fact, historical detail overtakes mythological allusion. Chaereas is no longer compared to Paris or any other mythical lover, but rather, as befits his new warrior role, he is likened to military men. He is a potential Leonidas or Othyrades.

Book 8 begins with Τύχη about to accomplish a παράδοξον that was σκυθρωπόν in nature. Chaereas is going to evacuate the island and take all the noble Persian wives with him, but he is going to leave Callirhoe on Aradus, just as Theseus left the sleeping Ariadne on Naxos. Aphrodite, however, thought that this would be too harsh and did not approve. Aphrodite, it seems, had forgiven Chaereas for having badly treated Callirhoe, her gift to him. This gift was more precious and beautiful than Helen, the gift she had given Paris Alexander. Since Chaereas, through his suffering, had made amends to Eros, all was forgiven.

Chariton himself states that the last book will focus on the truth that will come to light and on the reunification of the couple. After the couple is reunited and Φήμη has reported to all the people on Aradus that the general has recovered his wife, both lovers tell each other their adventures.[40] Immediately afterward they embrace each other and ἀσπάσιοι λέκτροιο παλαιοῦ θεσμὸν ἵκοντο (*Od.* 23.296 in 8.1.17). This line is of course very suitable, since Odysseus and Penelope, like Chaereas and Callirhoe, had been separated by the sea and by adventures.

From Aradus Chaereas and his troops sail to Cyprus,⁴¹ Paphos, and there they go to the temple of Aphrodite and pay honor to the goddess. On Cyprus Statira, the Persian queen, sees that the odds have turned against her, and lays all misfortune at the feet of Τύχη. Callirhoe, seeing the depressed state of the queen, quickly disabuses her of the idea that she is a prisoner of war. Chaereas then arranges for the queen to be safely returned to her husband. Before the queen is returned to her husband, Callirhoe entrusts her with a letter for Dionysius, in which she instructs Dionysius to raise their son, tells him that he should not remarry in order that the child may never know a stepmother, and that he should send their son to Syracuse to visit his grandfather. In the meanwhile, the king mourns the loss of his wife: Στάτειραν πρόφασιν, σφῶν δὲ αὐτῶν κήδε' ἕκαστος (8.5.2) echoing line 19.302 of the *Iliad*, Πάτροκλον πρόφασιν, σφῶν δ' αὐτῶν κήδε' ἑκάστη, referring to the mourning of the Greek women for Patroclos.

At the same time that Statira is restored to Artaxerxes, Dionysius is deprived of Callirhoe. This loss of and seeming betrayal of Callirhoe forces Dionysius to say: Οὕτω κοῦφον ἐστιν ὁ Ἔρως καὶ ἀναπείθει ῥᾳδίως ἀντερᾶσθαι (8.5.4). Poor Dionysius can find solace only in his child: θεασάμενος δὲ τὸ παιδίον καὶ πήλας ταῖς χερσίν, an adaptation of *Il.* 6.474, αὐτὰρ ὅ γ' ὃν φίλον υἱὸν ἐπεὶ κύσε πῆλέ τε χερσίν. The line recalls the moment when Hector played with Astyanax before he joined Achilles in mortal combat. The use of this Homeric line clearly shows that Chariton is no longer using Homer as mythological background but rather as literary decoration.

Dionysius leaves Babylon and returns as quickly as possible to Miletus, where he will take solace in the likenesses of Callirhoe. These "likenesses" were the statues that Dionysius had offered to Aphrodite in her temple at Miletus. As previously stated, this mention of the statues parallels the Ariadne myth of Paeon in that in both Paeon and Chariton Ariadne dies near or leaves the sanctuary of Aphrodite; in her stead a child, in both instances a male, and lifelike statues are left.

While Statira and Dionysius are undergoing their trials and tribulations, Callirhoe and Chaereas make their way back to Syracuse. When they reach their homeland all the Syracusans gather around her and compare her, for the last time, to Aphrodite, a suitable comparison in that Callirhoe reappears, or is reborn, from the sea just as Aphrodite had been. The novel ends with Callirhoe thanking Aphrodite and asking the goddess that she let her and Chaereas live together and that they not be separated from each other.

Book 8 reverses the trend of books 5, 6, and 7 by incorporating into the narrative numerous mythological allusions and Homeric lines. The action of the book is nonstop, and Eros quickly brings an end to this love story. It appears that Chariton wants to mention every myth one more time before he finishes his story; he mentions Ariadne and Paris Alexander and alludes to Helen, Penelope, Odysseus, Hector, Astyanax, Patroclos, Achilles, Eros, and, of course, Aphrodite. Chariton includes Homer in this last book; he supplies a line from the *Iliad* adapted in such a manner that Chariton seems to be telling his reader, "I just wanted to let you know, one more time, that I know my Homer."

Analysis of *Chaereas and Callirhoe* shows that Chariton wrote a work with a predominantly historical background. The mythical element, however, is sizable and cannot be disregarded. It takes many forms, such as allusion, quotation, and simile. One might even say that the social and historical conditions have a mythical quality about them. For example, women are included in the assemblies, a woman conquers a barbarian king, and altogether too much importance is awarded to the demos (cf. Williamson 1986, 38).

The use of myth in *Chaereas and Callirhoe* is primarily limited to the depiction of character through mythological comparison. Chariton compares Callirhoe to Aphrodite in order to show that the heroine of the novel is a beautiful young woman who, at least in the beginning of the novel, is a virgin and cherishes her virginity. The novelist also likens Callirhoe to Helen, the nymphs, Medea, and Ariadne. The last of the mythological analogues is very important, because Chariton uses the adventures of Ariadne to direct parts of the action of the plot.

Chariton uses Achilles, Nireus, Hippolytus, and Alcibiades as models upon which to base his depiction of Chaereas. The persona of the hero, however, is not, at least in the first half of the novel, developed as extensively as is the character of Callirhoe. In the first four books Chariton attempts to show that a dichotomy exists in the person of Chaereas, but this superficial characterization gives way to a more detailed one in the last four books. In the second half of the novel the author depicts Chaereas's character more through his acts than through mythological reference. In fact, historical characters displace the mythological as models for Chaereas.

In books 5 through 7 the mythological elements, such as references to myths found in the Homeric corpus, and the use of lines transposed from the *Iliad* or the *Odyssey* lessen in frequency. It seems that Chariton can deviate only so far from the historical nature of his work, through his use of myth, before having to reintroduce historical elements into the novel. Book 8, however, makes up for the lack of the mythological in the preceding three books by including numerous mythological allusions, some based on the myth of Ariadne, and by having Aphrodite, the moving force behind the start of the novel, appear as the catalyst for the end of the novel.

Xenophon, History, and Mythological Allusions

The date of the Xenophon's *Ephesiaca* seems more firmly fixed than Chariton's in the second century A.D. Xenophon mentions in 2.13 and 3.11 an *eirenarch* of Cilicia, a political and military office not known to have existed before the reign of Hadrian (A.D. 117–38).[1] The word *eirenarch*, however, is found in inscriptions dated to A.D. 116 or 117 (Reardon 1971, 336). Xenophon also seems to have imitated Chariton, thereby making it probable that his novel dates later than *Chaereas and Callirhoe*.[2]

Mythological elements in the *Ephesiaca* are subtle and scarce. It seems that Xenophon may have wanted to use myth, as shown by the mythological opening of the novel, but did not carry out his original intention (Steiner 1969, 134). By limiting allusions to myth Xenophon instead endows the protagonist with godlike qualities and replaces "mythic reputation with moral flawlessness."[3] Nor does this novelist set his novel in a specific historical time period like Chariton, but rather places it in a more recent time, thereby differing substantially from his novelistic predecessor. It is important to note, however, that although Xenophon may place his novel in a time period closer to his own time than Chariton did, he nevertheless gives his work historiographical qualities. It has already been mentioned that the earlier ancient novels, in general, were more historical in nature.[4] The main historical element in this novel, the inclusion of the eirenarch, may imply that Xenophon wants to set his novel in a time contemporary to that of his readers; this may be due to the possibility that no novelist can completely separate himself from the world in which he lives, and, as a result, there will be occasional references to the author's own time.

In this chapter I approach the use of myth and its interrelation with history in the *Ephesiaca* in several ways. The first approach is an examination of the development of character through myth. Xenophon seems to compare Habrocomes, the hero of the novel, with Hippolytus and Bellerophon. Artemis serves as the paradigm for Antheia, the heroine of the *Ephesiaca,* which is in keeping with the Hippolytus aspect of Habrocomes' character, since Hippolytus was devoted to Artemis. The second is an analysis of the oracle that portends trials and tribulations for the young couple. The third is an overview of the separation, adventures, and reunion of the couple, which demonstrates how Xenophon bases some of his narrative on the Hippolytus nature of Habrocomes.

HABROCOMES AND HIPPOLYTUS

The *Ephesiaca* begins with Xenophon supplying the parentage of Habrocomes, the hero of the novel. His father is Lycomedes and his mother is Themisto. The name Lycomedes[5] is found in the *Iliad* 17.345–46, where Homer says that Lycomedes is dear to Ares, a god whose name appears three times in this novel (1.9; 2.13; 3.3). Lycomedes is also the name of the king of Scyrus, the regent who, according to Plutarch (*Thes.* 35), is responsible for the death of Theseus. Apollodorus (3.13.8) and Pausanias (1.17.6; 10.26.4) also mention that Thetis at one time came to Lycomedes' kingdom to entrust to Lycomedes her son Achilles. There Achilles disguised himself as a girl in order that he might escape being drafted for the Trojan War. Another Lycomedes was a very important leader of the Arcadian League in the 370s B.C. (cf. Xen. *Hell.* 7.1.25 and Diod. 15.59.1).

Themisto's name is mythological in nature (Hägg 1971b, 44.). She was the daughter of Hypseus, an early Thessalian king, and the wife of Athamas, mother of Leucon,[6] Erythius, Schoeneus, and Ptoüs. She killed herself after inadvertently murdering Schoeneus and Ptoüs in an attempt to dispose of the sons of Ino, another wife of Athamas. This story is found in Hyginus *Fab.* 1, 4, and 157 and is based on the *Ino* of Euripides. Athamas had a brother named Cretheus, the king of Iolcus, who was married to Demodice. She fell in love with Phrixus, the son of Athamas by a previous marriage, and when he did not respond to Demodice's amorous advances she told Cretheus that Phrixus had attempted to violate her. This aspect of the story may foreshadow the Hippolytus-Bellerophon aspect of Habrocomes' relationship with Manto, the daughter of Apsyrtus, and the use of the *Ino* may hint at the stage-based facet of Habrocomes.[7]

In Greek mythology, Manto, the daughter of Teiresias, had been instructed by Apollo to found a colony in Asia Minor, which turned out to be Colophon. Manto had a son by the name of Mopsus, who left Colophon to settle other colonies, one of which happened to be Tyre, the home of Manto, the daughter of Apsyrtus. In the *Ephesiaca*, the character Manto falls in love with Habrocomes and confides to Rhode, the slave of Habrocomes and Antheia, that she loves Habrocomes, and she urges her to help win him over.

Leucon, a fellow-slave of Rhode, reveals Manto's intentions to Habrocomes, but Habrocomes swears that Manto will never be able to persuade him. Manto retaliates by writing a letter in which she states that she loves him, and she begs him not to spurn or humiliate her; if he refuses, all will suffer. Habrocomes also replies by letter that what Manto wants can never be. During this exchange of letters, Apsyrtus plans to marry his daughter to Moeris, but she tells him that Habrocomes had attempted to rape her. This deceit explicitly connects the story of Habrocomes with that of Hippolytus: both are falsely accused of attempting rape, are devoted to Artemis, spurned Love, and have been implicated through letters. In addition, letters and slaves play important roles in the *Hippolytus* and the *Ephesiaca*: Phaedra makes her love known through a letter and her nurse, and Manto uses her slaves and a letter in her attempt to seduce Habrocomes.

This deceit of Manto also recalls the Homeric narrative involving Bellerophon, who had been sent to the court of King Proetus, where the king's wife, Stheneboea, falls in love with him.[8] She had approached Bellerophon and made known her illicit love to him, but he refused to reciprocate, thereby forcing Stheneboea to tell Proetus that Bellerophon had attempted to rape her. Proetus, not wanting to invoke the wrath of Zeus, does not punish Bellerophon at his court, but rather sends him to his father-in-law, the king of Lycia, with a sealed letter in which he asks the king of Lycia to kill the bearer of the letter. This letter is mentioned by Homer in *Il.* 6.168–69 as σήματα λυγρά . . . ἐν πίνακι πτυκτῷ θυμοφθόρα πολλά. Although the content of the letter is different, Xenophon uses a word with Homeric undertones, πινακίδα (2.5.4), to describe the letter.

Moeris and Manto marry and Apsyrtus gives them a great number of wedding gifts, among which are included Antheia, Rhode, and Leucon. Manto, her new husband, and the others then set off to Moeris's home in Antioch, where Manto gives Antheia to a goatherd to be deflowered. The goatherd, however, when he learns of Antheia's misfortunes, pities her and promises that he will never harm her. In keeping with the Euripidean tone of the novel, Antheia's situation recalls that of Electra in the play of the same name. In the meanwhile Apsyrtus finds out the truth about Habrocomes, places him in charge of his household, and promises a free citizen's daughter for a wife; Habrocomes prefers to have Antheia.

Antheia, on the other hand, falls into the hands of the robber Hippothous,[9] who decides to offer her as sacrifice to Ares. The ritual of the sacrifice is unique: the victim is to be hung from a tree and struck with a javelin. This sort of ritual would be more appropriate for Habrocomes, since he has been likened to Hippolytus, the son of an Amazon known to worship Ares (Festugière 1954, 11). Antheia manages to escape being sacrificed to Ares, thanks to Perilaus, the eirenarch of Cilicia, who shows up at the nick of time, kills the robbers, and rescues her.

At the beginning of the first book of the novel, after the parents of Habrocomes have been identified, Xenophon proceeds to describe the youth.

μέγα δέ τι χρῆμα [ὡραιότητι σώματος ὑπερβαλλούσῃ] κάλλους
οὔτε ἐν Ἰωνίᾳ οὔτε ἐν ἄλλῃ γῇ πρότερον γενομένου. οὗτος ὁ
Ἀβροκόμης ἀεὶ μὲν καὶ καθ᾽ ἡμέραν εἰς κάλλος ηὔξετο, συνήνθει
δὲ αὐτῷ τοῖς τοῦ σώματος καλοῖς καὶ τὰ τῆς ψυχῆς ἀγαθά·
παιδείαν τε γὰρ πᾶσαν ἐμελέτα καὶ μουσικὴν ποικίλην ἤσκει, καὶ
θήρα δὲ αὐτῷ καὶ ἱππασία καὶ ὁπλομαχία συνήθη γυμνάσματα.
ἦν δὲ περισπούδαστος ἅπασιν Ἐφεσίοις, ἀλλὰ καὶ τοῖς τὴν ἄλλην
Ἀσίαν οἰκοῦσι, καὶ μεγάλας εἶχον ἐν αὐτῷ τὰς ἐλπίδας ὅτι πολίτης
ἔσοιτο διαφέρων. προσεῖχον δὲ ὡς θεῷ τῷ μειρακίῳ· καί εἰσιν
ἤδη τινὲς οἳ καὶ προσεκύνησαν ἰδόντες καὶ προσηύξαντο.
ἐφρόνει δὲ τὸ μειράκιον ἐφ᾽ ἑαυτῷ μεγάλα καὶ ἠγάλλετο μὲν καὶ
τοῖς τῆς ψυχῆς κατορθώμασι, πολὺ δὲ μᾶλλον τῷ κάλλει τοῦ
σώματος· πάντων δὲ τῶν ἄλλων, ὅσα δὴ ἐλέγετο καλά, ὡς
ἐλαττόνων κατεφρόνει καὶ οὐδὲν αὐτῷ, οὐ θέαμα, οὐκ ἄκουσμα

ἄξιον Ἀβροκόμου κατεφαίνετο· καὶ εἴ τινα ἢ παῖδα καλὸν
ἀκοῦσαι ἢ παρθένον εὔμορφον, κατεγέλα τῶν λεγόντων ὡς οὐκ
εἰδότων ὅτι εἷς καλὸς αὐτός. Ἔρωτά γε μὴν οὐδὲ ἐνόμιζεν εἶναι
θεόν, ἀλλὰ πάντη ἐξέβαλεν ὡς οὐδὲν ἡγούμενος, λέγων ὡς οὐκ ἄν
ποτε οὐ<δὲ> εἷς ἐρασθείη οὐδὲ ὑποταγείη τῷ θεῷ μὴ θέλων· εἰ
δέ που ἱερὸν ἢ ἄγαλμα Ἔρωτος εἶδε, κατεγέλα, ἀπέφαινέ τε
ἑαυτὸν Ἔρωτος παντὸς καλλίονα καὶ κάλλει σώματος καὶ
δυνάμει. καὶ εἶχεν οὕτως· ὅπου γὰρ Ἀβροκόμης ὀφθείη, οὔτε
ἄγαλμα <καλὸν> κατεφαίνετο οὔτε εἰκὼν ἐπῃνεῖτο (1.1.1–6).[10]

Even though the Xenophon never mentions the name of Artemis, it
appears that Habrocomes has dedicated himself to her. Therefore, if any
myth is alluded to in this passage, it is the myth of Hippolytus.[11]
Habrocomes' conduct strongly resembles that of Hippolytus in Euripides'
tragedy, an obvious source for much of the initial plot. For example,
Euripides, in the opening speech of his play, has Aphrodite note that
Hippolytus λέγει κακίστην δαιμόνων πεφυκέναι / ἀναίνεται δὲ λέκτρα
κοὐ ψαύει γάμων (13–14). Habrocomes, like Hippolytus, denigrates the
divinity of Love and rejects the accoutrements of Love. Hippolytus rejects
marriage and the marriage couch, while Habrocomes rejects Eros and the
love that he brings. Moreover, the illicit love that Phaedra has for
Hippolytus is paralleled by Manto's love of Habrocomes.[12]

ANTHEIA AND ARTEMIS

Eros, like Euripides' Aphrodite, cannot stand being rejected and accordingly seeks vengeance on Habrocomes: he makes him fall in love with
Antheia, the daughter of Megamedes[13] and Euippe,[14] at a festival in honor
of Artemis. In the festival the youths, separated according to sex, proceed
to the temple of Artemis, located about a mile away from the city, in this
order: πρῶτα μὲν τὰ ἱερὰ καὶ δᾷδες καὶ κανᾶ καὶ θυμιάματα ἐπὶ
τούτοις ἵπποι καὶ κύνες καὶ σκεύη κυνηγετικά, ἔτι καὶ πολεμικά, τὰ δὲ
πλεῖστα εἰρηνικά (1.2.4).[15] At the head of the maidens is Antheia, who
is fourteen, very beautiful, and exquisitely dressed: κόμη ξάνθη, ἡ πολλὴ
καθειμένη, ὀλίγη πεπλεγμένη, πρὸς τὴν τῶν ἀνέμων φορὰν κινουμένη.
ὀφθαλμοὶ γοργοί, φαιδροὶ μὲν ὡς κόρης, φοβεροὶ δὲ ὡς σώφρονος·
ἐσθὴς χιτὼν ἁλουργής, ζωστὸς εἰς γόνυ, μέχρι βραχιόνων καθειμένος,
νεβρὶς περικειμένη, γωρυτὸς ἀνημμένος, τόξα ὅπλα, ἄκοντες φερόμενοι,
κύνες ἑπόμενοι (1.2.6).[16]

Since Antheia is wearing a tunic, girdle, and fawnskin, has arrows, and is accompanied by dogs, Xenophon has created a graphic analogue of the girl to Artemis. The position she holds in the procession further strengthens her association with Artemis.[17] The divine nature of Antheia is further emphasized when the spectators of the procession think that she is Artemis in person or that she has been made by the goddess to appear in her own image (1.2.7).

The love of the couple cannot be quickly sated, since the genre demands that the couple suffer.[18] Habrocomes and Antheia fall ill, and consequently Antheia's parents, alarmed at the state of their child, summon diviners and priests to find out what ails their daughter: εἰς τέλος εἰσάγουσι παρὰ τὴν Ἀνθίαν μάντεις καὶ ἱερέας, ὡς εὑρήσοντας λύσιν τοῦ δεινοῦ. οἱ δὲ ἐλθόντες ἔθυόν τε ἱερεῖα καὶ ποικίλα ἐπέσπενδον καὶ ἐπέλεγον φωνὰς βαρβαρικάς, ἐξιλάσκεσθαί τινας λέγοντες δαίμονας, καὶ προσεποίουν ὡς εἴη τὸ δεινὸν ἐκ τῶν ὑποχθονίων θεῶν (1.5.6–7).[19] All this divination and glossolalia are of no avail,[20] and the mention of chthonic deities by the diviners is characterized by Xenophon as being pretense. A closer reading of the description of the procession which Antheia led (πρῶτα μὲν τὰ ἱερὰ καὶ δᾷδες καὶ κανᾶ καὶ θυμιάματα ἐπὶ τούτοις ἵπποι καὶ κύνες καὶ σκεύη κυνηγετικά, ἔτι καὶ πολεμικά, τὰ δὲ πλεῖστα εἰρηνικά [1.2.4]) makes clear that torches and incense were used. This paraphernalia may hint at the possibility that the Artemisian procession had chthonic symbols (Rogers 1991, 110; Picard 1922, 297).

THE ORACLE AND POSSIBLE HISTORY

Since the diviners are of no use, the parents of both youths send embassies to the temple of Apollo in Colophon for an oracle. The response is:

Τίπτε ποθεῖτε μαθεῖν νούσου τέλος ἠδὲ καὶ ἀρχήν;
ἀμφοτέρους μία νοῦσος ἔχει, λύσις ἔνθεν ἀνυστή.
δεινὰ δ' ὁρῶ τοῖσδεσσι πάθη καὶ ἀνήνυτα ἔργα·
ἀμφότεροι φεύξονται ὑπεὶρ ἅλα λυσσοδίωκτοι,
δεσμὰ δὲ μοχθήσουσι παρ' ἀνδράσι μιξοθαλάσσοις
καὶ τάφος ἀμφοτέροις θάλαμος καὶ πῦρ ἀίδηλον,
καὶ ποταμοῦ † Νείλου † παρὰ ῥεύμασιν Ἴσιδι σεμνῇ
σωτείρῃ μετόπισθε παραστῇς ὄλβια δῶρα.
ἀλλ' ἔτι που μετὰ πήματ' ἀρείονα πότμον ἔχουσι. (1.6.2).[21]

It was not uncommon for Ephesians to ask questions of the oracle of Apollo at Colophon or, more precisely, at Claros (Picard 1922, 123). Unlike the female priestess at Delphi, the priest of the Clarian oracle was male. He would issue Apollo's answer in hexameter verse and would not answer in the affirmative or negative as did the Delphic priestess (Parke 1967, 122; see also 30ff. and 137ff.).

The Roman historian Tacitus supplies one of the few references to the Clarian oracle: Germanicus, while in Asia, had attempted to visit Samothrace but could not do so because of unfavorable weather. He went instead to Colophon:

> *adpellitque Colophona ut Clarii Apollonis oraculo uteretur. Non femina illic, ut apud Delphos, sed certis e familiis et ferme Mileto accitus sacerdos numerum modo consulantium et nomina audit; tum in specum degressus, hausta fontis arcani aqua, ignarus plerumque litterarum et carminum, edit responsa versibus compositis super rebus quas quis mente concepit. Et ferebatur Germanico per ambages, ut mos oraculis, maturum exitum cecinisse (Ann. 2.54).*[22]

It is strange that the Xenophon's oracle is so clear-cut and understandable, while the response mentioned by Tacitus seems to have been equivocal and ambiguous. Aelius Aristides records in his *Sacred Tales* (3.12) an oracle given to him by the Clarian oracle regarding his health, which stated that Asclepius would cure and heal him in the famous city of Telephus, which is located near the streams of the Caicus.[23]

Aristides' and Xenophon's oracles have some elements in common: illness, cures, divinities, and bodies of water. Not all of the Clarian responses, however, were so clear (cf. Germanicus's). For example, when Oenomaus, a Cynic philosopher, went to Claros to ask commerce-related questions, he was given this response: *In the land of Trachis lies the fair garden of Herakles [sic] containing all things in bloom for all to pick on every day, and yet they are not diminished, but with rains continually their weight is replenished.*[24] It seems that this response was so vague that Oenomaus became angry and depressed, which led him to write his *Exposure*, a tell-all book about the oracle. It appears that he got even angrier when he found out that the same response had been given numerous times to numerous people.

HABROCOMES AND ANTHEIA

When the response of the oracle is made known to both Habrocomes' and Antheia's parents, a wedding is planned for the couple. The parents, however, are fearful of the oracle, since it predicts misfortune for the youths. Nevertheless, the parents interpret (παραμυθήσασθαι [1.7.2]) the oracle and then allow the couple to marry. What exactly does παραμυθήσασθαι mean? According to Liddell and Scott, it can mean "to explain." The oracle the parents had requested had to be explained, just as every oracle must be. In addition, Xenophon is telling his audience that he will explain the contents of the oracle via the story of Antheia and Habrocomes that comprises their separation, adventures, and reunion. Xenophon already has shown that Antheia's and Habrocomes' parents have some sort of mythological background; now he must construct a story full of mythological allusions.

On their wedding night Antheia and Habrocomes are taken to the bridal suite, where there is a canopy embroidered with mythical figures: παίζοντες Ἔρωτες, οἱ μὲν Ἀφροδίτην θεραπεύοντες (ἦν δὲ καὶ Ἀφροδίτης εἰκών), οἱ δὲ ἱππεύοντες Ναβαταίαις στρουθοῖς, οἱ δὲ στεφάνους πλέκοντες, οἱ δὲ ἄνθη φέροντες. ταῦτα ἐν τῷ ἑτέρῳ μέρει τῆς σκηνῆς, ἐν τῷ ἑτέρῳ Ἄρης ἦν οὐχ ὡπλισμένος, ἀλλ᾽ ὡς πρὸς ἐρωμένην τὴν Ἀφροδίτην κεκοσμημένος, ἐστεφανωμένος, χλαμύδα ἔχων. Ἔρως αὐτὸν ὡδήγει, λαμπάδα ἔχων ἡμμένην (1.8.2–3).[25] By describing this canopy Xenophon momentarily relates the story on the embroidery to the story taking place in the narrative. The Erotes are bringing in ἄνθη, Antheia as a *figura etymologica,* and Eros himself is bringing in an Ares, Habrocomes, who is prepared for love and not war. Xenophon is emphasizing this literary plot by alluding to a myth that comprises an unfaithful marriage and the adulterous affair of Ares and Aphrodite.[26] The author puts the finishing touch on the transformation of the two characters into mythical personae when he has Habrocomes tell Antheia that she is τῶν πώποτε λαλουμένων εὐτυχεστέρα (1.9.3); or in other words, she can be included among these women who are recalled in stories.[27]

The few and subtle mythological elements in the *Ephesiaca* appear mostly in the early part of the novel. There are even fewer historical elements. Eros is the chief divinity in the novel since the plot depends for momentum upon his dislike of Habrocomes, but in Xenophon, in fact, the divinities that are mentioned are those gods that played important roles in Xenophon's time, whereas in Chariton the gods "smack of literary personification" (Hägg 1983, 26). The gods in Xenophon have greater religious importance than they do in Chariton, and this may cause one to think that Xenophon is of a more "religious cast of mind than his predecessor, and seems to want to make of his story a patently religious document" (Reardon 1991, 35).

It has been argued that Xenophon was a deeply religious writer[28] particularly in his depiction of the wanderings of Antheia and their parallels to the wanderings in the myth of Io, which perhaps served as a subtext for the plot of the novel.[29] Perhaps Xenophon would have been "lost for his plot" (Witt 1971, 249) without the Io myth. It is true that if one searches long enough for allusions to particular myths in the novel, one will find them, just as I have done with the Euripidean influence on the *Ephesiaca* in the form of the myths of Hippolytus, Electra, Alcestis, and Ino.[30]

Altogether, mythological allusions play a minimal role in Xenophon, and history even less. A possible explanation for the scarcity of mythological elements may be that the *Ephesiaca*, as we have it, has come to down to us in an abridged form.[31] The *Suda* tells us: Ξενοφῶν, Εφέσιος, ἱστορικός. Εφεσιακά· ἔστι δὲ ἐρωτικὰ βιβλία ί περι Ἀβροκόμου καὶ Ἀνθίας· καὶ Περὶ τῆς πόλεως Ἐφεσίων· καὶ ἄλλα (Ed. A. Adler, III, 495). Of the ten books mentioned, we have only five. There is the possibility, therefore, that we do have an abridged version of the original novel. This would explain why the novel appears to be so choppy in places, why people who never were introduced show up in the plot, why the parents decide to send the newly wedded couple on a sailing trip, why Habrocomes ends up going to Sicily, and a host of other oddities. The extant novel, therefore, may be abridged, what we have only a skeletal framework of the original, which may have had more mythological stories and allusions and possibly historical references. In the first part of the novel, Xenophon mentions Eros, Hippolytus, and the canopy with Ares and Aphrodite, but then the mythological aspect of the novel disappears. Even if the novel is not in an abridged form, the ratio between the historical and the mythological does support my thesis that the historical gave way to the mythological. Much more mention is made of divinities, and there are many more mythological allusions or mythological pedigrees than there are historical data.

Longus, Myth, and History

On the basis of internal criteria, Longus may be said to have written *Daphnis and Chloe* in the second century A.D. Two factors aid in the dating of Longus: his name and the wall-painting mentioned in the prologue of the novel. Longus's cognomen could be identified with that of a Mytilenean family that may have taken "its gentile name" from Pompey the Great and that included in its members a consul by the name of Pompeius Longus (cos. suff. A.D. 49) (Perry 1967, 350 n. 17). Longus, the writer, might have been a member of this Mytilenean family. The second point is the particular use of wall-painting employed by Longus, a picturesque technique that can be dated to Roman imperial times. The rural landscape of the wall-painting found in the prologue was customarily used in the second century, and literary treatments of such wall-paintings can also be found among writers of the Second Sophistic, such as Dio Chrysostom, Lucian, Alciphron, Aelian, and Philostratus. (Vieillefond 1987, cix).

LONGUS AS ΝΥΜΦΑΓΈΤΗΣ: THE MYTH OF CHLOE

Goethe said that *Daphnis and Chloe* must be constantly reexamined and studied.[1] The amount of scholarship shows that there is agreement with

44

him.[2] Much of the research has focused on origin (Valley 1926, Rohde 1937, Lavagnini 1950, Schönberger 1960, Hunter 1983) and religion (Chalk 1960, Merkelbach 1960, 1988);[3] less emphasis has been placed on etiology (Turner 1960). In this essay I examine the aitia,[4] and determine whether they are included for structure or for other reasons.

The novel relates the love of Daphnis,[5] the son of Myrtale and Lamon,[6] and Chloe,[7] the daughter of Nape[8] and Dryas;[9] the action takes place on Lesbos. The boy was found as an infant being suckled by a goat, and the girl was discovered in a Nymphaeum.[10] Their true identities are not known. When they become teenagers, Eros commands them to tend his flocks. They obey and spend their days tending flocks, weaving garlands for the nymphs, culling flowers, playing on panpipes, and making cages for grasshoppers (cf. Theoc. 1.52). Both eventually fall in love: she after seeing him nude,[11] and he after winning a contest for which the prize was a kiss from Chloe.[12]

Aition #1: One day Daphnis tells Chloe the story of the wood-dove.

There was once, maiden, a very fair maid who kept many cattle in the woods. She was skillful in music, and her herds were so taken with her voice and pipe, that they needed not the discipline of the staff or goad, but sitting under a pine and wearing a coronet of the same she would sing of Pan and Pine, and her cows would never wander out of her voice. There was a youth that kept his herd not far off, and he also was fair and musical, but as he tried with all his skill to emulate her notes and tones, he played a louder strain as a male, and yet sweet as being young, and so allured from the maid's herd eight of her best cows to his own. She took it ill that her herd was so diminished and in very deep disdain that she was her inferior at the art, and presently prayed to the Gods that she might be transformed to a bird before she did return home. The Gods consent, and turned her thus into a mountain bird, because the maid did haunt there, and musical, as she had been. And singing still to this day she publishes her heavy chance and demands her truant cows again.[13]

Immediately afterward pirates kidnap Daphnis and steal his cattle. Chloe rescues them by playing on panpipes a tune known to the cattle, who recognize the tune, jump overboard to get back to shore, and cause the ship to sink and the pirates to drown. Daphnis makes it back to shore riding on two oxen.[14] Book 1 ends containing only a generic myth.

Aition #2: Book 2 begins with the couple wanting to sate their passions, but they do not know how. Luckily, an old man called Philetas[15] visits them and says that Eros appeared and related the myth of Eros.[16] He also instructs them, to no avail, in the ways of love.[17] This tutelage is explicit: Ἔρωτος γὰρ οὐδὲν φάρμακον, οὐ πινόμενον, οὐκ ἐσθιόμενον, οὐκ ἐν ᾠδαῖς λεγόμενον, ὅτι μὴ φίλημα καὶ περιβολὴ καὶ συγκατακλιθῆναι γομνοῖς σώμασι (2.7).[18] The couple, however, πάνυ ἐτέρφθησαν ὥσπερ μῦθον οὐ λόγον ἀκούντες; that is, they are mistaken in thinking that what Philetas told them was a tale (μῦθος) and not instruction (λόγος).

In an attack by a band of Methymnaeans, Chloe is taken. Daphnis seeks the help of the nymphs, who reveal that Pan will aid him. Help comes in the form of a dream, in which Pan forces the enemy captain to return Chloe because Pan wished ἐξ ἧς Ἔρως μῦθον ποιῆσαι (2.27; cf. Hdt. 6.105). Pan's revelation dictates the plot of the novel: Longus will create a new myth, the metamorphosis of Chloe.

To honor Pan and the nymphs, and to give thanks for Chloe's rescue, there is a party that Philetas and his son Tityrus[19] attend. There Lamon tells the story of Syrinx (panpipes aition).

This pan-pipe was heretofore no organ, but a very fair maid, who had a sweet and musical voice. She had fed goats, played together with the Nymphs, and sang as now. Pan, while she in this manner was tending her goats, playing and singing, came to her and endeavoured to persuade her to what he desired, and promised her that he would make all her goats bring forth twins every year. But she disdained and derided his love, and denied to take him to be her sweetheart who was neither perfect man nor perfect goat. Pan follows her with violence and thinks to force her. Syrinx fled Pan and his force. Being now weary with her flight, she shot herself into a grove of reeds, sunk in the fen, and disappeared. Pan for anger cut up the reeds, and finding not the maid there, and then reflecting upon what had happened, joined together unequal quills, because their love was so unequal, and thus invented this organ. So she who then was a fair maid is now become a musical pipe.

In response to the story Chloe and Daphnis mimic it. So ends the second book; for the first time an actual myth is told.

Aition #3: Book 3 begins in winter with the Mytileneans marching, under the command of Hippasus,²⁰ against the Methymnaeans. This state of hostility is quickly settled. During this time, Daphnis visits Chloe's home on the pretext of bird-catching and is so successful that he is invited in by Dryas. He joins in a Dionysian feast, where tales are told (μυθολογήσαντες [3.9]). The next day the lovers argue as to why Daphnis had visited Chloe, a debate where Longus describes Chloe as καθάπερ Ἠχώ (3.11), thus he hints at the next aition. This allusion is strengthened by the line δέδοικα μὴ ἐγὼ πρὸ ταύτης τακῶ (3.10): Daphnis fears Echo's fate.

In the spring the youths return to the fields, to the nymphs, and to their passions.²¹ Daphnis's erotic fever burns greater than ever, especially when he sees the animals mating. He even imitates, to no avail, these actions on Chloe. Luckily a woman by the name of Lycaenium,²² Chromis's wife,²³ teaches the art of love to Daphnis, who learns eagerly and willingly. She, however, warns that what he has done may cause Chloe some pain and perhaps some shedding of blood. He, therefore, does not put to use his new skills; instead he relates Echo's myth.

> There are of the Nymphs, my dear girl, more kinds than one. There are the Meliae of the Ash, there are the Dryades of the Oak, there are the Heleae of the Fen. All are beautiful, all are musical. To one of these Echo was daughter, and she mortal because she came of a mortal father, but a rare beauty, deriving from a beauteous mother. She was educated by the Nymphs, and taught by the Muses to play on the hautboy and the pipe, to strike the lyre, to touch the lute, and in sum, all music. And therefore when she was grown up and in the flower of her virgin beauty, she danced together with the Nymphs and sung in consort with the Muses, but fled from all males, whether men or Gods, because she loved virginity. Pan sees that, and takes occasion to be angry at the maid, and to envy her music because he could not come at her beauty. Therefore he sends a madness among the shepherds and goatherds, and they in a desperate fury, like so many dogs and wolves, tore her all to pieces and flung about them all over the earth her yet singing limbs. The Earth in observance of the Nymphs buried them all, preserving to them still their music property, and they by an everlasting sentence and decree of the Muses breathe out a voice. And they imitate all things now as the maid did before, the Gods, men, organs, beasts. Pan himself they imitate too when he plays on the pipe; which when he

hears he bounces out and begins to post over the mountains, not so much to catch and hold as to know what clandestine imitator that is that he has got.

In the summer suitors come to Chloe's parents to ask for her hand in marriage. Daphnis wants to do the same, but poverty stands in the way. The Nymphs help him obtain money, which he takes to Dryas, who promises him Chloe. Lamon, thinking his son deserves better, doesn't agree; he asks that they wait until his master, Dionysophanes,[24] visits them in the fall.[25]

While all await the arrival, Lampis,[26] one of Chloe's rejected suitors, causes mayhem by destroying a garden under Lamon's care.[27] The destruction of the garden is the worst possible crime in this idyllic setting. Since most of the characters in this novel are in one way or another connected with vegetation or pastoralia, a destruction of vegetation would be a destruction of the force that gives them life. This, in fact, has caused Anderson (1984, 8) to consider this novel a restatement of the "original fertility myth." The destruction of the gardens, however, does not have any ramifications, because Astylus, Dionysophanes' son, arrives earlier than his father and remedies the situation. In the garden there are a fane and altar dedicated to Dionysus; there is also a statue in honor of Pan. Included in Longus's description of this garden is the aition of the spring Daphnis: πηγή τις ἦν, ἣν εὖρεν ἐς τὰ ἄνθη Δάφνις. ἐσχόλαζε μὲν τοῖς ἄνθεσιν ἡ πηγή, Δάφνιδος δὲ ὅμως ἐκαλεῖτο πηγή (4.4).[28]

Astylus has brought with him Gnathon, a parasite,[29] who falls in love with Daphnis and asks his master to give him Daphnis. He cites mythological examples, ἐρωτικὴν μυθολογίαν (4.17), and uses them to prove that there is nothing wrong with homosexual love or love for a shepherd: Aphrodite loved Anchises; Apollo loved Branchus; Zeus loved Ganymede. The hero and Lamon, however, hear what Gnathon has planned and take preventative measures.

Dionysophanes' arrival and Gnathon's plot force the revelation of the true identity of Daphnis, who turns out to be Dionysophanes' son. Lampis, thinking that the class difference between Daphnis and Chloe would prevent their marriage, carries off Chloe, but Gnathon, hoping to redeem himself, rescues the maiden. Book 4 concludes with the revelation of the identity of Chloe's parents, the wedding of the couple, a description of altars built to Eros the Shepherd and Pan the Soldier, and Daphnis testing his erotic skills on Chloe.

The major aitia are four in number. In Book 1 there is the generic story of the wood-dove. Book 2 contains the panpipes aition, and book 3 that of Echo. In book 4 Longus does not supply a specific aition or metamorphosis, unless it relates the aition or myth of Chloe.

AITIA

After a half-day of rustic activities the hero and heroine decide to rest; at that time Chloe hears a wood-dove and asks Daphnis μαθεῖν ὅ τι λέγει, to which Daphnis answers (μυθολογῶν) with the story of the wood-dove.

Ἦν οὕτω, παρθένε, παρθένος καλή, καὶ ἔνεμε βοῦς πολλὰς οὕτως ἐν ὕλῃ. ἦν δὲ ἄρα καὶ ᾠδική, καὶ ἐτέρποντο αἱ βόες ἐπ᾽ αὐτῆς τῇ μουσικῇ, καὶ ἔνεμεν οὔτε καλαύροπος πληγῇ οὔτε κέντρου προσβολῇ, ἀλλὰ καθίσασα ὑπὸ πίτυν καὶ στεφανωσαμένη πίτυϊ ᾖδε Πᾶνα καὶ τὴν Πίτυν, καὶ αἱ Βόες τῇ φωνῇ παρέμενον. παῖς οὐ μακρὰν νέμων βοῦς καὶ αὐτὸς καλὸς καὶ ᾠδικὸς φιλονεικήσας πρὸς τὴν μελῳδίαν, μείζονα ὡς ἀνήρ, ἡδεῖαν ὡς παῖς, φωνὴν ἀντεπεδείξατο, καὶ τῶν βοῶν ὀκτὼ τὰς ἀρίστας ἐς τὴν ἰδίαν ἀγέλην θέλξας ἀπεβουκόλησεν. ἄχθεται ἡ παρθένος τῇ βλάβῃ τῆς ἀγέλης, τῇ ἥττῃ τῆς ᾠδῆς, καὶ εὔχεται τοῖς θεοῖς ὄρνις γενέσθαι πρὶν οἴκαδε ἀφικέσθαι. πείθονται οἱ θεοὶ ποιοῦσι τήνδε τὴν ὄρνιν ὄρειον καὶ μουσικὴν ὡς ἐκείνη. καὶ ἔτι νῦν ᾄδουσα μηνύει τὴν συμφοράν, ὅτι βοῦς ζητεῖ πεπλανημένας (1.27).

This myth lays out the elements shared by the next two myths: 1) questioning or supplication: μαθεῖν ὅ τι λέγει; 2) identification (sex and beauty): παρθένος καλή; 3) profession: ἔνεμε βοῦς πολλὰς; 4) skill: ἦν δὲ ἄρα καὶ ᾠδική, καὶ ἐτέρποντο αἱ βόες ἐπ᾽ αὐτῆς τῇ μουσικῇ, καὶ ἔνεμεν οὔτε καλαύροπος πληγῇ οὔτε κέντρου προσβολῇ; 5) reference to a divinity (Pan): καθίσασα ὑπὸ πίτυν καὶ στεφανωσαμένη πίτυϊ ᾖδε Πᾶνα καὶ τὴν Πίτυν; 6) introduction of rival or lover: παῖς οὐ μακρὰν νέμων βοῦς καὶ αὐτὸς καλὸς καὶ ᾠδικὸς; 7) rejection of rival or lover: ἄχθεται ἡ παρθένος; 8) prayer to gods for help: εὔχεται τοῖς θεοῖς; 9) acquiescence of the gods: πείθονται οἱ θεοί; 10) metamorphosis: οἱ θεοὶ ποιοῦσι τήνδε τὴν ὄρνιν. In the aition of the wood-dove there is an allusion to the myth of Pitys. The line καθίσασα ὑπὸ πίτυν καὶ στεφανωσαμένη πίτυϊ ᾖδε Πᾶνα καὶ τὴν Πίτυν has two references to the myth of Pitys, who was "killed by Pan's rival Boreas" (Hunter 1983, 53). The story of Pitys is found in Nonnus 42.259 and may be alluded to in Theoc. *Id.* 1.1–3.[30] This aition does not exist in a vacuum, because it depends on the questioning of Daphnis by Chloe, and on the allusions to the myth of Pitys incorporated in it. The latter is an important aspect of the aition, for it makes Pan the divinity of the aitia.[31]

In book 2 Philetas had promised Chloe that he would play the panpipe. He could not do what Chloe asked, however, since he did not have his own instrument with him; he sent Tityrus home to fetch the pipe. In the meanwhile Lamon told them a story, ἐπηγγείλατο . . . ἀφηγήσασθαι μῦθον (2.33), to keep them entertained; Lamon's story is the second major aition of the novel.

Αὕτη ἡ σύριγξ τὸ ἀρχαῖον οὐκ ἦν ὄργανον, ἀλλ' παρθένος καλὴ καὶ τὴν φωνὴν μουσική. αἶγας ἔνεμεν, Νύμφαις συνέπαιζεν, ᾖδεν οἷον νῦν. Πάν, ταύτης νεμούσης, παιζούσης, ᾀδούσης, προσελθὼν ἔπειθεν ἐς ὅ τι ἔχρῃζε καὶ ἐπηγγέλλετο τὰς αἶγας πάσας θήσειν διδυματόκους. ἡ δὲ ἐγέλα τὸν ἔρωτα αὐτοῦ, οὐδὲ ἐραστὴν ἔφη δέξασθαι μήτε τράγον μήτε ἄνθρωπον ὁλόκληρον. ὁρμᾷ διώκειν ὁ Πὰν ἐς βίαν. ἡ Σύριγξ ἔφευγε καὶ τὸν Πᾶνα καὶ τὴν Βίαν. φεύγουσα, κάμνουσα ἐς δόνακας κρύπτεται, εἰς ἕλος ἀφανίζεται. Πὰν τοὺς δόνακας ὀργῇ τεμών, τὴν κόρην οὐχ εὑρών, τὸ πάθος μαθὼν καὶ τοὺς καλάμους κηρῷ συνδήσας ἀνίσους, καθ' ὅτι καὶ ὁ ἔρως ἄνισος αὐτοῖς, τὸ ὄργανον νοεῖ, καὶ ἡ τότε παρθένος καλὴ νῦν ἐστι σύριγξ μουσική (2.34).

This story shares eight of the ten elements of the first aition. The first is the request by Chloe that Philetas play a tune. παρθένος καλὴ is the second element, the identification of the main character of the aition. αἶγας ἔνεμεν is her profession, the third element, and ᾖδεν οἷον νῦν describes her musical skill, the fourth element. There can be no clearer examples of the fifth element, the introduction of the divine, and of the sixth, the introduction of the lover: Πάν . . . προσελθὼν ἔπειθεν ἐς ὅ τι ἔχρῃζε καὶ ἐπηγγέλλετο τὰς αἶγας πάσας θήσειν διδυματόκους. ἡ δὲ ἐγέλα τὸν ἔρωτα αὐτοῦ, οὐδὲ ἐραστὴν ἔφη δέξασθαι μήτε τράγον μήτε ἄνθρωπον ὁλόκληρον. ὁρμᾷ διώκειν ὁ Πὰν ἐς βίαν. The refusal of the lover, ἡ Σύριγξ ἔφευγε, is the seventh element. ἡ τότε παρθένος καλὴ νῦν ἐστι σύριγξ μουσική, the metamorphosis, is the eighth element.

There is no imprecation to the gods or the granting of wishes by the gods in this version of the story. In most of the other myths concerning Syrinx,[32] however, there is a prayer to divinities for succor. Ovid (*Met.* 1.689–712), for example, differs from Longus in several ways. He characterizes Syrinx as a nymph, while Longus makes her mortal. The second difference is that Ovid has Syrinx praying to her nymph-sisters to help her in her flight from Pan, while Longus makes no mention of prayers.

In book 3 Longus writes that Chloe had heard an unusual sound (an echo). Since she had never experienced this phenomenon before (ἡ δὲ Χλόη τότε πρῶτον πειρωμένη τῆς καλουμένης ἠχοῦς [3.22]), she asked (ἐπυνθάνετο τοῦ Δάφνιδος) Daphnis what the cause was. He responded (ἤρξατο αὐτῇ μυθολογεῖν τὸν μῦθον) with the story of Echo.

Νυμφῶν, ὦ κόρη, πολὺ <τὸ> γένος, Μελίαι καὶ Δρυάδες καὶ Ἕλειοι, πᾶσαι καλαί, πᾶσαι μουσικαί. καὶ μιᾶς τούτων θυγάτηρ Ἠχὼ γίνεται, θνητὴ μὲν ἐκ πατρὸς θνητοῦ, καλὴ δὲ ἐκ μητρὸς καλῆς. τρέφεται μὲν ὑπὸ Νυμφῶν, παιδεύεται δὲ ὑπὸ Μουσῶν συρίττειν, αὐλεῖν, τὰ πρὸς λύραν, τὰ πρὸς κιθάραν, πᾶσαν ᾠδήν. ὥστε καὶ παρθενίας εἰς ἄνθος ἀκμάσασα ταῖς Νύμφαις συνεχόρευε, ταῖς Μούσαις συνῇδεν· ἄρρενας δὲ ἔφευγε πάντας καὶ ἀνθρώπους καὶ θεούς, φιλοῦσα τὴν παρθενίαν. ὁ Πὰν ὀργίζεται τῇ κόρῃ, τῆς μουσικῆς φθονῶν, τοῦ κάλλους μὴ τυχών, καὶ μανίαν ἐμβάλλει τοῖς ποιμέσι καὶ τοῖς αἰπόλοις. οἱ δὲ ὥσπερ κύνες ἢ λύκοι διασπῶσιν αὐτὴν καὶ ῥίπτουσιν εἰς πᾶσαν γῆν ἔτι ᾄδοντα τὰ μέλη. καὶ τὰ μέλη <ἡ> Γῆ χαριζομένη Νύμφαις ἔκρυψε πάντα καὶ ἐτήρησε τὴν μουσικήν· καὶ <ᾇ> γνώμῃ Μουσῶν ἀφίησι φωνὴν καὶ μιμεῖται πάντα, καθάπερ τότε ἡ κόρη, θεούς, ἀνθρώπους, ὄργανα, θηρία. μιμεῖται καὶ αὐτὸν συρίττοντα τὸν Πᾶνα. ὁ δὲ ἀκούσας ἀναπηδᾷ καὶ διώκει κατὰ τῶν ὀρῶν, οὐκ ἐρῶν τυχεῖν ἀλλ' ἢ τοῦ μαθεῖν, τίς ἐστιν ὁ λανθάνων μιμητής. (3.23)

The components found in the first two aitia are also present here. The questioning of Daphnis has already been mentioned. Daphnis replies: Νυμφῶν, ὦ κόρη, πολὺ <τὸ> γένος, Μελίαι καὶ Δρυάδες καὶ Ἕλειοι, πᾶσαι καλαί, πᾶσαι μουσικαί. καὶ μιᾶς τούτων θυγάτηρ Ἠχὼ γίνεται, θνητὴ μὲν ἐκ πατρὸς θνητοῦ, καλὴ δὲ ἐκ μητρὸς καλῆς. Immediately after this the profession and musical ability of the maiden are given: μὲν ὑπὸ Νυμφῶν, παιδεύεται δὲ ὑπὸ Μουσῶν συρίττειν, αὐλεῖν, τὰ πρὸς λύραν, τὰ πρὸς κιθάραν, πᾶσαν ᾠδήν. The profession of Echo is different; she is a musician and not a shepherdess. The introduction of the divine and of the lover and the rejection of the lover are included in the line ὁ Πὰν ὀργίζεται τῇ κόρῃ, τῆς μουσικῆς φθονῶν, τοῦ κάλλους μὴ τυχών. Although there is no distinct prayer for help there is divine aid: τὰ μέλη <ἡ> Γῆ χαριζομένη Νύμφαις ἔκρυψε πάντα καὶ ἐτήρησε τὴν μουσικήν. The last element, the metamorphosis, is described as: <ἃ> γνώμῃ Μουσῶν ἀφίησι φωνὴν καὶ μιμεῖται πάντα, καθάπερ τότε ἡ κόρη, θεούς, ἀνθρώπους, ὄργανα, θηρία. μιμεῖται καὶ αὐτὸν συρίττοντα τὸν Πᾶνα. ὁ δὲ ἀκούσας ἀναπηδᾷ καὶ διώκει κατὰ τῶν ὀρῶν, οὐκ ἐρῶν τυχεῖν ἀλλ᾽ ἢ τοῦ μαθεῖν, τίς ἐστιν ὁ λανθάνων μιμητής.

Longus calls special attention to the metamorphosis of Echo because the version that he gives does not appear in any other extant source.[33] This may mean that the story has some sort of deeper meaning than the obvious attempt of Daphnis to explain the echo. Longus includes among the genealogical identification of Echo three types of nymphs: Μελίαι καὶ Δρυάδες καὶ Ἕλειοι. The Μελίαι are, according to Hesiod (*Theog.* 182–85), nymphs born from the blood of Uranus. The Δρυάδες are tree-nymphs, whom Ovid includes in stories that tell the story of Echo or describe the dismemberment of mythological characters. For example, in the third book of the *Metamorphoses* the Dryades and other assorted nymphs lament the death of Narcissus (3.505–7). In the sixth book (451–54) Ovid compares Philomela to the Dryades; Philomela, of course, is a member of a family that will suffer from the disfiguring of Philomela and the dismemberment of Itys.[34] In the eleventh book (11.49) Ovid writes that the wild beasts of the forest, the flinty rocks, the trees, the rivers, and the naides et dryades mourned the dismembered Orpheus.

The Ἕλειοι are also included in Daphnis's list. There is a problem, however, with the identification of these nymphs because they are not mentioned in any other extant ancient literature.[35] ἡ Ἐλεία, however, a title of Artemis in Cos and epithet, may help clarify the inclusion of the names of the nymphs at the outset of the myth of Echo (cf. Schwyzer 1923, 251). The first two sets of nymphs are associated with myths that are particularly bloody and gruesome. The Meliai were born from the blood of the castrated genitals of Uranus; the Meliai, therefore, are suitably included in Daphnis's account because he had just learned from Lycaenium erotic skills that would cause blood to flow from Chloe's genitals. More importantly, the violence done to Uranus foreshadows the violence that Echo will suffer. The Dryades are also associated with myths that deal with blood and violence, in particular the rending of flesh. The sparagmos of Orpheus, therefore, foreshadows the rending of Echo; Orpheus's eternal musical contribution to the world hints at the musical or audial inheritance Echo will leave to the world: καὶ <ἃ> γνώμῃ Μουσῶν ἀφίησι φωνὴν καὶ μιμεῖται πάντα, καθάπερ τότε ἡ κόρη, θεούς, ἀνθρώπους, ὄργανα, θηρία. μιμεῖται καὶ αὐτὸν συρίττοντα τὸν Πᾶνα. The epithet of Artemis reinforces and reminds the reader of the fact that Chloe, just like all of the maidens in the aitia, is a virgin, like Artemis, but will undergo some sort of violence.

The first three aitia of the novel deal with metamorphosis and foreshadows the aition or metamorphosis of Chloe's womanhood. They also imply an antithesis of innocence and virginity in their violence and sex, about which it has been said that "the increasing savagery of the three stories foreshadows the loss of Chloe's virginity" (Hunter 1983, 54). The story of Chloe also shares some of the ten structural components found in the three aitia. (1) The questioning that introduces the myth is Longus's searching out of an exegete of the painting he saw while hunting in Lesbos: ἀναζητησάμενος ἐξηγητὴν τῆς εἰκόνος (Preface). (2) The identification of the maiden occurs when Dryas follows a sheep into a cave, where he finds it suckling a baby girl: θῆλυ ἦν τοῦτο τὸ παιδίον (1.5). (3) The profession of the maiden is given when her father dreams that Eros commands that Dryas's daughter should tend Eros's flock: κελεῦσαι λοιπὸν ποιμαίνειν . . . τὴν δὲ τὸ ποίμιον (I.7). (4) The musical ability of Chloe is mentioned many times, but the first time it is mentioned is when she attempts to imitate Daphnis's beauty, which she thought emanated from the beautiful music he produced with his syrinx: καὶ ἐδόκει καλὸς αὐτῇ συρίττων πάλιν, καὶ αὖθις αἰτίαν ἐνόμιζε τὴν μουσικὴν τοῦ κάλλους, ὥστε μετ᾽ ἐκεῖνον καὶ αὐτὴ τὴν σύριγγα ἔλαβεν, εἴ πως γένοιτο καὶ αὐτὴ καλή (1.13). (5) The divine is not introduced into the novel at any one particular point, for it appears many times, in many forms, and in many ways: Eros appears in a dream and in Philetas's story within a story; nymphs in pictures, dreams, caves; Pan in dreams and myths. (6) The introduction of the lover occurs in the myth of Chloe before the introduction of Chloe herself: Ἐν τῷδε τῷ ἀγρῷ νέμων αἰπόλος Λάμων τοὔνομα, παιδίον εὗρεν ὑπὸ μιᾶς αἰγῶν τρεφόμενον (1.2). (7) The refusal of the lover comes at the end of Book 3 not as an actual fleeing, but rather as metaphor. Daphnis has acquired his erotic arts and has been promised Chloe's hand in marriage, but Chloe refuses to have sex.

There stood one apple-tree that had all its apples pulled; all the boughs were now bare, and they had neither fruit nor leaves, but only there was one apple that swung upon the very top of the spire of the tree; a great one it was and very beautiful, and such as by its rare and rich smell would alone outdo many together. It should seem that he that gathered the rest was afraid to climb so high, or cared not to come by it. And peradventure that excellent apple was reserved for a shepherd that was in love. When Daphnis saw it, he mantled to be at it, and was even wild to climb the tree, nor would he hear Chloe forbidding him. But she, perceiving her interdictions neglected, made in anger towards the flocks.

The elements of prayer for divine aid are found throughout the novel, for example, the prayer of Daphnis for rescue from the Methymnaeans (2.24). The prayer for help is answered by Pan, who warned the captain of the Methymnaeans to let Chloe go because he wanted παρθένον ἐξ ἧς Ἔρως μῦθον ποιῆσαι (2.27). The loss of Chloe's virginity or her metamorphosis from maiden into a sexual adult may appear to be the last structural element. It is not. The metamorphosis which with Chloe should be primarily associated is the overall metamorphosis that has occurred in the novel: Chloe has gone from being one of the παιδία ἐκκείμενα in the preface to being the subject of the overall myth of the novel.

LONGUS AND THUCYDIDES: A NEW INTERPRETATION

1. Ἐν Λέσβῳ θηρῶν ἐν ἄλσει Νυμφῶν θέαμα εἶδον κάλλιστον ὧν εἶδον· εἰκόνος γραφήν, ἱστορίαν ἔρωτος. Καλὸν μὲν καὶ τὸ ἄλσος, πολύδενδρον, ἀνθηρόν, κατάρρυτον· μία πηγὴ πάντα ἔτρεφε, καὶ τὰ ἄνθη καὶ τὰ δένδρα· ἀλλ' ἡ γραφὴ τερπνοτέρα καὶ τέχνην ἔχουσα περιττὴν καὶ τύχην ἐρωτικήν· ὥστε πολλοὶ καὶ τῶν ξένων κατὰ φήμην ᾔεσαν, τῶν μὲν Νυμφῶν ἱκέται, τῆς δὲ εἰκόνος θεαταί. 2. Γυναῖκες ἐπ' αὐτῆς τίκτουσαι καὶ ἄλλαι σπαργάνοις κοσμοῦσαι, παιδία ἐκκείμενα, ποίμνια τρέφοντα, ποιμένες ἀναιρούμενοι, νέοι συντιθέμενοι, λῃστῶν καταδρομή, πολεμίων ἐμβολή. Πολλὰ ἄλλα καὶ πάντα ἐρωτικὰ ἰδόντα με καὶ θαυμάσαντα πόθος ἔσχεν ἀντιγράψαι τῇ γραφῇ. 3. Καὶ ἀναζητησάμενος ἐξηγητὴν τῆς εἰκόνος τέτταρας βίβλους ἐξεπονησάμην, ἀνάθημα μὲν Ἔρωτι καὶ Νύμφαις καὶ Πανί, κτῆμα δὲ τερπνὸν πᾶσιν ἀνθρώποις, ὃ καὶ νοσοῦντα ἰάσεται, καὶ λυπούμενον παραμυθήσεται, τὸν ἐρασθέ-

ντα ἀναμνήσει, τὸν οὐκ ἐρασθέντα προπαιδεύσει. 4. Πάντως γὰρ
οὐδεὶς ἔρωτα ἔφυγεν ἢ φεύξεται, μέχρις ἂν κάλλος ᾖ καὶ ὀφθαλμοὶ
βλέπωσιν. Ἡμῖν δ' ὁ θεὸς παράσχοι σωφρονοῦσι τὰ τῶν ἄλλων
γράφειν. (Prooemium to *Daphnis and Chloe*)[36]

Many scholars view the allusion to Thucydides' archaeologia in
Longus's prooemium as one of many learned references in the text.[37] I
think that Longus intends more than a show of erudition. I suggest that by
recalling the historian, Longus not only stays within the tradition of
opening a novel historiographically,[38] but also demonstrates that even
though conversant with historiography he will not be writing a historical
account. Instead he uses history to help him alter the genre. Proof of this
modification appears in the second and third books of the novel when
Longus renders τερπνότερα, the serious Thucydidean account dealing
with Mytilene and Methymna.[39] Precedents for novel historiographical
introductions are found in *Chaereas and Callirhoe* and in the *Ephesiaca*.[40]
Chariton writes: Χαρίτων Ἀφροδισιεύς, Ἀθηναγόρου τοῦ ῥήτορος
ὑπογραφεύς, πάθος ἐρωτικὸν ἐν Συρρακούσαις γενόμενον διηγήσομαι
(1.1.1). He identifies himself and his place of origin and says that he will
relate an amorous account.[41] In the opening to *Ephesiaca* Xenophon
Ephesius writes: Ἦν ἐν Ἐφέσῳ ἀνὴρ τῶν τὰ πρῶτα ἐκεῖ δυναμένων,
Λυκομήδης ὄνομα. τούτῳ τῷ Λυκομήδει ἐκ γυναικὸς ἐπιχωρίας Θεμι-
στοῦς γίνεται παῖς Ἁβροκόμης (1.1).[42] He does not identify himself but
gives the parentage of the novel's hero. Although this may not seem to
reflect historiography, it does parallel the opening of a historical text:
Δαρείου καὶ Παρυσάτιδος γίγνονται παῖδες δύο μὲν Ἀρταξέρξης,
νεώτερος δὲ Κῦρος (*An*. 1.1). Xenophon Ephesius imitates his namesake
by giving the names of the hero's parents and by echoing γίγνονται
παῖδες with γίνεται παῖς.

Just as Chariton echoes the opening lines of histories and Xenophon
reflects the work of his namesake, Longus pays homage to his literary
predecessors. He does not start his work with the expected "I am X, hail
from Y, and shall write about Z." Instead he comments that he will be
writing (presumably his novel) in response to a picture he saw while
hunting in Lesbos. He writes that the document is a κτῆμα τερπνὸν πᾶσιν
ἀνθρώποις (*pr*. 3).

Longus's juxtaposition of κτῆμα and τερπνὸν has caused scholars to ask
if and why Longus alludes to the archaeologia of Thucydides (in particular 1.22.4). Several answers have been suggested: Turner (1960, 118)

proposes that Longus wants to reveal that he has a serious purpose in mind, a purpose as serious as that of Thucydides, which is to make "people understand human life" by producing "something of universal significance ('a possession for all men')." He sees the inclusion of myth as facilitating the conveyance of the novel's purpose to the reader. For Turner the aim of this book is didactic in nature and serves as a guide for the eventual maturation of the reader. The reader should be able to integrate harmoniously life's events, some of which can be disturbing and most of which are common to all, by reading the story of Daphnis and Chloe. Longus's plan, therefore, correlates to Thucydides' goal of providing a source through which people can predict the future by understanding and examining past human behavior.

McCulloh (1970, 31) views the reference to the historian as "external validation through association with historiography." He continues: Longus repeats the key word "possession," reverses the role of delight, keeps the instructional utility of the past for the future, and adapts the justificatory principle of the perennial and universal recurrence of the subject chosen for analysis (32). Hunter interprets (1983, 49), correctly so, the literary echoes as Longus affiliating himself with Herodotus: by stressing the element τὸ τερπνόν within an allusion to Thucydides, Longus aligns his work with that of Herodotus, whom ancient scholars saw as the object of Thucydides' attack in 1.22.

MacQueen (1990, 64 and 158) suggests that the Thucydidean terminology in the prooemium is intrusive in nature: the framework of the novel is pastoral and the historical breaks the "frame of reference." Longus's approach to "serious historiography" is continued in the first passages of the novel proper, but, MacQueen warns, "Longus invites us to think about history but will not allow us to mistake what we are reading for history."

Thucydides writes that in his work τὸ μυθῶδες is excluded, and that perhaps as a result the work will be less pleasing to its audience. He also prefers to write a κτῆμα ἐς αἰεί rather than something that will be momentarily pleasing. Finally, the historian proceeds to the causes for the outbreak of the war between the Greek city-states. In the narrative, therefore, Thucydides goes from the fabulous, τό μυθῶδες, and what leads to it, to a work of true worth, κτῆμα ἐς αἰεί, and ends up with the causes of the Peloponnesian War. The outline may then be formulated as myth-intrinsic worth-cause (history).

Longus reverses this progression. He begins by writing that he has seen, εἶδον (*pr.* 1), a picture that told a story. Longus uses the term ἱστορία for the content of the painting⁴³ and clarifies the term by writing that he will tell his readers the stories (myths) found in the painting and dedicate them to the mythological characters of Eros, Pan, and nymphs. It is the specific insertion of the word ἱστορία that makes clear Longus's approach: he wants to make the factual in his novel resemble myth and thereby distances himself from Thucydidean stylistics.

Before the dedication of the work, however, Longus declares that his work is more than just a literary exercise: κτῆμα δὲ τερπνὸν πᾶσιν ἀνθρώποις, ὃ καὶ νοσοῦντα ἰάσεται καὶ λυπούμενον (*pr.* 3). The novelist then proceeds to relate the myth of Daphnis and Chloe. Longus's outline, therefore, is cause (history)-intrinsic worth-myth, a modified reversal of Thucydides.⁴⁴

In order to make sure that the reader understands that he is using historiographical elements, Longus also reports on what must be done in order to write history or to research the necessary material. The method consists of seeing (εἶδον) or having firsthand experience of the data; in this case it is the γραφήν (*pr.* 1) that tells the lovers' ἱστορία, or ἔργα.⁴⁵ A written response (ἀντιγράψαι, *pr.* 2) should then be produced. If firsthand experience of the subject matter cannot be attained, secondhand knowledge must be sought (ἀναζητησάμενος, *pr.* 3), such as reports (φήμην, *pr.* 1). The finished product should be written down (γράφειν) in some form (βίβλους, *pr.* 3). Longus also notes that this is not easy work (ἐξεπονησάμην).⁴⁶

Longus continues his narrative by including immediately after the prooemium more Thucydidean echoes: Πόλις ἐστι τῆς Λέσβου Μιτυλήνη, μεγάλη καὶ καλή· διείληπται γὰρ εὐρίποις ὑπεισρεούσης τῆς θαλάσσης, καὶ κεκόσμηται γεφύραις ξεστοῦ καὶ λευκοῦ λίθου. Νομίσαις οὐ πόλιν ὁρᾶν ἀλλὰ νῆσον. Ἀλλὰ ἦν ταύτης τῆς πόλεως Μιτυλήνης ὅσον ἀπὸ σταδίων διακοσίων ἀγρὸς ἀνδρὸς εὐδαίμονος, κτῆμα κάλλιστον (1.1–2).⁴⁷ Longus seems compelled to call attention to the word κτῆμα. He already used it in the prooemium and made clear that his "possession" would be one that was "a pleasing possession for all men," in contrast to the κτῆμα⁴⁸ found in Thucydides. In addition to the use of κτῆμα, Longus further emphasizes the connection with the historian by mentioning Mytilene. The purpose of these additional allusions needs to be explained. I suggest that Longus wants to apply his reversal of the Thucydidean progression to the account (3.1–50) of Mytilene's revolt from Athens and its war with Methymna. Longus, in other words, will change the serious tone of the historical conflict into something τερπνοτέρα in the novel's account of the skirmish between Methymna and Mytilene.

Since it has been established that Longus employs Thucydidean phraseology in his prooemium, I shall now comment on some of the allusions (some direct borrowings) to Thucydides in order to show that it is the Mytilenean-Methymnaean narrative that Longus wishes to transform:[49]

(1) L † 1.22.1: ὁ μὲν κινδύνου παρὰ τοσοῦτον ἐλθὼν

T 3.49.4: παρὰ τοσοῦτον μὲν ἡ Μυτιλήνη ἦλθε κινδύνου:

In L 1.22.1 Longus relates Dorcon's escape from the dogs with the help of Chloe and his rival, Daphnis, while T 3.49.4 tells of the rescue of Mytilene by the second trireme dispatched by Diodotus. There seems to be no parallel between the two narratives, except perhaps that destruction is averted by rivals in the nick of time. In †2.19.1 there is a similar echo, τότε μὲν δὴ παρὰ τοσοῦτον Δάφνις ἦλθε κακοῦ; in the passages leading up to this line the villagers rescue Daphnis from the Methymnaeans. In addition to T 3.49.4, this phraseology also appears in √ T 7.2.4: παρὰ τοσοῦτον μὲν Συράκουσαι ἦλθον κινδύνου; once again, the theme of averting destruction is present.

(2) L *2.14.1: κλυδώνιον

T 2.84.3: κλύδωνι:[50]

In 2.14.1 Longus writes that a wave caused by the wind blowing (κινηθέντος . . . τοῦ πνεύματος) from the mountains pushed the boat into the open sea. In 2.84.3 Thucydides explains that it was a wind (ὡς δὲ τό τε πνεῦμα κατήει) that caused the heavy seas that made Phormio signal his ships to attack. Although troubled seas caused by the wind are a a common occurrence, nevertheless a parallel exists.

(3) αὐτερέταις (L *2.20.1) may allude to αὐτερέται (T 1.10.4, 3.18.4)

when combined with ἐπέπλει τοῖς (L *2.20.1); this combination occurs in numerous places in Thucydides.[51] There are also instances where there may be possible echoes (most dealing with military action of some sort).[52]

In *Daphnis and Chloe* the military narrative pertaining to the war between Mytilene and Methymna is limited to 2.12.1–3.3.1.,[53] and the majority of the words that are Thucydidean in nature appear in this section of the novel. Moreover, ἀδεῶς ἐπιμίγνυσθαι καὶ κατὰ γῆν κατὰ θάλασσαν in *3.2.3 confirms that Longus had Thucydides in mind (the line from Thucydides reads οὐ᾿ δ᾿ ἐπιμιγνύντες ἀδεῶς ἀλλήλοις οὔτε κατὰ γῆν οὔτε διὰ θαλάσσης [1.2.2]). Since it is clear that Longus verbally echoes Thucydides, I would like to suggest that Longus had Thucydides' text as a model for his narrative of the Lesbian conflict. Longus, however, transforms this well-known episode of the Peloponnesian War in his novel.

Thucydides writes that Mytilene, along with all of Lesbos, with the exception of Methymna, rebelled from Athens because they feared the abuse of Athenian power: οὐ γὰρ εἰκὸς ἦν αὐτοὺς οὓς μὲν μεθ᾿ ἡμῶν ἐσπόνδους ἐποιήσαντο καταστρέψασθαι, τοὺς δὲ ὑπολοίπους, εἴ ποτε ἄρα δυνηθεῖεν, μὴ δρᾶσαι τοῦτο (3.10.6).[54] No such grandiose justification is given in the novel for the military action between the two Lesbian cities. Rather, the cause of hostilities between the cities finds its origin in a Methymnaean hunting trip on Mytilenean land (2.12–3.2). The hunters suffer the loss of their ship, because the vine that they used to fasten the ship to the shore was eaten by a goat. As retaliation they beat Daphnis, and consequently some of Daphnis's compatriots attempt to help him. All participants end up giving their accounts of the event to an arbiter, who finds in favor of Daphnis; the Methymnaeans seek recourse in their own town.

This quasi-judicial episode in the novel parallels the famous policy debate between Cleon and Diodotus in Thucydides 3.37–48. It may be argued that Longus does not recall the debate between Cleon and Diodotus in the trial scene in the second book. If the general premise is accepted that Longus is altering Thucydides by including the mythical in his novel and producing a work that will serve to instruct and at the same time please the audience, it should be agreed that Longus modifies the debate on Mytilene. Evidence of this is the οἶκτος at 3.17.1 (τούτοις ἐπεδάκρυσεν ὁ Δάφνις καὶ εἰς οἶκτον ὑπηγάγετο τοὺς ἀγροίκους πολύν), which Longus writes after Daphnis has finished his defense. It is οἶκτος, compassion, which moves Philetas to invoke Pan and nymphs to witness that Daphnis is blameless. Thucydides, conversely, has Cleon warn the Athenians not to yield to pity (ἢ οἴκτῳ ἐνδῶτε, 3.37.2) or to make a mistake on account of pity (μηδὲ . . . οἴκτῳ . . . ἁμαρτάνειν, 3.40.2–3). Diodotus also employs this word when he argues against Cleon (μήτε οἴκτῳ πλέον νείμαντες, 3.48.1). It is compassion, however, that moves Philetas to call upon the gods (the mythological) and thereby changes the serious tone of Thucydides. The historical narrative continues with the Athenians sending out a second ship to rescind the first decree and concludes with the line παρὰ τοσοῦτον μὲν ἡ Μυτιλήνη ἦλθε κινδύνου (3.49.4), which is the basis for Longus's τότε μὲν δὴ παρὰ τοσοῦτον Δάφνις ἦλθε κακοῦ (2.19.1).

In keeping with Longus's transposed historical technique, the novel modifies the tenor of Thucydides' serious and important account. There is no real justification for the outbreak of hostilities in the novel. It may be said that the Methymnaeans, angered by the verdict favorable to Daphnis, did lose a great amount of money with the loss of their ship. The simplicity of the resolution of the skirmish, however, demonstrates that the war could not have been that important:

> Τὸν μὲν οὖν κήρυκα τοῖς Μυτιληναίοις ὁ Ἵππασος ἀποστέλλει, καίτοιγε αὐτοκράτωρ στρατηγὸς κεχειροτονημένος, αὐτὸς δὲ τῆς Μηθύμνης ὅσον ἀπὸ δέκα σταδίων στρατόπεδον βαλόμενος τὰς ἐκ τῆς πόλεως ἐντολὰς ἀνέμενε. καὶ δύο διαγενομένων ἡμερῶν ἐλθὼν ὁ ἄγγελος τήν τε ἁρπαγὴν ἐκέλευσε κομίσασθαι καὶ ἀδικήσαντα μηδὲν ἀναχωρεῖν οἴκαδε. πολέμου γὰρ καὶ εἰρήνης ἐν αἱρέσει γενόμενοι τὴν εἰρήνην εὑρίσκειν κερδαλεωτέραν. ὁ μὲν δὴ Μηθυμαίνων καὶ Μυτιληναίων πόλεμος ἀδόκητον λαβὼν ἀρχὴν καὶ τέλος οὕτω διελύθη. (3.2.4–3.3.1)[55]

If the conflict had been on the scale of the war in Thucydides' history, more than a simple diplomatic solution would have been necessary.

In the opening of the third book Longus concludes his account of the skirmish, and it seems that he wants to drive home the point that he is reworking Thucydides. Longus does so by including in 3.1.1–3.3.1 an abundance of historical and military terminology: ἐπίπλουν, νεῶν, ἁρπαγὴν, ὅπλα κινεῖν, καταλέξαντες ἀσπίδα τρισχιλίαν καὶ ἵππον πεντακοσίαν, στρατηγὸν, ἐξορμηθεὶς, ὡς ἐπεισπεσούμενος ἀφρουρήτοις ταῖς πύλαις, σταδίους, κῆρυξ ἀπαντᾷ σπονδὰς κομίζων, αὐτοκράτωρ στρατηγός, σταδίων, στρατόπεδον, ἄγγελος, πολέμου, κτλ. The militaristic tone set by these words and phrases, however, is changed by the simplistic resolution offered by Longus.

Longus adapts the historical account in the following manner. First, he takes a serious and weighty historical episode and reverses its somber tenor by reducing it in the novel to a squabble over a lost ship. Second, he interjects into the military narrative the mythological figures and stories of the nymphs, Syrinx, and the god Pan. The insertion of the episode involving Pan is a clear reference and reverse correlation to the τὸ μυθῶδες of the archaeologia. In his epiphany to Bryaxis Pan declares ἀπεσπάσατε δὲ βωμῶν παρθένον ἐξ ἧς Ἔρως μῦθον ποιῆσαι θέλει (2.27.2), which is specifically what Thucydides wants to avoid in his history. Thucydides does not want to include the mythical lest he run the risk of making his work an ἱστορία τερπνοτέρα, as Herodotus, the object of the attack in the archaeologia, had done (specifically in his account of Pan's epiphany to Pheidippides [Hdt. 6.105]).

Turner (1960, 117) writes that Longus is a "highly conscious artist with clear ideas about the purpose of his art, and he has left us a preface explaining them—or rather hinting at them, for the full meaning of his words is not immediately apparent." Indeed the "full meaning" of the prooemium is not apparent until one realizes that Longus is playing an intertextual game. The reader must understand that by alluding to Thucydides Longus transforms the historian's approach to writing history, orients his work to the "pleasing" nature of Herodotus's writing style, and therefore composes a work that is both a κτῆμα τερπνὸν πᾶσιν ἀνθρώποις and a κτῆμα ἐς αἰεί.[56]

4

Thematic Myths, Pan, and Achilles Tatius

Achilles Tatius was thought to have composed his *Leucippe and Clitophon* as late as the fifth century A.D., papyri assure a middle- to late-second-century A.D. date (Perry 1967, 348 n. 12). The first papyrus fragment to be published was Oxyrynchus papyrus no. 1250, which is dated to the early fourth century. After more scholarly analysis, the novel was then dated to the third, and afterward to the late second century (Sinko 1940–46, 40f.). A papyrus at Milan firmly establishes the composition date to the second century A.D. (Vogliano 1938).

Although Longus is somewhat anomalous in respect of his predecessors, in his novel the change from a historical background to a mythological and romantic background is nevertheless apparent. The mythological and romantic elements in *Daphnis and Chloe* take precedence over quasi-historical information, and if historical data are supplied, the inclusion of such information can be attributed to the actuality that no author can completely separate himself from contemporary social circumstances. Longus removes all realistic elements from the world in which he sets his novel, thereby creating a utopian world: an Arcadian Lesbos that traces its lineage to the idyllic and pastoral world of Theocritus. The two novelists who write after Longus, Achilles Tatius (hereafter Tatius) and Heliodorus, do not duplicate the utopian and comprehensively mythological design of *Daphnis and*

Chloe.¹ Instead they place their characters and stories in a more realistic (not historical) world, incorporating myth, however, for the development of the characters and plots.²

In this chapter I shall not identify characters with mythological figures, since that has already been done, but shall attempt to demonstrate that myth or mythical allusion directs the action of each book and consequently the plot of the novel. Although Tatius includes numerous references to mythological beings and animals in the first book,³ he nevertheless imparts historical qualities to the beginning of his novel.⁴ He writes: Σιδὼν ἐπὶ θαλάσσῃ πόλις· Ἀσσυρίων ἡ θάλασσα· μήτηρ Φοινίκων ἡ πόλις· Θηβαίων ὁ δῆμος πατήρ (1.1.1).⁵ Tatius then proceeds to supply a description of a painting located in the temple of Astarte in Sidon: Εὐρώπης ἡ γραφή· Φοινίκων ἡ θάλασσα· Σιδῶνος ἡ γῆ. ἐν τῇ λειμὼν καὶ χορὸς παρθένων. ἐν τῇ θαλάσσῃ ταῦρος ἐπενήχετο, καὶ τοῖς νώτοις καλὴ παρθένος ἐπεκθητο, ἐπὶ Κρήτην τῷ ταύρῳ πλέουσα (1.1.2–3).⁶

The narrator then enters into a dialogue with a young man who is admiring the painting and tells the narrator that he suffered something similar to the story told in the painting. His story, the young man says, may seem to be mythological, but it is really true (εἰ καὶ μύθοις ἔοικε [1.2.2–3]). The young man then narrates his adventure: the love story of Leucippe and Clitophon.⁷

The historical qualities of the opening sections of the novel are based on Herodotus, much in the way Longus uses Thucydides. Tatius starts his novel with the abduction of a woman (Europa), which is the same motif (Io) used by Herodotus to begin his history. Herodotus writes that the Phoenicians were to blame for the troubles between the Greeks and the Persians because they stole Io, the daughter of Inachus, and in turn the Greeks, probably Cretans, carried off Europa, the daughter of the king of Tyre. Accordingly, similar elements in both narratives cause the plot to unfold. In both works Europa is stolen, Crete and Phoenicia are mentioned, and the action is centered in or around Sidon and Tyre.

Book 1: Eros plays a very important role in the novel, particularly in book 1.⁸ Tatius relates in 1.1.13 that in the painting there are *erotes* leading the bull, which hints at the possibility that Eros is responsible for the abduction of Europa: he is responsible for the amorous adventures the characters of the novel will undergo. In fact, he is to blame, because he makes the leading characters fall in love. Thus Eros and myths dealing with love, whether fortunate or unfortunate, will dictate the action in the first book of the novel.⁹

The erotic myths in this book can be divided into two groups: those having fortunate or unfortunate outcomes. For example, Tatius's inclusion of the myth of Apollo's one-sided, ill-fated love affair with Daphne (1.5.5 and 1.8.2) is followed by some lines from Hesiod: Τοῖς δ' ἐγὼ ἀντὶ πυρὸς δώσω κακόν, ᾧ κεν ἅπαντες / τέρπωνται κατὰ θυμόν, ἑὸν κακὸν ἀμφαγαπῶντες (Works and Days 57–8).[10] They foreshadow the numerous ill-fated or treacherous love stories and myths that Tatius will relate. First mentioned are the Sirens, the bird-headed females who cause men to fall in love with their voices but also bring about their doom.[11] Tatius includes the husband-killer and filicide Eriphyle to foreshadow Clitophon's infidelity, which is also insinuated in the myth of Philomela, and later in the inclusion of Procne's name. The myth of Stheneboea seems to have been inserted in order to illustrate what Clitophon should do; that is, he should imitate Bellerophon and not surrender to sexual temptation. The story of Aerope probably indicates that Leucippe, like the daughter of Catreus, will be sold in a foreign land. The rest of the alluded to myths—those of Agamemnon, Chryseis, Achilles, Briseis, Helen, Penelope, Phaedra, Hippolytus, and Clytemnestra—give witness to the certainty that Leucippe's and Clitophon's amorous adventures will not have smooth sailing.

In his listing of exempla, Tatius is closely following literary tradition, such as that found in Ovid, Ars Am. 2.373ff. and Juvenal 6.643ff. Ovid exonerates Helen and blames her husband, pities Medea and condemns Jason, and understands that Procne killed her own son because she had to avenge herself and her sister. Ovid also writes that so long as Agamemnon was faithful, Clytemnestra was chaste, but when she heard about his dalliances with Chryseis, Briseis, and Cassandra, she invited Thyestes' son to her bed. Juvenal lists Medea, Procne, the Belidae, Eriphyle, and Clytemnestra as wicked women whom men should avoid. These examples of female exempla show that Tatius is following an established literary tradition of giving caveats about women through female archetypes and their myths. The novelist, however, aside from using the myths to lend structure to his plot, also includes in his list a semimythical character: Candaules. By incorporating the king of Lydia the novelist is not only giving a new slant to the exercise, but may also be acknowledging his debt to Herodotus's work, where he found the impetus for his own narrative.

In the middle of the first chapter (1.10–12) Tatius once again invokes the figure of Eros, as he had previously done,[12] and places him in a philosophical setting.[13] To demonstrate fully the faculties of Eros, Tatius alludes to the myth of Aurora in the description of the garden, where Clitophon makes his first amorous advances toward Leucippe (1.15.8). In the garden, the narrator says, there are flowers, vegetation, and fauna of all different types; the creatures in the garden are of particular interest because the cicadas sing of Aurora and her marriage-bed, while the swallows sing of the banquet of Tereus.

The power of Eros over humans, plants, animals, vegetation, and even bodies of water is also made clear at the end of book 1. After Clitophon has insinuated to Leucippe, by way of exempla, that he has some sort of erotic feelings for her, Satyrus,[14] a slave of Clitophon whose name is appropriate for the bosky environment, adds his own exempla to those of his master. He discloses that Eros has dominion not only over birds, but also over snakes, plants (palms), stones, and even bodies of water:

Γίνεται δὲ καὶ γάμος ἄλλος ὑδάτων διαπόντιος. καὶ ἔστιν ὁ μὲν ἐραστὴς ποταμὸς Ἠλεῖος, ἡ δὲ ἐρωμένη κρήνη Σικελική. διὰ γὰρ τῆς θαλάσσης ὁ ποταμὸς ὡς διὰ πεδίου τρέχει. ἡ δὲ οὐκ ἀφανίζει γλυκὺν ἐραστὴν ἁλμυρῷ κύματι, σχίζεται δὲ αὐτῷ ῥέοντι, καὶ τὸ σχίσμα τῆς θαλάσσης χαράδρα τῷ ποταμῷ γίνεται· καὶ ἐπὶ τὴν Ἀρέθουσαν οὕτω τὸν Ἀλφειὸν νυμφοστολεῖ. ὅταν οὖν ᾖ <ἡ> τῶν Ὀλυμπίων ἑορτή, πολλοὶ μὲν εἰς τὰς δίνας τοῦ ποταμοῦ καθιᾶσιν ἄλλος ἄλλα δῶρα. ὁ δὲ εὐθὺς πρὸς τὴν ἐρωμένην κομίζει, καὶ ταῦτά ἐστιν ἔδνα ποταμοῦ. (1.18.1–2)[15]

The Arcadian myth of Alpheus and Arethusa, which involves traveling over bodies of water and the gift-giving of the sea to those in love, foreshadows one of the more gruesome episodes in the novel.

This gruesome episode is in book 5, where Chaereas and some ne'er-do-wells have kidnapped Leucippe and are trying to escape with their booty while Clitophon is in hot pursuit. In order to stop the pursuit, the kidnappers behead Leucippe (her second *Scheintod*) and dump only her body into the sea while presumably keeping the head on board the ship. Clitophon begs that the ship be stopped and the body be picked up. Once the body is on board Clitophon cries out: Νῦν μοι, Λευκίππη, τέθνηκας ἀληθῶς θάνατον διπλοῦν, γῇ καὶ θαλάσσῃ διαιρούμενον· τὸ μὲν γὰρ λείψανον ἔχω σου τοῦ σώματος, ἀπολώλεκα δὲ σέ. οὐκ ἴση τῆς θαλάσσης πρὸς τὴν γῆν ἡ νομή· μικρόν μοί σου μέρος καταλέλειπται ἐν ὄψει τοῦ μείζονος· αὕτη δὲ ἐν ὀλίῳ τὸ πᾶν σου κρατεῖ. ἀλλ᾽ ἐπεί μοι τῶν ἐν τῷ προσώπῳ φιλημάτων ἐφθόνησεν ἡ Τύχη, φέρε σου καταφιλήσω τὴν σφαγήν (5.7.8–9).[16] The sea presents as a final gift to Clitophon the partial remains of Leucippe.

Book 1 has Eros and the myths associated with him dictating the overall structure of the book and of the novel. He is the prime mover of the novel and causes the adventures and misadventures that the hero and heroine undergo. The other myths in this book are supplied in order to show what types of infidelities will occur and what the proper comportment of Clitophon should be. Some of the myths even point to what will occur in the forthcoming books. Eros is the prominent divinity in this book, but by the end of it a new divinity, Pan, starts to gain in significance. Although Pan is alluded to only twice, in the form of the slave Satyrus and in the myths that deal with Arcadia, he will eventually become the principal god with whom most of the myths are associated.

Book 2 begins with Leucippe singing line 16.823 of the *Iliad*. Once she has finished her performance all retire to dinner, where various aitia of wine are put forth:

ἦν γὰρ ἑορτὴ προτρυγαίου Διονύσου τότε. τὸν γὰρ Διόνυσον Τύριοι νομίζουσιν ἑαυτῶν, ἐπεὶ καὶ τὸν Κάδμου μῦθον ᾄδουσι. καὶ τῆς ἑορτῆς διηγοῦνται πατέρα μῦθον, οἶνον οὐκ εἶναί ποτε παρ᾽ ἀνθρώποις ὅπου μήπω παρ᾽ αὐτοῖς, οὐ τὸν μέλανα τὸν ἀνθοσμίαν, οὐ τὸν τῆς Βιβλίας ἀμπέλου, οὐ τὸν Μάρωνος τὸν Θράκιον, οὐ Χῖον ἐκ Λακαίνης, οὐ τὸν Ἰκάρου τὸν νησιώτην, ἀλλὰ τούτους μὲν ἅπαντας ἀποίκους εἶναι Τυρίων οἴνων, τὴν δὲ πρώτην παρ᾽ αὐτοῖς φῦναι τῶν μητέρα. (2.2.1–2)[17]

The mention of these four different types of wine is programmatic: the myths associated with each type of wine will dictate what will occur in this book: Eros and wine (Dionysus) will kindle the love affair of Leucippe and Clitophon; Conops, Panthea's slave and Leucippe's guardian, will be beguiled by Satyrus, who employs the same method with which Odysseus fooled Polyphemus; the aition of the discovery of purple dye will be associated, through Athenaeus, with Chian wine; the effects produced by Icarius's wine will parallel the aphrodisiac given in Leucippe in a later book.

In the passage above there are four aitia for wine. The author tells the reader that in the beginning there was no wine (οὐκ εἶναί ποτε παρ᾽ ἀνθρώποις) and then proceeds to mentioned different types: ὅπου μήπω παρ᾽ αὐτοῖς, οὐ τὸν μέλανα τὸν ἀνθοσμίαν, οὐ τὸν τῆς Βιβλίας ἀμπέλου, οὐ τὸν Μάρωνος τὸν Θράκιον, οὐ Χῖον ἐκ Λακαίνης, οὐ τὸν Ἰκάρου τὸν νησιώτην. Tatius finally reveals that all wines are dervied from Tyrian vines: ἀλλὰ τούτους μὲν ἅπαντας ἀποίκους εἶναι Τυρίων οἴνων, τὴν δὲ πρώτην παρ᾽ αὐτοῖς φῦναι τῶν μητέρα.

References to Biblian wine are found in *Works and Days* 587 and in Theocritus 14.15. Hesiod remarks that βίβλιος οἶνος should be drunk when flowers are blooming, cicadas are singing, goats are their fattest, women are most wanton, and men are most feeble. He gives no aition for the origin of this wine but makes it quite clear that this wine should be drunk when everything, especially women, is ripe for the picking. Theocritus has Aeschines, the protagonist of the idyll, declaring his love for a maiden while sharing Biblian wine with said maiden, who does not love him in return (cf. the drinking scene in book 2).

Maron, the priest of Apollo whom Odysseus spared when he destroyed Ismarus and slaughtered its inhabitants, presented wine as a gift to Odysseus, who in turn gave it to the Cyclops. As is well known, the monster got drunk on this wine, thereby allowing Odysseus and his men to blind the creature and to escape. This myth is important, because in the novel the guardian of Leucippe, Conops, is put to sleep by a drink administered to him by Satyrus (2.23). More importantly, this Conops is called Cyclops. Satyrus likewise drugs Conops (2.23.3 and 2.23.27) in order for his master to have an ill-fated sexual escapade with Leucippe, and in order for his master and mistress to escape the wrath of Panthea, Leucippe's mother. Athenaeus relates that the third type of wine (οὐ Χῖον ἐκ Λακαίνης) is of the best kind,[18] and that this line on wine comes from the Aristophanic saying "from a Laconian cup." But it may also be a subtle reference to the *ekphrasis* on the aition of purple dye in 2.11, that is, if Tatius was using either Athenaeus as a source or Athenaeus's source (cf. Gaselee 1969, 59 n. 3). In 2.11 Tatius gives his reader a short account of the discovery of purple dye, which involves a shepherd (or herdsman), a dog, and a seashell; he also specifies that this dye is used to color Aphrodite's robe (2.11.4). Athenaeus, however, does not limit his comments on Chios to the wine that it produces, for he also writes that Alexander the Great ἤθελεν γὰρ τοὺς ἑταίρους ἅπαντας ἀλουργὰς ἐνδῦσαι στολάς. ἀναγνωσθείσης δὲ τῆς ἐπιστολῆς Χίοις παρὼν Θεόκριτος ὁ σοφιστὴς νῦν ἐγνωκέναι ἔφη τὸ παρ᾽ Ὁμήρῳ εἰρημένον· ἔλλαβε πορφύρεος θάνατος καὶ μοῖρα κραταιή (11.540a). The Homeric passage refers to Diomedes, whom Athena had enthused with her power, but more importantly, many polyptotic forms of πορφύρεος are found in the sections dealing with the aition of wine and with the description of Calligone's wedding dress (2.11). The threads connecting Chian wine with the aition of purple dye in 2.11 are very tenuous, but the supposition that Tatius knew that Chios was known for more than its wine cannot be ignored.

The last type of wine included in Tatius's list recalls the unlucky myth of Icarius. He is the luckless soul to whom Dionysus first presented the gift of wine. He, however, gave it in an undiluted state to ignorant Athenian shepherds, who, when they felt the full effects of the wine, thought that Icarius had attempted to poison them.[19] The shepherds sought vengeance on Icarius and beat him to death with clubs. Dionysus, not wanting to let this offense go unpunished, consequently made all the Athenian maidens go mad.

This madness visited upon the Athenian maidens portends the induced madness that Gorgias the Egyptian soldier inflicts upon Leucippe through an aphrodisiac (4.15). The undiluted aphrodisiac that the soldier gives Leucippe, however, is a mistake, just like the misunderstood effects of wine: ἤρα δὲ τῆς σῆς γυναικός. ὢν δὲ φύσει φαρμακεὺς σκευάζει τι φάρμακον ἔρωτος καὶ πείθει τὸν διακονούμενον ὑμῖν Αἰγύπτιον λαβεῖν τὸ φάρμακον καὶ ἐγκαταμεῖξαι τῷ τῆς Λευκίππης ποτῷ. λανθάνει δὲ ἀκράτῳ χρησάμενος τῷ φαρμάκῳ, καὶ τὸ φίλτρον εἰς μανίαν αἴρεται (4.15.3–4).[20] Thus the intended madness in the Athenian maidens has a parallel in the madness caused by the love-philter.

After listing the types of wine, Tatius proceeds to give an Attic account (2.2.3) of the origin of this beverage: Dionysus once visited a herdsman who was very hospitable to him, and in turn the god gave his host a cup of wine. After drinking the wine the herdsman describes its effects, and in response Dionysus shows him what the source of the wine was. The Tyrians use this myth as the justification for celebrating the gift of wine and for thanking Dionysus.

Clitophon's father, in keeping with the mood of the party, brought out a cup, which resembled the famous goblet of Glaucus of Chios, in which to serve the gift of the god (2.3.1). On the goblet were Eros and Dionysus, who symbolize the effects that wine can produce: not only inebriation but also an increase in libido brought on by the alcohol. Clitophon and Leucippe eventually succumb to the power of both Eros and Dionysus.

Tatius includes a few other myths in book 2. He has Clitophon say to Leucippe that he feels as if he has become her slave, just as Heracles became the slave of Omphale (2.6.2–3), which is an ironic statement because Leucippe (as Lacaena) will become his slave. This allusion to Heracles sets the groundwork for the mistaken abduction of Calligone by Callisthenes (2.14–18).

Sostratus, Leucippe's father, in order to win the gods' favor in war and to fulfill an oracle, sends a delegation to make sacrifice in Tyre at the altar of Heracles. This oracle is also found in the *Anthologia Palatina*, with some textual variations. The anthology lemma (14.34) is as follows.

1 Νῆσός τις πόλις ἐστὶ φυτώνυμον αἷμα λαχοῦσα,
2 ἰσθμὸν ὁμοῦ καὶ πορθμὸν ἐπ' ἠπείροιο φέρουσα·
3 ἔνθ' ἀπ' ἐμῆς ἔσθ' αἷμα ὁμοῦ καὶ Κέκροπος αἷμα·
4 ἔνθε Ἥφαιστος ἔχει χαίρει γλαυκῶπιν Ἀθήνην·
5 κεῖθι θυηπολίην πέμπειν κελόμην Ἡρακλεῖ.²¹

The oracle in the second book of the novel (2.14.1) is almost identical to the lemma of the anthology.

1 Νῆσός τις <πόλις> ἐστὶ φυτώνυμον αἷμα λαχοῦσα,
2 ἰσθμὸν ὁμοῦ καὶ πορθμὸν ἐπ' ἠπείροιο φέρουσα,
3 ἔνθε Ἥφαιστος ἔχων χαίρει γλαυκῶπιν Ἀθήνη·
4 κεῖθι θυηπολίην σε φέρειν κέλομαι Ἡρακλεῖ.

The version of the oracle in the novel, however, leaves out πόλις in the first line,²² does not include the third line of the anthology lemma, reads ἔχων instead of ἔχει in the fourth line, and in the fifth line has σε φέρειν κέλομαι instead of πέμπειν κελόμην. The point of this part of this chapter is that the third line of the anthology lemma contributes something to the elaboration and understanding of the novel and perhaps should be restored to the corrupt text of the novel.

At 1.3.4f. Clitophon, who is engaged to his half-sister Calligone, has a dream that causes him some anxiety.

ὄναρ ἐδόκουν συμφῦναι τῇ παρθένῳ τὰ κάτω μέρη μέχρις ὀμφαλοῦ, δύο δὲ ἐντεῦθεν τὰ ἄνω σώματα· ἐφίσταται δή μοι γυνὴ φοβερὰ καὶ μεγάλη, τὸ πρόσωπον ἀγρία· ὀφθαλμὸς ἐν αἵματι, βλοσυραὶ παρειαί, ὄφεις αἱ κόμαι. ἅρπην ἐκράτει τῇ δεξιᾷ, δᾷδα τῇ λαιᾷ. ἐπιπεσοῦσα οὖν μοι θυμῷ καὶ ἀνατείνασα τὴν ἅρπην, καταφέρει τῆς ἰξύος, ἔνθα τῶν δύο σωμάτων ἦσαν αἱ συμβολαί, καὶ ἀποκόπτει μου τὴν παρθένον. περιδεὴς οὖν ἀναθορὼν ἐκ τοῦ δείματος, φράζω μὲν πρὸς οὐδένα, κατ᾽ ἐμαυτὸν δὲ πονηρὰ ἐσκεπτόμην.[23]

The first part of the dream is easily understood: Clitophon sees himself engaged in sex. The second part of the dream, in which the snaky-haired woman forcefully divides the couple, is more difficult to interpret and raises several interesting questions. Who is the woman? Why has she stopped the young couple from having sex? Why does the woman in the dream have snaky hair? These questions are not answered by the hero or by any other character, nor will they be answered until the reader of the novel decodes, examines, and interprets the oracle in 2.14.1 in view of *Anth. Pal.* 14.34.

Immediately after Clitophon has this ominous dream a letter arrives from his uncle Sostratus saying that he is sending his wife, Panthea, and daughter, Leucippe, to Sidon for safekeeping. As expected, the two cousins fall in love, and although Clitophon falls deeply in love with Leucippe, he realizes that this love can never be, because his father has already arranged his marriage to Calligone.

Hippias, Clitophon's father, also has a dream that compels him to hasten the wedding plans, but as he prepares to initiate the wedding an eagle swoops down and carries off the nuptial sacrifice. This foreboding act forces Hippias to postpone the wedding, to call in soothsayers to advise him, and then to agree with the seers who recommend that Zeus must be appeased by an offering of a midnight seaside sacrifice (a bull).

While all these dreams and harbingers of doom are frightening Hippias, a certain Byzantine, by the name of Callisthenes, takes it upon himself to kidnap the daughter of Sostratus. He has never seen Leucippe but has heard that she is very beautiful. This rumored beauty so vanquishes Callisthenes that he is compelled to ask Sostratus for Leucippe's hand in marriage. The character of Callisthenes (much like the character of the legendary Hippocleides: Hdt. 6.129–30) causes Sostratus to refuse to agree to the marriage; Callisthenes consequently decides to kidnap Leucippe and make her his wife by force.

The legal basis for this kidnapping turned marriage is based on Byzantine law (cited at 2.13.3): νόμου γὰρ ὄντος Βυζαντίοις, εἴ τις ἁρπάσας παρθένον φθάσας ποιήσει γυναῖκα, γάμον ἔχειν τὴν ζημίαν.[24] Since the law allows Callisthenes to do what he intends, he goes to Sidon to make Leucippe his wife. He even has the perfect excuse to go to Sidon: he has been appointed a θεωρός, an ambassador, to fulfill an oracle.

When the women of Sidon, among whom is Calligone, are making their midnight sacrifice of a bull to Zeus, Callisthenes and some of his cohorts come upon the celebrants and steal Calligone by mistake. This theft of Calligone seems to have been foreshadowed by the painting of Europa mentioned at the start of the novel (1.1.2–3). Calligone, whose abduction occurs as she sacrifices a bull at the seaside to Zeus, parallels Europa, who was kidnapped at the seaside by Zeus in the shape of a bull. Scholars have long recognized that the theft and rape of Europa depicted in the painting foreshadow the elopement of Leucippe and Clitophon and more importantly the abduction of Clitophon's sister, Calligone.[25] What has not been observed, however, is the importance of the foreshadowing supplied by the novel oracle based on the verses of the lemma preserved in *Anth. Pal.* 14.34.

The line from the anthology (quoted *supra*) not included in Tatius's oracle, discusses the types of people who were at Tyre: Athenians (Κέκροπος αἷμα) and Tyrians (ἀπ᾽ ἐμῆς ἔσθ᾽ αἷμα). It is suitable that sacrifice should be made to Heracles at Tyre since he is the patron deity of the Tyrians. The absence of the third line of the oracle of the novel, however, has never been adequately examined or explained. Jacobs (1821) was able to restore the corrupt first line of the oracle in the novel using the preserved verses in the anthology but does not comment on the discrepancy. Gaselee (82 n. 1) writes that the third line of the riddle is of "doubtful meaning." Vilborg (1955, 51), in his commentary on Tatius, writes: "In the anthology, there is one more line . . . omitted by A.T., probably because he did not need it for his aims." Even the most recent critical edition of this romance (Garnaud 1991, 45 n. 1) only mentions that the oracle is included in the *Anthologia Palatina*.

Both the oracle and the riddle are a bit strange in that they have Hephaestus embracing or holding sweet Athena. Hephaestus, the "violent obstetrician" (Burkert 1985, 143) of the androgenetic goddess, attempted to force himself violently on Athena in the Acropolis at Athens, but he was not successful. Instead he prematurely ejaculated and from his semen Erichthonius was born.

According to Apollodorus (3.14.6), some say that Erichthonius was the son of Hephaestus and Atthis, while others claim that he was the son of Hephaestus and Athena.[26] The latter genealogy is related as follows: Hephaestus, forsaken by Aphrodite, falls in love with Athena, who is then pursued by Hephaestus for sexual purposes. There is an attempted rape of Athena, but Hephaestus, for some reason or other, is unable to violate the virgin goddess. Instead Hephaestus ejaculates on her, and Athena in disgust proceeds to wipe away the semen with wool that she then throws on the ground. From this semen-permeated wool springs Erichthonius, half serpent, half man. Pausanias (1.24.7) also associates Athena with the serpent Erichthonius when he writes in his description of the statue of Athena in the Parthenon: πλησίον τοῦ δόρατος δράκων ἐστίν· εἴη δ' ἂν Ἐριχθόνιος οὗτος ὁ δράκων.

The versions of the birth of Erichthonius that have Hephaestus as the father of the snake divinity seem to be later accounts.[27] Robertson (1985, 231–95, in particular 258–69) speculates that Prometheus may have lusted after Athena and consequently may have been the father of Erichthonius.[28] For our purposes it does not matter who the father of the child was, or even who the child was. The overall structure of the myth is what is important: a male attempts to rape a virgin, intercourse is prohibited, and snakes are mentioned in one way or another.

The bizarre parts of this oracle need to be decoded in terms of the individual elements of the overall structure of the myth. Tatius himself supplies one interpretation of the oracle in 2.14.5–10: the expression of Hephaestus embracing Athena is meant to be interpreted as an allusion to the connection between the olive and fire and the connection between an olive grove and the mild volcanic eruptions that supply the necessary soil ingredients. A nonagricultural decoding, however, must take into account that in the original oracle (in the line not included in the text of the novel) the snaky Cecrops is mentioned and that there is an allusion to the attempted rape of Athena by Hephaestus.

Tatius intended his readers to recall the mythological references contained in the epigram, which originally contained the line now missing in the current text of the novel, and then to fit them into the narrative flow of the novel: in 2.23 Satyrus has arranged for Leucippe and Clitophon to bring their love to fruition. Clitophon is to slip into Leucippe's room after Satyrus has drugged Conops, but all does not go as planned, for when Clitophon is about to make love to Leucippe, her mother, Panthea, has a dream in which she sees her daughter being murdered by a robber: ἐδόκει τινὰ λῃστὴν μάχαιραν ἔχοντα γυμνὴν ἄγειν ἁρπασάμενον αὐτῆς τὴν θυγατέρα καὶ καταθέμενον ὑπτίαν, μέσην ἀνατεμεῖν τῇ μαχαίρῃ τὴν γαστέρα, κάτωθεν ἀρξάμενον ἀπὸ τῆς αἰδοῦς (2.23.5).[29] This scene brings to mind the dream (1.3.4) in which Clitophon sees himself grown, from the waist down, into one body with Calligone. A woman, as mentioned above, then appears who cuts the two bodies apart. The description of the woman in Clitophon's dream would be a fitting portrait of Leucippe's mother and of her intended action when she bursts into her daughter's room. Note that the woman in Clitophon's dreams has snaky hair, while in the oracle the snaky Cecrops is mentioned.

In the dream Panthea sees a robber splitting her daughter in two, metaphorical rape, while the oracle makes mention of the myth of Hephaestus and Athena. Thus the decoded oracle fits perfectly into the plot: Clitophon will attempt to consummate illegally his love for Leucippe just as Hephaestus had tried to have illicit sex with Athena, and the snaky-haired woman who will prevent any coital activity purposely recalls the complete original epigram. This is of course what happens. Clitophon enters Leucippe's room and is about to have sex with her, when Panthea, looking like a frightful Gorgon, bursts into the room and stops the young couple from consummating their love.

In conclusion: Tatius extensively employs foreshadowing in his novel, for example, the painting of Europa and the kidnapping of Calligone. The oracle, as originally preserved in the *Anth. Pal.*, also supplies the foreshadowing of Clitophon's failed attempt at intercourse with Leucippe. The present-day text of *Leucippe and Clitophon*, however, has the oracle but omits the third line of the original oracle that foreshadows the scene involving Panthea. Since readers could not have been expected to be familiar with such an obscure oracle and all of its lines, it is obvious that the omission of the third line is not Achilles Tatius's doing, but rather a loss in textual transmission like πόλις in the first line. Once Panthea discovers that a man has been in Leucippe's room, she is determined to find out who the culprit and his accomplices are, thereby forcing everyone associated with the amorous plans of Clitophon and Leucippe to flee: Clitophon, Leucippe, Satyrus, Clio (Leucippe's maid), and some assorted friends take the next available boat out of Tyre. Before the great escape, however, Leucippe asks Satyrus that he help her avoid her mother's wrath. She implores him in the name of the country gods, thereby linking him even closer with Pan: "Δέομαι," says Leucippe, "πρὸς θεῶν ξένων καὶ ἐγχωρίων, ἐξαρπάσατέ με τῶν τῆς μητρὸς ὀφθαλμῶν, ὁποιβούλεσθε" (2.30.1).[30]

On the fleeing ship the fugitives encounter a certain Menelaus, who relates his own tragic love story (2.34).[31] It seems that he accidentally killed his lover, who is compared to Patroclos, in a hunting accident. In 2.35.4 Clitophon tells Menelaus, who is arguing in behalf of homosexual love, that the beauty of males disappears no sooner than it has blossomed. It is a beauty that resembles the draught of Tantalus that at the very act of drinking disappears. Menelaus rebuts by noting in Homeric terms that it was Ganymede, a beautiful male youth, whom Zeus took up to Olympus, and not a woman (2.36.3). He continues his argument by listing women (Alcmene, Danae, and Semele) whom Zeus loved but who never shared his abode in Olympus, but Zeus loved Ganymede so much that he even replaced Hebe.

Clitophon rejoins that although Zeus never took any of these women up to Olympus, it was their beauty that not only brought Zeus down from Olympus but even made him undergo metamorphosis: Europa caused him to become a bull, Antiope forced Zeus to become a satyr, Semele saw Zeus as a golden beam. If this is to enough proof of the king of the gods' love and preference for women, Clitophon also hints at the noble offspring generated from these liaisons, in particular Perseus. What is more important here is that Menelaus, like his mythological namesake, is going to Egypt, since it is Egypt where the mythological Menelaus finds his phantom wife.

This book continues the trend of counting on myth for structure. The arrangement of the myths divides the book into two sections; the first myths deal with wine, and the second set of myths deals with love, both heterosexual and homosexual. The first myths encountered deal with the origin of wine, and the different aitia program the action of the first half of the book. Biblian, with its sensual connotation, denotes the ever-increasing love of Leucippe and Clitophon. The wine of Maron foreshadows the battle of wits between Conops, Panthea's slave and Leucippe's guardian, and Satyrus and Conops's eventual sedation. Chian wine links itself to the aition of the discovery of purple dye. Icarius's wine not only parallels the aphrodisiac given to Leucippe in a later book, but also completes the circle started by the inclusion of the Biblian: Biblian is an aphrodisiac and so is the drug given to Leucippe. In between the wine aitia and the myths dealing with love, an oracle is also used to arrange the structure of the chapter. This oracle uses the myth of Hephaestus and his attempted rape of Athena to anticipate the sexual encounter of Leucippe and Clitophon, foiled by Panthea. The second set of myths appears in a philosophical debate. Clitophon and Menelaus argue the merits of heterosexual versus homosexual love by recalling the loves of Zeus. Since Tatius heavily emphasizes the king of the gods and the myths associated with him in the second half of the book, it is no surprise that the first myth he employs in the third book deals with Zeus; in other words, the erotic debate not only employs these myths as exempla, but also serves to bridge the action between the end of book 2 and that of the beginning of the following book. In 2.30 we see, once again, the divinity of Pan making an appearance through the person of Satyrus. As in the first book a binary structure is found: Eros and his accoutrements show up in the earlier parts of both books, while in the latter parts materialize Pan, the madness he invokes, and the power of unrestrained sexuality with which he is associated.

Is there a historical allusion in book 2 in keeping with Tatius's custom including a historical element in his exempla? Yes. Callisthenes, the kidnapper of Calligone, wants to marry Leucippe, but Sostratus, Leucippe's father, refuses to allow this marriage, because he does not approve of Callisthenes' loose living: ὁ δὲ βδελυττόμενος τοῦ βίου τὴν ἀκολασίαν ἠρνήσατο (2.13.2). In book 1 there was a single historical allusion, Candaules, and in this book there seems to be a parallel between Callisthenes and Herodotus's Hippocleides (6.128–9); neither has the respect of his prospective father-in-law, and both lose their finacées because of their styles of living.

Book 3 begins with a shipwreck, and among the survivors are Leucippe and Clitophon, who manage to come ashore at Pelusium, where there is located a statue of Zeus of Mount Casius. In the statue's hand there is sculpted a pomegranate, generative in nature (Harlan 1965, 107ff.), and perhaps an omen of the first *Scheintod*, the disembowelment of Leucippe (Bartsch 1989, 55ff.). The pomegranate (beautiful on the outside, not so on the inside) may also have been used in sophistic argumentation, which further strengthens the contention that Tatius was well versed in literature (Anderson 1979).

Near the statue there are two paintings by Evanthes.[32] One painting shows Andromeda chained and ready to be sacrificed to the sea monster. The other depicts a chained Prometheus with an eagle tearing at his liver. Andromeda is beautifully painted except for her wrists: τὰς δὲ χεῖρας εἰς τὴν πέτραν ἐξεπέτασεν, ἄγχει δὲ ἄνω δεσμὸς ἑκατέραν συνάπτων τῇ πέτρᾳ· οἱ καρποὶ δὲ ὥσπερ ἀμπέλου βότρυες κρέμανται (3.7.4).[33] This description of the wrists and hands may seem to be overobserved, but what can one expect from a painter whose son may owe his reputation to the vine? This painting of Andromeda has been decoded as foreshadowing the trials and tribulations that Leucippe will undergo (Bartsch 1989, 57). Prometheus and his lacerated liver also point to this fact.

Included in the painting are the rescuers of both mythological prisoners, who have already been encountered in the previous book: Heracles and Perseus. Heracles was tied in with the sacrifice at Tyre, and he now

will rescue Prometheus from eternal suffering. Perseus was the only offspring mentioned by name in the listing of women who had been born
children to Zeus. The slayer of the Gorgon, depicted with a strange rapier,
will now prevent Andromeda from becoming the sacrificial victim offered
to the sea monster.

Book 3 derives its plot from Evanthes' paintings. In fact the narrative of
this chapter faithfully follows the scenes depicted on the paintings.
Leucippe is kidnapped by robbers (cf. Panthea's dream) and pegged to the
ground with all her limbs stretched in the same manner as Andromeda.[34]
The heroine is then disemboweled before the very eyes of Clitophon:[35]
εἶτα λαβὼν ξίφος βάπτει κατὰ τῆς καρδίας καὶ διελκύσας τὸ ξίφος εἰς
τὴν κάτω γαστέρα ῥήγνυσι (3.15.4).[36]

In a manner recalling the death of Leucippe in Panthea's dream:
ἐδόκει τινὰ λῃστὴν μάχαιραν ἔχοντα γυμνὴν ἄγειν ἁρπασάμενον αὐτῆς
τὴν θυγατέρα καὶ καταθέμενον ὑπτίαν, μέσην ἀνατεμεῖν τῇ μαχαίρᾳ
τὴν γαστέρα, κάτωθεν ἀρξάμενον ἀπὸ τῆς αἰδοῦς (2.23.5).[37] The location of Leucippe's wound is in the same general area as the wound in-
flicted upon Prometheus by the eagle, and the exotic quality of Perseus's
sword finds its counterpart in the stage-knife used by Menelaus to fake the
death of Leucippe.[38]

In keeping with the Herodotean tenor of the first two books, Tatius
introduces the myth of the Phoenix bird (2.25), an episode right out of
Herodotus 2.73 (cf. Gaselee 1917, 187 n. 1). The Phoenix is said by
Tatius to carry the corpse of its father from Ethiopia to Egypt in a sepulcher. The bird is described as about the same size as a peacock but superior
in plumage. It lives in Ethiopia, but upon its death the male offspring of
the Phoenix constructs a sepulcher, places his dead father in it, and carries
the casket to Heliopolis in Egypt for burial. In Heliopolis one of the priests
of the Sun examines the bird to make sure that it is an authentic Phoenix.
The bird helps in its identification by allowing himself to be thoroughly
examined, even to the extent that the bird allows his private parts to be
scrutinized.

Herodotus's account agrees with but varies from Tatius's narrative in a
number of ways. He states that the bird comes with the corpse of his father
from Arabia and not from Ethiopia. Egypt as the place of burial is the same
in both accounts, but in Herodotus there is no physical examination by
the priests of the Sun to validate the Phoenix's lineage and identity. It
seems that it is not enough for Tatius that a bird has constructed a

movable coffin for its parent and brought it all the way from Ethiopia to Heliopolis for burial.³⁹

Book 4: Before the account of the Phoenix, Tatius construes a military overtone. Charmides, the general who rescued Clitophon and his group from the robbers, plans to attack the camp of the robbers. There is more, however, since Charmides has fallen in love with Leucippe and schemes to have his way with the heroine. This military ambiance dovetails with the myths that begin the fourth book. In this book the myth of Aphrodite and Ares sets the agenda. Charmides loves (Aphrodite) Leucippe but has to make war (Ares) on the robbers. The general himself detects the dilemma he is in.

ἐν πολέμῳ δὲ τίς ἐπιθυμίαν ἀναβάλλεται; στρατιώτης δὲ ἐν χερσὶν ἔχων μάχην οἶδεν εἰ ζήσεται; τοσαῦται τῶν θανάτων εἰσὶν ὁδοί. αἴτησαί μοι παρὰ τῆς Τύχης τὴν ἀσφάλειαν, καὶ μενῶ. ἐπὶ πόλεμον νῦν ἐξελεύσομαι βουκόλων· ἔνδον μου τῆς ψυχῆς ἄλλος πόλεμος κάθηται. στρατιώτης με πορθεῖ τόξον ἔχων, βέλος ἔχων. νενίκημαι, πεπλήρωμαι βελῶν· κάλεσον, ἄνθρωπε, ταχὺ τὸν ἰώμε-νον·⁴⁰ ἐπείγει τὸ τραῦμα. ἅψω πῦρ ἐπὶ τοὺς πολεμίους· ἄλλας δᾷδας ὁ Ἔρως ἀνῆψε κατ᾽ ἐμοῦ (4.7.3–4).⁴¹

The only cure Charmides can find is to pray that he has sex with Leucippe before he engages in battle with the enemy: Ἀφροδίτη με πρὸς Ἄρεα ἀποστειλάτω (4.7.5). The general's lust, however, is not sated, since Leucippe suffers an epileptic-like fit, like Anthea's induced by an aphrodisiac, which prevents the general from having sex with the maiden.⁴²

The rest of this book comprises a battle between Charmides' forces and those of the enemy, the routing of the general's forces, the death of the general, and the destruction of the enemy's forces by a larger contingent of men sent by the satrap of Egypt.⁴³ In this book Eros plays no role but is supplanted by his mother, Aphrodite. Pan does not appear and need not, since this book is dedicated solely to sexual and military strategies.

After the episode involving love and war we find the hero and heroine in Alexandria. They enter the city by the Sun Gate and notice that at the opposite end of the town is the Moon Gate and between the two portals there is a labyrinth of columns, streets, people, and temples. Coinciding with their arrival to the city is a festival to Zeus (Serapis) in which the ritual torches are so many in number and so bright that they remove the darkness caused by the oncoming night. Straightaway the scene has been set for a transformation from light (the Sun Gate) to darkness (the Moon Gate). This polarity sets the theme for book 5.

Book 5: Chaereas, the man who had cured Leucippe of her madness, falls in love with her and contrives to kidnap her. He invites Leucippe, Clitophon, and Menelaus to dinner on the pretext of celebrating his birthday. On the way to his home, located near the lighthouse at Pharos, a hawk strikes Leucippe's head, an ill omen. As the characters are searching for an explanation for this incident, they come upon a painting depicting the rape of Philomela.[44] The painting tells the complete myth of Philomela, Procne, and Tereus, except for the metamorphoses of these people into birds.

The painting is interpreted by Clitophon, who gives a nearly identical version of the myth. His rendering starts with the metamorphoses, provides the reasons for Tereus's lust and the means he employs to rape and mutilate Philomela, supplies a description of the weaving of Philomela, relates the gruesome banquet, and ends with the transformation of humans into birds. The avian ring-structure of Clitophon's version ends with the party guests postponing their visit to Chaereas for one day.

The one-day delay does not prevent Chaereas from carrying out his designs. He kidnaps Leucippe and stops the pursuing Clitophon by staging the second simulated death of Leucippe. Chaereas escapes with Leucippe, and Clitophon, through the machinations of Satyrus, is engaged to marry Melite, a widow from Ephesus. The prenuptial discussions are held in the temple of Isis in order that the goddess may witness their engagement. The wedding, however, will not be held in Egypt, but rather in Melite's hometown of Ephesus, where Artemis is the patron deity. Since Isis is associated with the Underworld, and Artemis is associated with Selene, the moon, and with Hecate, with whom Leucippe was compared,[45] the transformation from light to darkness is accomplished by degrees. At the beginning of this book the Sun and his powers were emphasized, but now toward the end the Moon and the divinities associated with it come to the fore.

On the sea voyage to Ephesus Melite attempts to seduce Clitophon, who refuses because he wants to remain faithful to Leucippe. In a rhetorical outburst Melite tries to win over Clitophon by citing her own exempla of mythological figures such as Aphrodite, Eros, Poseidon, the Nereids, and Amphitrite, who are connected with the sea and its creative powers. The learned disquisition of Melite is of no avail.

The divinities are not the only ones who undergo transformation in this book. Leucippe, who up until now had been a nobly born and free person, loses her freedom and becomes a slave and a follower of the moon goddesses. The transformation from normal person to witch has been planned from the first chapter of the novel. In 1.4.3. Leucippe is said to resemble Selene; in 2.7 Leucippe casts a spell on the bee-stung hand of Clio and on the healthy lips of Clitophon; in 3.18.3 Leucippe is mistaken for Hecate; and in 5.17 she is identified as Lacaena, a woman from Thessaly, the genetrix of Greek witches.[46] The transformation is complete when Melite asks Leucippe to supply her with herbs with which she can make Clitophon have sex with her (5.22–26.12). The description of Leucippe picking herbs is especially meaningful, because she does this in the moonlight; witchery and the moon goddesses are united: διανυκτερ-εύσειν γὰρ ἔλεγεν εἰς τὸν ἀγρὸν βοτανῶν ἔνεν χάριν, ὡς ἐν ὄψει τῆς σελήνης αὐτὰς ἀναλάβοι (5.26.12).[47]

The aphrodisiac of Lacaena is never used, because Thersander, Melite's husband, reappears after having been missing for several years. Thus ends book 5, in which transformations program the action. At the beginning the polarity between the Sun and Moon gates reveals the changes that will take place: divine attributes go from those identified with the sun to those related to the moon; Leucippe the nobly born becomes a slave; Leucippe is depicted as a witch and as a servant of the moon goddess.

Book 6: Transformation as a motif is not limited to book 5. From the very outset of the sixth book Tatius recalls this motif by having Clitophon dress up in women's clothing in order to escape from jail, but not before Melite and Clitophon have sex. Thersander, the husband of Melite, has sent him there on the charge of adultery. Melite supplies the clothes for Clitophon's transvestism, and when he is in drag Melite compliments him, saying that he reminds her of a picture of Achilles she once saw. The painting, of course, must have depicted the time Achilles spent at the court of King Lycomedes of Scyros while dressed as a woman (Pyrrha).

The theme is intensified by the myth of Iphigenia in 6.2.3. The prison guard, who was to have kept a close eye on his prisoner, is flabbergasted when he looks inside the jail and realizes that Clitophon has escaped and in his stead is Melite. Tatius writes that this change is θέαμα . . . παρα-δοξότατον, τῆς κατὰ τὴν ἔλαφον ἀντὶ παρθένου παροιμίας (6.2.3–4). Metamorphosis also shows up in the scene (6.7.4) in which Thersander attempts to seduce Leucippe, whom he has also imprisoned. Leucippe, when she perceives Thersander's intentions, bursts into tears. If these tears solidified, then the earth καινὸν ἂν εἶχεν ἤλεκτρον (6.2.3). The old ἤλεκτρον obviously refers to the amber produced by the tears of Phaethon's sisters, who, while they were mourning the death of their brother, also underwent metamorphosis (cf. Gaselee 1917, 317 n. 1).

The metamorphosis motif undergoes a reversal in 6.19.6, where Leucippe tells Thersander, after many attempts at seduction, that she would love him only if he became Clitophon. No transformation actually takes place; rather, the underlying motif is revealed: only metamorphosis can allow Thersander to achieve what he wishes, just as Clitophon had changed, superficially, from a man into a woman in order to escape his imprisonment. Thersander refuses to become Clitophon, but he does change into what he did not expect or want: the master of Leucippe becomes her slave, a metaphor for love.

This book relies upon metamorphosis and the myths associated with it for structure. Clitophon becomes a woman (myth of Achilles), Melite the free woman becomes a prisoner (myth of Iphigenia), Leucippe cries tears superior to those shed by the Heliades, and Thersander the master of Leucippe becomes the slave of Leucippe. This book derives its program of change from the fifth, where one of the overall themes was the transformation of Leucippe into a witch.

Book 7 does not follow the myth-inspired structure of the previous six but takes on a completely different tenor. While the previous divisions included love, pirates, shipwrecks, and all the other components expected in a novel, book 7 concentrates on only one of the elements found in the ancient Greek novels: the trial. In the trial scenes Tatius unleashes his sophistic nature, employing diverse legal terminology and manipulation. The trial nature of this book, however, foreshadows the mythologically inspired trials that Leucippe and Melite must undergo in the following book.

Book 8: The last book renews the dependency on myth for structure. Thersander argues that in order to prove the innocence and virginity of Leucippe (she had been accused of violating Artemis's temple, where only slaves and virgins are allowed to enter) she must undergo the trial of the panpipes (8.3.3). It seems that there is a grotto behind the shrine to Artemis, where only virgins may enter. After a lengthy description of the panpipes and aition in which they came to be, it is revealed that in the grotto are panpipes that Pan gave to Artemis as a gift.[48] These panpipes can prove the virginity of a maiden in the following manner: the maiden whose virginity is in question is placed in the grotto, and the doors of the cave are closed behind her; if the maiden is a virgin, the panpipes are heard and the girl comes out wreathed with pine;[49] if she is not, the panpipes are silent and in its stead a cry is heard and the maiden disappears. On the third day after the girl's cry is heard, the chief priestess of the cult of Artemis opens up the grotto and finds the panpipes lying on the ground but no maiden. Leucippe undergoes the test and is vindicated.

Leucippe is not the only woman who undergoes a test. Thersander accuses Melite of having had sex with Clitophon while he was presumed dead and therefore demands that she be tested in the waters of the river Styx. The test is as follows:

ὅταν τις αἰτίαν ἔχῃ Ἀφροδισίων, εἰς τὴν πηγὴν εἰσβᾶσα ἀπολού-
εται· ἡ δὲ ἐστιν ὀλίγη, καὶ μέχρι κνήμης μέσης. ἡ δὲ κρίσις·
ἐγγράψασα τὸν ὅρκον γραμματείῳ μηρίνθῳ δεδεμένον περιεθ-
ήκατο τῇ δέρῃ. κἂν ἀψευδῇ τὸν ὅρκον, μένει κατὰ χώραν ἡ πηγή.
ἂν δὲ ψεύδηται, τὸ ὕδωρ ὀργίζεται καὶ ἀναβαίνει μέχρι τῆς δέρης
καί τὸ γραμματεῖον ἐκάλυψε (8.12.8–9).[50]

Melite passes the test on a technicality. She did commit adultery because she had sex with Clitophon while he was in prison, before he dressed up as a woman, but Thersander accused her of committing adultery while he was presumed dead. This technicality allows Melite to enter into the Styx with the reply to accusation carefully worded: I did not commit adultery while Thersander was away.

The two tests are similar in nature, tests of sexual promiscuity, and connected to Pan. The creation of the panpipes and the myth of Syrinx has been discussed in the chapter on Longus. The myth of the trial by water is as follows: Rhodopis, a chaste attendant of Artemis, had sworn that she would never enjoy the fruits of Aphrodite. Aphrodite, as in the case of Hippolytus, heard this oath and, became enraged, consequently planned the ruination of Rhodopis. She made Euthynicus, an Ephesian and Rhodopis fall in love with each other. The two made love in a cave while Artemis was away, and when she returned and found out that Rhodopis had betrayed her, she turned her into a spring. Tatius does not explain Rhodopis's change in name to Styx, but we can find the connection between the Styx and Pan in Herodotus. The historian tells us that in the Arcadian town of Nonakris the waters of the Styx are found (6.74). The connection between Pan, *the* Arcadian deity, and the waters of the river Styx may possibly be found in the last use of Herodotus by Tatius.

This last book of the novel receives its atmosphere from the legal tone of the previous book, which is full of legal maneuvers and machinations and sets the stage for the trials and tribulations of Leucippe and Melite.[51] The mythological elements in the last book are in nature Pan-myths and signal the preeminence of this Arcadian deity at the end of the novel.

In *Leucippe and Clitophon* myths thoroughly guide the plot of each book and dictate the development of character. Eros and the myths associated with this divinity set the romantic groundwork not only of the first book, but also of the entire novel. In the second book the four aitia of the wines prescribe the sensual atmosphere of the book, foreshadow the drugging of Conops, and furnish a setting for a dialogue on the merits of heterosexual and homosexual love. The paintings of Evanthes arrange the plot of the third, while Love and War, in the mythological guise of Ares and Aphrodite, ordain the action of the fourth. Books 5 and 6 deal with transformation, specifically the transformation of Leucippe, which is paralleled by the change in scenery from light to darkness. Book 7 deals with trials and legal maneuvers, and it foreshadows the mythologically based trials of Leucippe and Melite in book 8.

5

The Analogue of the Hero
of Heliodorus's *Aethiopica*

Heliodorus's novel has been dated to the third or fourth century A.D.[1] It is very difficult, if not impossible, to date accurately this novel. Emperor Julian in his eulogy of the Emperor Constantius (written in A.D. 357), however, seems to parallel Heliodorus's account of the siege of Syene (book 9) with his account of the third siege of Nisibis "by the Persian King Sapor II in A.D. 350" (Sandy 1982, 4). Two hypotheses are possible: Heliodorus imitated Julian, and therefore he must have written after A.D. 357, or Julian imitated Heliodorus, and therefore Heliodorus wrote before A.D. 357. Although this quandary has not been settled, most scholars believe that Julian borrowed from Heliodorus (Lightfoot 1988; Maróth 1979; Szepessy 1976).

The *Aethiopica* is the longest and most complicated and creative of all the ancient Greek novels. It starts, contrary to the rules of novelistic composition, in medias res, and employs throughout its narrative foreshadowing, flashback, and story lines borrowed from Homer and the tragic corpus. The epics supply the largest number of story lines, but tragedy supplies the second largest amount.[2] In this chapter I argue that the subtext created by the tragedy story lines supply the reader with the tragic and mythical analogue and identity of Theagenes,[3] the hero of the novel.[4]

The narrative structure and technique of the *Aethiopica* are intriguing in their construction. Heliodorus, it has been suggested, models the overall structure of the novel on Homer's *Odyssey;* by paralleling the epic with the novel he makes the details, actions, and narrative of books 1 through 5 and 6 through 10 of the *Aethiopica* analogous to books 1 through 12 and 13 through 24 of the *Odyssey*.[5] Theatrical elements also appear in the novel; in fact, the narrative may possibly be borrowed from the stage, with each character presenting "his own story in full view" (Sandy 1982, 33).

One of the most prominent narrative techniques is found in the duplicity of the character Calasiris, which has a tremendous impact on the development and exposition of the plot (see Winkler 1982). Indeed, it has been proposed that the duplicitous nature of Calasiris correlates to the double motivational components of many of the events of the novel. A novel analysis of this work focuses on the conclusion and explores the "unpredictability of the path" that leads to the end (Morgan 1989b, 319). The quality of the narrative once again depends on the manipulated rehearsal of events by the characters and author.[6]

The novelty of the narratological constituents of the *Aethiopica* has not been the only focus of scholarly research; historical events and the attendant social circumstances in Heliodorus have also been investigated. The historical research on Heliodorus is justified, since the novelist from the very beginning of his narrative incorporates numerous historical allusions or details into his story. For example, he locates the opening scene of the novel in the Heracleiotic mouth of the Nile (1.1), proceeds to disclose that the leading characters of the novel are in an area called the Land of the Herds (1.5), strengthens the historical allusion by borrowing from Herodotus (5.16), and then links the topographical data to Athenian judicial information.[7] The attribution of some possibly authentic detail to a novel, as previously mentioned, possibly stems not from a premeditated plan of composing history, but rather from the inescapable certainty that an author cannot compose in a vacuum and so may turn to contemporary or historical minutiae. This is not to say that Heliodorus cannot be used as a source for information about Heliodorus's world.[8]

The historical characteristics of the novel can be divided into two categories: (1) coincidental details that are pertinent to the circumstances at hand, for example, the setting of the opening scene must take place somewhere, and what better place, following the dictates of novelistic writing, for a shipwreck to occur than in Egypt? Heliodorus makes the setting historical by identifying the site with a verifiable historical name:

the Heracleiotic mouth of the Nile (1.1). (2) The author also calls upon and uses literary sources to lend a historical flavor to his work,[9] but the use of these sources is not meant to convey the notion that Heliodorus is writing a historical work; rather, he is supplying his reader with verifiable details to which the reader can relate. At the same time, the novelist is showing that he is conversant with historical works.

Historical sources are outnumbered by the Homeric lines that abound in the *Aethiopica*.[10] The addition of quotations from the Homeric epics serves the same purposes as the borrowing from historical sources: to embellish the work, to show the novelist's erudition, and to make the work acceptable to an audience that is thoroughly familiar with the Homeric corpus. Heliodorus, in other words, is carrying on the novelistic tradition (see Garson 1975).

The sources used by Heliodorus are not limited, however, to historical or epic works. He cites Hesiod's *Theogony* and *Works and Days*, the Homeric *Hymn to Hermes*, Plato's *Phaedo* and *Gorgias*, Moschos's *Megara*, Aratus's *Phaenomena*, and Lucian's *On Dancing* in the novel.[11] Although the Homeric epics supply the largest number of borrowings, tragedy is a close second as a source for Heliodorus.[12]

A TRAGIC OPENING AND
THEATRICAL INTENT

The opening scene of the novel takes place at daybreak, and its first actors quickly appear (ἄνδρες ἐν ὅπλοις λῃστρικοῖς, men in piratical gear [1.1.1]); they survey a scene staged not only for them but also for the reader: a beach full of dead and half-dead bodies. This is not a typical battle scene, for included among the gore are the remains of a feast turned deadly: tables, some overturned and held by dead men, some used as weapons in an unexpected battle, others used as hiding places to no avail. The casualties lay scattered in various poses: one brought down by an axe, another beaten to death with a club, yet another burned to death. The majority of the dead are slaughtered by arrows.

Heliodorus concludes this opening scene with a brief summation employing stage terms: καὶ μυρίον εἶδος ὁ δαίμων ἐπὶ μικροῦ τοῦ χωρίου διεσκεύαστο, οἶνον αἵματι μιάνας, καὶ συμποσίοις πόλεμον ἐπιστήσας, φόνους καὶ πότους, σπονδὰς καὶ σφαγὰς ἐπισυνάψας, καὶ τοιοῦτον θέατρον λῃσταῖς Αἰγυπτίοις ἐπιδείξας (1.1.6).[13] As if the phrases μυρίον εἶδος and τοιοῦτον θέατρον λῃσταῖς Αἰγυπτίοις ἐπιδείξας are not explicit enough to make clear that Heliodorus is putting on a stage production, he further reinforces the dramatic quality by writing: οἱ γὰρ δὴ κατὰ τὸ ὄρος θεωροὺς ἑαυτοὺς τῶνδε καθίσαντες οὐδὲ συνιέναι τὴν σκηνὴν ἐδύναντο (they stood on the mountainside like an audience, nor were they able to comprehend the scene [1.1.7]).[14]

The second act of our novelistic tragedy reveals that the hero and heroine of the novel are Theagenes and Charicleia, and although the novelist does not identify Theagenes and Charicleia by name, he compares the female to a goddess (θεὸς εἶναι ἀναπείθουσα [1.2.1]) and describes the male as the victim of an assault that has made him even more handsome. In the same chapter the mythical analogue of Charicleia is mentioned in more specific terms: the Egyptians conjecture that she is either Artemis or Isis (1.2.6). It is more probable that Heliodorus wants the reader to associate the young girl with Artemis, for no other goddess is more often depicted with a quiver, bow, and arrows.

A MISSING ANALOGUE

The question that arises is, if Charicleia's analogue is Artemis, what then is the mythical analogue of Theagenes? Although Heliodorus is most definitely writing a romance novel that incorporates epic and tragic elements into its structure, he also seems to be playing a game with his reader: he wants the reader to investigate and discover the analogue of the hero through means of the stage elements in the narrative.[15] Heretofore, scholarship has focused on the enigma of Charicleia's true identity.[16]

A survey of the tragic passages and allusions that may aid in the discovery of Theagenes' analogue is therefore in order. The first definite clue is found at 4.10.5: ἀλλ᾽ ἐπειδήπερ ἅπαξ ἔρωτος, ἐπήσθου καὶ φανείς σε Θεαγένης ᾕρηκε, τοῦτο γὰρ ὀμφή μοι θεῶν ἐμήνυσε, σὺ μὲν ἴσθι μὴ μόνη καὶ πρώτη τὸ πάθος ὑποστᾶσα ἀλλὰ σὺν πολλαῖς μὲν γυναιξὶ τῶν ἐπισήμων σὺν πολλαῖς δὲ παρθένοις τῶν τὰ ἄλλα σωφρόνων.[17] This passage, based on line 439 from Euripides' Hippolytus, ἐρᾷς; τί τοῦτο θαῦμα; σὺν πολλοῖς βροτῶν, superficially associates Theagenes with Hippolytus in the following manner: in the opening scene of the novel, as previously mentioned, the analogue of the wounded young man next to the maiden resembling Artemis is not supplied. The girl is proclaimed to be Artemis or Isis, but the young man is disregarded for the time being. The young couple is then captured by brigands and taken to their hideout where they meet a Greek called Cnemon. It is at this moment (1.8) in the narrative that the leading characters' names are actually revealed by the characters themselves.

HIPPOLYTUS AS THEAGENES' ANALOGUE

Cnemon, the fellow captive of the hero and heroine, in a long story (1.9–17) reveals to Theagenes and Charicleia that he is an exile from Athens. His exile stems from the plots and lies of his stepmother Demainete and her slave Thisbe. Demainete fell in love with her stepson and attempted to seduce him, but Cnemon spurned her advances, and she, like the Euripidean Phaedra, plotted his doom. To make a long story short, Demainete, with the help of Thisbe, contrived the downfall of her stepson but attained only his exile.[18]

This incident is interesting, because although Cnemon played Hippolytus to Demainete's Phaedra,[19] it is about Theagenes that Calasiris relates at 4.10.5 the lines based on the *Hippolytus*. It would only make sense that Calasiris should have spoken these lines in reference to Cnemon, but since he did not, it seems that Heliodorus is calling attention to this borrowing from the *Hippolytus* and, more importantly, attributing this mythical allusion to Theagenes and not to Cnemon.[20] The intertwining of the mythical and true adventures of Cnemon, and the transference of these experiences by Calasiris to Theagenes, is the first example of Heliodorus's clues to the analogue of Theagenes.

At the camp of the brigands, Thyamis, the chief robber, falls in love with Charicleia and plans to marry her but is not able to, because of an attack by a rival band. During the battle he returns to the cave where he hid Charicleia in order to kill her but mistakenly kills Thisbe (1.30–31), who has managed to get to Egypt after having caused the death of Demainete. In the hands of the dead Thisbe is a tablet containing a letter to Cnemon, in which Thisbe relates what has happened in Athens since his absence.

The murder of Thisbe by Thyamis may call to mind the mythological story of Pyramus and Thisbe, the tragic Assyrian lovers. Aside from the similarity in names, in both stories a cave is mentioned and people thought dead are actually alive. More importantly, Thisbe parallels the actions of the nurse in the myth of Hippolytus. She planned to help her mistress seduce her stepson and communicated important information through a letter. This letter, however, served the opposite purpose to that of the letter in the myth, for it conveyed information that exonerated rather than accused. Once again the myth of Hippolytus has been brought to the fore.

The second clue to Theagenes' analogue is found in the amorous episode involving Arsace (7.2–8.15), the wife of Oroondates, the satrap of Memphis. Theagenes at first refuses the sexual advances of Arsace and agrees to have sex with her only if she puts a stop to the marriage of Charicleia to a servant. Arsace agrees to do so only to her detriment, because her husband is made aware of what she is plotting. When Arsace attempts to keep Theagenes to his promise, he refuses to carry out his end of the bargain. She consequently orders the torture of Theagenes, who is soon joined by Charicleia on the trumped-up charge that she had killed her once-future mother-in-law. Oroondates, however, aware of what his wife was up to, orders through a letter[21] that the young couple be brought to him. When these orders are made known, Arsace kills herself and the news of the suicide is reported to the young couple in Euripidean language: τέθνηκεν Ἀρσάκη βρόχον ἀγχόνης ἀψαμένη (8.15.2). The line closely echoes the report given by the chorus to Theseus when he inquires about his wife: βρόχον κρεμαστὸν ἀγχόνης ἀνήψατο (Hippolytus 802).

The identification of the mythical analogue of Theagenes is now almost complete. The Euripidean passage at 4.10.5 began to assimilate Theagenes as Hippolytus, and the analogue was further strengthened by the clear-cut allusions to the Hippolytus myth in the love affair of Demainete and Cnemon and by the absolving letter of Thisbe. The announcement of the death of Arsace in Euripidean phraseology also reinforces the Theagenes-Hippolytus analogue: if Arsace is Phaedra, Theagenes must be Hippolytus.

On the way to Oroondates the pair of lovers are taken as the first prisoners of war by the forces of the Ethiopian king Hydaspes. In Meröe, the capitol of Ethiopia, Theagenes and Charicleia are prepared to be sacrificed according to an ancient Ethiopian custom that demands that the first prisoners of war should be sacrificed to Selene and Helios. The sacrificial victims, however, have to be virgins, and Heliodorus therefore includes tests of virginity in his novel: Charicleia and Theagenes must prove their innocence by holding onto a grate that will burn all but the pure. The couple passes the test with flying colors and therefore are judged suitable for sacrifice.

As they are led to the sacrifice, Charicleia produces a ribbon and other tokens that can prove that she is the daughter of the king and queen of

Ethiopia and thereby saves herself from being slaughtered. Theagenes, on the other hand, does not fare as well. It does not matter an iota to the Ethiopians who he is or what he wants, and since his virginity has already been vouched for by the magic grate, he is led away to be sacrificed.

The hero, however, is bent on proving his true nature to the Ethiopians (and perhaps to the reader); especially after Persinna, the queen of the Ethiopians and mother of Charicleia, asks her daughter what the reader has long wondered: ἀλλ᾽ οὑτοσὶ τίς ποτέ ἐστι (10.18.1). Theagenes, in an attempt to avoid immolation by defining his worth, consequently wrestles a bull (10.28–30) and fights an unnamed giant (10.30–32).

These are the last two pieces of the puzzle to Theagenes's analogue: Hippolytus, in most versions of the myth, for example, Euripides' *Hippolytus*, also encounters a bull, though he does not fare as well as Theagenes. Unlike his mythological model, Theagenes does not die in his encounter with the animal, but rather he is judged all the more suitable to be sacrificed to the god Helios. Theagenes, however, is called to a second contest, in which he must fight a man whom Heliodorus describes as: τοσοῦτός τις τὸ μέγεθος καὶ οὕτως ὠγύγιος ἄνθρωπος ὥστε τὸ γόνυ τοῦ βασιλέως φιλῶν μικροῦ φανῆναι τοῖς ἐφ᾽ ὑψηλοῦ προκαθημένοις ἐξισούμενος (10.25.1).[22] I suggest that with this description Heliodorus is perhaps recalling the myth of another Hippolytus—the son of Ge and Uranus who was killed by Hermes. Apollodorus (*Bibl.* 1.6.2) writes that immediately before Artemis slew Gration, Hermes, while using Hades' cap of invisibility, killed the Giant Hippolytus. In the *Aethiopica* Heliodorus describes Theagenes thus: οἷα δὴ γυμνασίων ἀνὴρ καὶ ἀλοιφῆς ἐκ νέων ἀσκητὴς τήν τε ἐναγώνιον Ἑρμοῦ τέχνην ἠκριβωκώς (10.31.5).[23] The author therefore clearly links the description of the unnamed wrestler and Theagenes' devotion to Hermes with the myth of the Giant Hippolytus.

Heliodorus, however, would not write a sad ending to his story, and just as he had employed a theatrical device, in medias res, at the beginning of the novel, he uses another such device, the deus ex machina, to bring about a happy ending. It just so happens that Charicles, Charicleia's foster father, had made his way to Ethiopia, where he prevents the sacrifice of Theagenes. Charicles reveals everything to everyone, and all rejoice that the legitimate daughter of the royal couple has been returned and cele-brate that such a fine specimen of youth as Theagenes has been spared death. The novel then ends with Theagenes and Charicleia being wed and made priests of Helios.

CONCLUSION

Although the Hippolytus story is without doubt exploited in the *Aethiopica*, Heliodorus is not consistent and exclusive in his usage of this myth. For example, he casts Cnemon as Hippolytus and recalls the love story of Pyramus and Thisbe. The novelist, however, makes two clear allusions to Euripides' *Hippolytus* (4.10.5 and 8.15.2) that can be said to equate Theagenes with Hippolytus. It can also be argued that Heliodorus used other mythical analogues:[24] when describing Theagenes' speed of foot he alludes to Achilles (2.34),[25] and also to Odysseus through the scar from a boar's tusk on his leg (5.5). These assimilations, however, are not repeated, as is the Hippolytus imagery.

Heliodorus begins his novel in an innovative manner by using the technique of in medias res and thereby draws up a theatrical blueprint for his novel. He shows the reader a young couple on a beach and suggests that the maiden is Artemis, but leaves unclear the mythical analogue of the young man. Using the *Hippolytus* as the source for the clues that reveal the identity of Theagenes, the reader solves the question of the analogue of the young man on the beach: he is Hippolytus. The analogue is proper in that Hippolytus is the follower of Artemis and in that Theagenes and Hippolytus share common qualities and experiences. Theagenes is as chaste as Hippolytus, is associated with Artemis (Charicleia), and fights off the unwanted sexual attentions of a Phaedra (Arsace). A bull and an unnamed giant also play important parts in Theagenes' story. The Hippolytus facet of the novel is also clarified by the letter of Thisbe, the disastrous amorous adventures of Cnemon with his stepmother, and the borrowing of lines from Euripides' *Hippolytus*.[26]

Conclusion

This present study has primarily focused on the relationship between the diminution of historical detail and the increase of mythological and literary allusion in the development of the ancient Greek novel. I have generally concentrated on the various literary functions of myth introduced into the novel as the genre evolved, and specifically on the central part that literary allusions to myth serve in the later novels.

The introductory chapter explored the available data on the five canonical novels. Chariton, as one may recall, wrote the earliest extant ancient Greek novel, and the abundance of historical minutiae in *Chaereas and Callirhoe* suggests that Chariton was relying upon the major preexisting prose form to give his erotic work a respectable veneer. Other preexisting forms that serve as building blocks for the novel genre are epic, New Comedy, Alexandrian erotic poetry, and *periegesis*. A specific form, however, cannot be designated as *the* progenitor of the novel.

Although there are many common ingredients shared by all the novels, such as aristocratic couples, pirates, traveling, and false-deaths, this does not mean that the combination of this list of ingredients will always result in a novel. It may be more profitable, though more difficult, to examine the nature of the audience of these erotic novels. The middle class, the somewhat educated class, scribes, women, youths, the poor in spirit, and the intelligentsia have been put forth as possible readers. I have shown that clues to the nature of the audience of the ancient novel are found in the high literary complexity of the ancient Greek novel. The interplay between the literary allusions to myth and the subtle manner in which they were included in the novel can have been appreciated only by an extremely educated author writing for an equally educated audience. This is not to say that the ancient Greek novel could not have been read by people other than the intelligentsia, but it does suggest that the author was very learned and may have expected *some* of his readers to understand and appreciate the intricacies and nuances of literary allusion.

Myth and mythological allusions serve two functions in Chariton's novel; firstly, the author developed his major characters through analogue. Callirhoe was likened to Aphrodite, Ariadne, Artemis, Helen of Troy, the nymphs, and Medea. Chaereas was compared to Achilles, Nireus, Hippolytus, and Alcibiades. Since the analogues were mythological in nature, I examined Chariton's accuracy in his use of literary antecedents for his analogues. This examination led me to the conclusion that Chariton relied heavily upon literary predecessors for the depiction of his characters and for the formation of his plot. For example, the persona of Callirhoe is greatly dependent upon the mythological Ariadne found in Paeon's account of the Theseus myth. Identical narratological elements, verbal echoes, and a similar treatment of the mythological Ariadne imply that Chariton may have read either Plutarch's *Theseus*, where Paeon's version of the Theseus-Ariadne myth is located, or Paeon himself. If the novelist did read Plutarch, a revision in the dating of *Chaereas and Callirhoe* is necessary.

The second literary use of myth is plot structuring through Homeric quotation. Chariton introduced into the narrative lines and passages from the Homeric epics, which, at first glance, may seem to be decoration or erudition. A closer look at these borrowings shows that the Homeric lines and passages had to be reinterpreted in an intertextual manner: the original locations and backgrounds of the Homeric borrowings had to be considered when analyzing their new surroundings in the novel. Once this new interpretation is accomplished, it is quite plain to see that the Homeric quality of the novel was not ornamental, at least in the first four books. The very idea that this reinterpretation should occur may help to identify the audience of the ancient Greek novel: only an educated reader could see what Chariton's plan was, and only an educated reader could reinterpret the Homeric lines and passages.

Characterization through mythological analogue and plot structuring through Homeric borrowing occur most frequently in the first four books of the novel. In the second half of the work there is a noticeable drop in the employment of myth, Homer, and allusion. The diminution of mythological detail gives way to historical features, as witnessed by the importance given to the "Battle of Champions" passage. Overall, the historical nature of Chariton's opus overwhelms the mythological quality.

The mythological in Xenophon's *Ephesiaca* is minimal, and the historical almost nonexistent. The approaches taken to the analysis of this novel, characterization through myth, the oracle as history, and the adventures of Habrocomes and Antheia as having analogues in myths, however, point to the possibility that Xenophon may have based his plot on some Euripidean plays. Echoes of the *Ino*, the *Hippolytus*, and the *Electra* resonate throughout the play, with special emphasis on the *Hippolytus*.

Xenophon likens Antheia to Artemis and partially derives Habrocomes' character from the stories of Hippolytus, Bellerophon, and perhaps even the Joseph-Potiphar tale. Part of the *Ephesiaca*'s plot derives its narrative sequence from the *Hippolytus*: the women in love with Habrocomes, Manto and Kyno, mirror the actions of Phaedra. A second set of love stories, those of Hippothous and Hyperanthes, and Aegialeus and Thelxinoe, are included by Xenophon in order to counterbalance the actions of Manto and Kyno. The homosexual relationship of Hippothous and Hyperanthes, doomed from the start, parallels the adventures of the novel's hero and heroine, and the marriage of Aegialeus and Thelxinoe seems to be presented by Xenophon as the marriage par excellence that the young couple should emulate with due moderation.

Notwithstanding Witt's theory that Xenophon would have been at a loss without the myth of Io, mythological allusions are very limited in the *Ephesiaca*. This may be due to the possible abridgement of the novel, but one cannot be sure. What is certain is that the mythological details outnumber the historical aspects, which shows that even by the time of Xenophon, the genre was moving away from the custom that demanded that prose should be used only for the writing of history.

My chapter on Longus presented an analysis of the relationship between literary and mythological allusions and the aitia, and the function of the aitia and the story or myth of Chloe. There are problems, however, when examining *Daphnis and Chloe*, because it does not seem to resemble structurally its novelistic forerunners. This dissimilarity has caused some scholars to label this novel as a subgenre.

The analysis of this novel comprised inquiries into the possible historical characteristics of the novel, mythological allusions, and the importance and function of the aitia. The historical facet of *Daphnis and Chloe* is found in the preface, in which Longus inversely mirrors the archaeologia of Thucydides. The juxtaposition of Thucydidean phraseology with Longus's preface results in the conclusion that the novelist was acknowledging his literary predecessors, specifically Thucydides, but at the same time distancing himself from them. The words εἶδον, γραφήν, ἱστορίαν, φήμην, ἰδόντα, ἀντιγράψαι, ἀναζητησάμενος, ἐξηγητήν, βίβλους, βλέπωσι, and γράφειν form the procedure, according to Longus, by which one may go about writing history. The author, however, does not go on to write history but only wants to show that he knows how to write history. It is true that these words may also be applied to painting, but in light of the direct influence of Thucydides, these words have to be understood in historiographical terms. History, in fact, is not the only genre acknowledged in the preface, because the words ἡμῖν δὲ ὁ θεὸς παράσχοι σωφρονοῦσι τὰ τῶν ἄλλων γράφειν clearly recall the opening lines of the *Iliad*, *Odyssey*, and *Aeneid*.

Some characterization through mythological analogue is used in this novel. Daphnis is likened to Dionysus, and the aition of a spring called Daphnis is mentioned. Chloe is said to be a Bacchant and is subtly likened to Echo. Gnathon, the parasite of the novel, compares his situation through mythological exempla to those of Anchises, Branchus, and Ganymede. The important point of the literary allusion of the novel is that Longus relies upon Hellenistic authors, primarily Theocritus, as the source for his myths.

The phrase παρθένον ἐξ ἧς Ἔρως μῦθον ποιῆσαι is all-important, because it is the author's own statement of purpose. Longus wanted to write the myth of Chloe and decided to do so by giving his readers the aition of Chloe's change from a virgin to a sexually experienced wife. He supplied three aitia dealing with sex, which set the stage for the aition of Chloe. The aition is spread throughout the entire novel and reaches its climax in the last part of the fourth book. Included in the same book is the often overlooked aition of the spring called Daphnis, which may foreshadow the sexual union between the hero and heroine of the novel: Daphnis, like his namesake spring, finally ὕδωρ ἐπωχέτευσε (4.1) at the end of the novel.

Myth in *Leucippe and Clitophon* has a programmatic function. It directs the action of both the plot of the individual chapter and of the overall novel. The first instance of myth, the story of Europa, in the novel derives its impetus from a historical work: Herodotus seems to have served as the author upon whom Achilles Tatius, much like Longus and his use of Thucydides, based his introduction. The historical aspect of the introduction is not that apparent; nevertheless, it is there. It seems that Tatius, even though far removed from Chariton's time, followed the novelistic tradition of giving the opening to his work a historical flavor.

In *Leucippe and Clitophon* myths program the plot of each chapter and dictate the development of character. I did not analyze the development of character through mythological analogue, because Laplace had already done so. Instead I placed emphasis on the relationship between the inclusion of myths in each chapter and the progress of the narrative: Eros and the myths associated with him dictated the movement of the first book, and consequently of the entire novel. Four aitia on the wine set up the romantic relationship between Leucippe and Clitophon, likened the drugging of Conops to that of Polyphemus, and set the stage for a debate on heterosexual and homosexual love. In the third book Evanthes' paintings dictated the plot, and Love and War, in the mythological guise of Aphrodite and Ares, did the same for book 4. Metamorphosis was the theme of the fifth and sixth books, in particular the transformation of Leucippe, and it paralleled the change in the lighting of the scenery. The legalistic nature of the seventh book foreshadowed the trials of Leucippe and Melite in the final book.

Literary allusion played a great role in *Leucippe and Clitophon*. Tatius recalled Herodotus, Athenaeus, Theocritus, Homer, and the enigmatic oracle found in *Anthologia Palatina* 14.34; and through references to the mythological elements found in these authors' works, Tatius constructed a novel dependent solely upon myth for its narrative. Even when he employed a historian, namely Herodotus, he selected only mythological subjects, such as the story of Europa and the story of the Phoenix.

Finally, I focused on the analogous identity of Theagenes in the *Aethiopica*: the mythological analogue of the hero of the novel is found in the tragic subtext of the novel.[1] Heliodorus uses passages, lines, and myths found in the *Persians* of Aeschylus, the *Ajax* and *Oedipus Rex* of Sophocles, and the *Phoenicians*, *Medea*, *Hecuba*, *Heraclidae*, *Orestes*, and *Hippolytus* of Euripides to enable the reader to identify Theagenes. The *Hippolytus* supplies the majority of signs that point to the solution of the analogous identity.

Literary allusion is not limited to tragedy. Heliodorus also includes references to Hesiod, Homer, Plato, Aratus, and Lucian; even historical works are employed. The historical, however, is limited to affording some authenticity to the novel. In Heliodorus, myth reaches its ancient apex as a literary tool. In Chariton history gives the backdrop for the novel, sets the stage for the action, identifies the characters, and puts the reader at ease by supplying him with a literary genre, although new, that owes a great deal to history. Myth is marginal in Chariton. Xenophon, in possible imitation of Chariton, begins his work by identifying the leading characters of his novel in a historical manner. Longus breaks away from the historical approach to novelistic writing by preferring to show that he knows historical theory but opts, instead, to use idyllic myth as the source for his characters' delineation and for the structure of his novel. Achilles Tatius follows the lead of Longus and, like the author of *Daphnis and Chloe*, begins his work with an ekphrasis that has undertones of history but for the most part uses myth to lend structure.

Heliodorus does away with the historical or ekphrastic manner of opening a novel and chooses to use the stage techniques of in medias res (to begin) and deus ex machina (to end). Like the Sophistic novelists he employs myth, though more subtly. No longer are the characters constantly likened to mythological personae, no longer is Homer used to dictate plot or mythological context, no longer is the mythological element one of many components of the novel: mythical allusion is *the* constituent of the *Aethiopica*.

Appendixes

Appendix 1

The myths and legends in the *Iliad* and the *Odyssey* are the earliest recorded by the Greeks. Homer did not differentiate between the two, and it was Hesiod who first commented on the difference between fiction and truth. Hesiod wrote that the Muses are able to tell both the truth and lies as if they were the truth (*Theog.* 26–28). The Presocratics were next in line to offer some criticism of myths. Among the many Presocratics who criticized myth were Xenophanes of Colophon and Heraclitus of Ephesus. Hecataeus of Miletus, one of the earliest Ionian geographers, also criticized mythology. Xenophanes (fl. 530 B.C.) spurned Homeric and Hesiodic mythology and the religious tradition that grew out of the epics (cf. fr. 11). Heraclitus (fl. 500 B.C.) continued the attack on the mythology found in his predecessors, Homer and Archilochus, and noted τόν τε ῞Ομηρον ἔφασκεν ἄξιον ἐκ τῶν ἀγώνων ἐκβάλλεσθαι καὶ ῥαπίζεσθαι καὶ ᾿Αρχίλοχον ὁμοίως (fr. 42). Hecataeus (fl. 500 B.C.), in the introduction to his Γενεηλογίαι, wrote ῾Εκαταῖος Μιλήσιος ὧδε μυθεῖται· τάδε γράφω, ὥς μοι δοκεῖ ἀληθέα εἶναι· οἱ γὰρ ῾Ελλήνων λόγοι πολλοί τε καὶ γελοῖοι, ὡς ἐμοὶ φαίνονται, εἰσίν (fr. 1). Hecataeus, from the very start of his work, attempted to show that the ἀληθέα must not be confused with the λόγοι γελοῖοι and hence differentiated the fictional from the historical.

Herodotus followed Hecataeus in separating the fictional from the historical. Although Herodotus's work at times might seem to be purely fictional, he did write in the first lines of his *History* that he would record what had actually happened (1.1–5). He also related that he would arrive at the truth from his own observations, by research, and by writing down what he himself saw (2.99). Shortly after Herodotus, Thucydides wrote that, in regard to the speeches in his work, he would attempt to narrate what he thought the speaker would have said and what would have been fitting for the occasion of the speech. In regard to facts about the war, however, Thucydides had a different plan: τὰ δ' ἔργα τῶν πραχθέντων ἐν τῷ πολέμῳ οὐκ ἐκ τοῦ παρατυχόντος πυνθανόμενος ἠξίωσα γράφειν οὐδ' ὡς ἐμοὶ ἐδόκει, ἀλλ' οἷς τε αὐτὸς παρῆν καὶ παρὰ τῶν ἄλλων ὅσον δυνατὸν ἀκριβείᾳ περὶ ἑκάστου ἐπεξελθών (1.22.2).[1] He also made it clear that he would not include τὸ μυθῶδες (1.22.4) even though the finished product might not be as pleasing. Thucydides did not want to write a prize essay for the moment but rather a κτῆμά ἐς αἰεί (1.22.4), and this would necessarily eliminate any myth.

In the second book of the *Republic* Plato stressed that μύθοι, fictional stories, are the things first taught to children (377a); therefore, these myths should not hold opinions contrary to those expected from the children when they become adults (377b).[2] Accordingly, Plato suggested that there should be some sort of censorship of the myth-makers (377c) and that lists of acceptable myths should be created. These lists would include stories about respected heroes but not the myths and stories that harmed the image of the gods (377d). Plato, in other words, harked back to the ideas of the Presocratics who had denigrated the traditional myths; Plato recommended that the myths told to children espouse the fairest lessons of virtue (378e).

Aristotle also dealt with the subject of poetry as fiction and history as truth. In his *Poetics*, though not specifically examining myth in the modern sense of the word, he dictated that it is the poet's object not to tell τὰ γενόμενα but rather οἷα ἂν γένοιτο καὶ τὰ δυνατὰ κατὰ τὸ εἰκὸς ἢ τὸ ἀναγκαῖον (1451a37–b1).[3] The difference between a historian and a poet was not that a historian wrote in prose and a poet in verse, but that the historian tells τὰ γενόμενα, while the poet writes οἷα ἂν γένοιτο. He also advised that the myths (stories) that the poet wrote had become hackneyed, and therefore: οὐ πάντως εἶναι ζητητέον τῶν παραδεδομένων μύθων, περὶ οὓς αἱ τραγῳδίαι εἰσὶν ἀντέχεσθαι. καὶ γὰρ γελοῖον τοῦτο

ζητεῖν, ἐπεὶ καὶ τὰ γνώριμα ὀλίγοις γνώριμά ἐστιν, ἀλλ᾽ ὅμως εὐφρ-
αίνει πάντας (1451b23–27).[4]

On the Roman side of literature, Vergil seems to have shared Aristotle's notion that the myths had become worn out (*Georgics* 3.1–8). His
comments on the state of literature dealing with mythology would be
echoed by many other writers, for example, Martial in an epigram that
might have been aimed at Statius (4.49). Juvenal wrote that he did not
want to remain a listener all his days; he also wanted to have his say. He
was tired of listening to epics and tragedies such as the *Theseid* of Codrus,
the *Telephus*, and the *Orestes*. He knew his mythology, which by this time
had been worked to death (cf. 1.7–14).

The Romans also speculated about the historical and the fictional, as
the author of the *Rhetorica Ad Herennium* (written ca. 86–82 B.C.) shows.
He differentiated between the factual and the fictional and said that the
fictional and the factual can be mixed, but he noted that the two are not
the same: *Id quod in negotiarum expositione positum est tres habet partes:*
fabulam, historiam, argumentum. Fabula est quae neque veras neque veri simi-
les continet res, ut eae sunt quae tragoediis traditae sunt. Historia est gesta res,
sed ab aetatis nostrae memoria remota. Argumentum est ficta res quae tamen
fieri potui, velut argumenta commoediarum (1.13).

In the beginning of the fourth book of his *World History*, Diodorus
Siculus made plain the difficulties with which the mythographer had to
struggle. Firstly, the antiquity of the events that the mythographer would
write down in his work were hindering to research. Secondly, the numbers
and types of heroes, demigods, and men were too vast to allow a coher-
ent exposition of deeds and genealogies. Lastly, Diodorus complained that
the ancient mythographers themselves had been in disagreement and so
have handed down faulty and confusing compilations. On account of
these three factors, the greatest historians, Isocrates, Callisthenes, and
Theopompus, according to Diodorus, have not included myth in their
histories. Diodorus, in contrast to the greatest historians he cited, endeav-
ored to include the ancient legends. It is true that a pronouncement like
Diodorus's may be subjective and superficial, since some historians included the fantastic consciously (e.g., Duris) and others unconsciously
(e.g., Thucydides). Diodorus is saying that those who impress him as
historians are historians; those who do not are not. Though his comment
may say nothing about popular tradition, it does hint at what the educated
writer and reader expected.

Lucian, a contemporary of the earlier novelists, also ventured into the realm of fact and fiction. In his satiric *How to Write History*, Lucian recalls the faults of shoddier historians: they neglected to record events, they included excessive praise of individuals, and, what is more important, they did not separate history and poetry (7–8). These historians did not see that history must be useful and that this usefulness could be arrived at only through truth (9). In contrast to these historians, the best historians had two prerequisites before undertaking the writing of history: political acumen and the power of expression. Lucian did understand that myth would have to turn up in any historical work, but when it did he cautioned that καὶ μὴν καὶ μῦθος εἴ τις παρεμπέσοι, λεκτέος μέν, οὐ μὴν πιστωτέος πάντως, ἀλλ᾽ ἐν μέσῳ θετέος τοῖς ὅπως ἂν ἐθέλωσιν εἰκάσουσι περὶ αὐτοῦ· σὺ δ᾽ ἀκίνδυνος καὶ πρὸς οὐδέτερον ἐπιρρεπέστερος (60).[5]

In the second and third centuries A.D. many rhetoricians wrote on what history should be and what myth was. Rufus of Perinthus, a student of Herodes Atticus, noted in his ΤΕΧΝΗ ΡΗΤΟΡΙΚΗ that Ἱστορικὸν δὲ ἐν ᾧ διηγούμεθα πράξεις τινὰς μετὰ κόσμου ὡς γεγενημένας (β'). Hermogenes of Tarsus (second century A.D.), in his rhetorical handbook, echoed Plato when he wrote that myth was the first type of story to which children were exposed. He, however, after recalling the fact that myths were found in Hesiod and Archilochus (1.4–5), specified that myth had to be fictitious (ψευδῆ) (1.10), practical (χρήσιμον) (1.11), plausible (πιθανόν) (1.12), expandable (ἐκτείνεν), or concise (συστέλλειν) (1.17–18). Theon of Alexandria (second century A.D.) defined myth as a false story, but having some semblance of truth (3.1).

In sum: according to ancient Greek and Roman sources, myth preceded history and history employed myth. History was to be written in prose since it was factual, and myth was to be written mostly in verse since it was fictional. Parallel to this literary restriction of genre and content, it can be said that the factual had to be written in prose, and the fictional in verse. There are exceptions, however, to this history-prose and myth-verse practice (e.g., Apollodorus), and the ancient Greek novel that is purely fictional in content, though the earlier novels have some quasi-historical form, especially disregards the content-form maxim. This genre-specific attribute was probably the cause for the contempt and disregard that the ancient literary critics had for the novel. Lucian in *How to Write History*, in my opinion, best sums up the approach of the ancient novelists to myth.

Appendix 2

A fter the wedding the parents decide to send away the couple. On the journey Antheia swears by Artemis of the Ephesians that she will not live or look upon the sun if separated even for a short time from Habrocomes. One of their first stops is Rhodes, where the couple are mistaken for gods, and consequently the Rhodians offer sacrifice and celebrate their arrival as a festival. In Rhodes, at the temple of Helius, the couple offer a gold panoply inscribed with their names, and as it happens, pirates are made aware of the wealthy cargo of the newlyweds' ship and decide to take it. Corymbus, the chief of these pirates, leads the assault on the ship and orders the slaughter of everyone except Antheia and Habrocomes, who had begged him to spare their lives, and hands them over to Apsyrtus, his commander.[1] Corymbus in the meanwhile develops a violent passion for Habrocomes, and a fellow pirate by the name of Euxinus has the same feelings for Antheia. Corymbus and Euxinus confide to each other their loves and decide to help each other: Euxinus will reveal to Habrocomes Corymbus's feeling, and Corymbus will reveal Euxinus's feelings to Antheia. Both Habrocomes and Antheia, when they have been made aware of the pirates' plans, tell the pirates to give them time to think over their proposals.

While Habrocomes and Antheia are pondering the pirates' offers,

Apsyrtus takes them away from Corymbus and Euxinus and sets sail to Tyre, where the people think that Habrocomes and Antheia are gods. As mentioned above, however, Manto, the daughter of Apsyrtus, falls in love with Habrocomes.

Later on in the novel, Habrocomes meets up with Hippothous, who tells his traveling companion the sad story of his life: διηγήματα καὶ πολλὴν ἔχοντα τραγῳδία (3.1.4). The story not only seems to reinforce the tragic subtext of this novel, but also parallels the adventures of the hero and heroine. It seems that Hippothous is from Perinthus, where he had fallen in love with a young man named Hyperanthes.[2] The two Perinthians loved each other, unbeknownst to everyone else, but a man by the name of Aristomachus interfered in that love. Aristomachus took Hyperanthes away to Byzantium, on the pretext of wanting to be his tutor; Hippothous followed them there and killed Aristomachus. Afterward, Hippothous and Hyperanthes fled by ship to Asia, but as luck would have it the ship sank off the coast of Lesbos, and Hyperanthes drowned. To assuage his grief Hippothous set up an inscription which read: Ἱππόθοος κλεινῷ τεῦξεν τόδε <σῆμ'> Ὑπεράνθει, / οὗ τάφον ἐκ θανάτου ἀγαθὸν ἱεροίο πολίτου / ἐς βάθος ἐκ γαίης, ἄνθος κλυτόν, ὅν ποτε δαίμων / ἥρπασεν ἐν πελάγει μεγάλου πνεύσαντος ἀήτου (3.2.13).[3] After setting up the inscription he went to Asia Minor, where he became a robber.

Habrocomes, in turn, tells Hippothous all of his adventures but does not mention Antheia's name. Hippothous, in an attempt to console Habrocomes, reveals to him that he and his fellow robbers were about to sacrifice a girl to Ares but had not been able to because they had been interrupted. Habrocomes surmises that it had been Antheia, and consequently the two men set out to find her.

In the meantime, at Tarsus, Antheia had become friends with a certain fellow Ephesian named Eudoxos, who happened to be a doctor. He knew of the trials and tribulations that Antheia had undergone and swore by Artemis that he would not reveal any of Antheia's story. When Antheia sees that she will be forced to marry Perilaus, she asks Eudoxos for help, and he gives her a potion that when taken simulates death (Scheintod). Antheia, thinking that she has a lethal concoction, takes it in the bridal chamber and falls into a deep sleep. Perilaus then assumes that Antheia is dead and buries her. In the tomb, however, Antheia regains consciousness (cf. Callirhoe) and cries out that she has been made a sacrifice to Love and Death. Antheia, however, suffers even more misfortune: pirates find out that a girl had been richly buried, and consequently they plunder the tomb.

When Habrocomes finds out what has happened, he sets sail to catch up with the pirates but is shipwrecked off the Phoenician coast. There he is taken prisoner and sold to a retired soldier named Araxus. The old soldier has a wife by the name of Kyno (cf. Hägg 1971b, 42), who so lusts after Habrocomes that she tells him that she would even kill Araxus to sleep with him. Kyno forces Habrocomes, after much pressure, to agree to have sex with her, and on the night that they are to consummate her illicit love, Kyno kills Araxus. When Habrocomes finds this out he will have nothing to do with her, and she, in turn, angered by his refusal of sex, accuses him of having murdered her husband. Habrocomes is arrested and sent for trial to the prefect of Egypt. This part of the story once again emphasizes the Hippolytean nature of Habrocomes.

Habrocomes is then sent to Egypt, where he is ordered by the prefect[4] to be crucified. When Habrocomes hears this he consoles himself by thinking that it is for the best, since Antheia is dead. The crucifixion is attempted on the banks of the Nile, but it is futile, since the Nile sends a gust of wind that knocks the cross into the river. Habrocomes is then ordered to be burnt on a pyre, which proves as ineffective as the cross: the Nile surges onto the pyre and quenches the fire.[5] When this occurs the prefect orders Habrocomes to be kept under watch in order that he may find out the identity of this divinely protected man.

En route to Ethiopia, Antheia stops in Memphis and is attacked by Hippothous and his band. At the same time, the prefect of Egypt finds out the truth about Habrocomes and gives him his freedom, gifts, money, and promises to send him back to Ephesus. Habrocomes, for some unknown reason, chooses instead to take the money and gifts and to sail to Italy.

Antheia does not fare well as well as Habrocomes: she is almost raped by a guard named Anchilaus, who is killed by her before he can commit the act. In retribution Antheia is condemned to a gruesome death by being placed in a ditch with two fierce and ravenous dogs. Another guard, by the name of Amphinomus, however, rescues her.

To parallel the adventures of Antheia, Xenophon writes that when Habrocomes makes his way to Syracuse he meets there an old fisherman by the name of Aegialeus, who tells him a very interesting story. It seems that he and his future wife, Thelxinoe, had met at a festival in Sparta, promised each other undying love, and eloped even though Thelxinoe had originally been betrothed to a Spartan named Androcles. They both loved each other, but this love became threatened by some god who was envious of them. Aegialeus and Thelxinoe had consequently eloped on the night before Thelxinoe was to marry Androcles.[6] They had lived happily ever after in Syracuse, until the death of Thelxinoe. Aegialeus, however, after embalming her, talked with her, ate with her, and slept with her. She even consoled him (παραμυθεῖται 5.1.11; her body is called a παραμυθία for Aegialeus 5.1.12).[7] Habrocomes, however, did "not bolt out of the house immediately to avoid . . . a senile lunatic" (Schmeling 1980, 67), but having been consoled by Aegialeus's story, he lived with him and helped him in his fishing.

Antheia undergoes one more attempted rape at the hands of a certain Polyidus, but she escapes by taking asylum in the temple of Isis in Memphis. She asks the goddess to protect her, and when Polyidus hears this he pities her and promises not to do violence to her. On account of his promise, Antheia leaves the temple and goes to the temple of Apis, where she asks the god to give her a sign. The prophecy is that soon all will be well. All does not go well soon enough, because Antheia is sold to a brothel-keeper in Tarentum. Now that all three main characters are in roughly the same part of the world, Antheia in Tarentum, Hippothous in Tauromenium, and Habrocomes in Syracuse, the story comes to an end. Hippothous finds Antheia, rescues her from the brothel, and takes her to Rhodes, where she and Habrocomes are reunited.

Notes

1. There has been controversy surrounding the completeness of the *Ephesiaca*. Hägg (1966) seemed to have settled this quandary by demonstrating that what we have of Xenophon's novel is not an epitome, but rather the entire work. For a completely new approach to this problem see O'Sullivan (1995). On the dates of novels see Swain 1996, 422–25.

2. In Stephens and Winkler's collection (1995) there are found the fragmentary remains of an additional twenty-five novels. I am not including in the list of the five canonical works the works by Pseudo-Lucian, Lucian, Pseudo-Callisthenes, the anonymous author of *Apollonius King of Tyre* (this novel was written in Latin), Antonius Diogenes, and Iamblichus, because they do not conform to the traditional plot of the novel. The plots usually follow this form: boy meets girl, they fall in love, undergo numerous adventures and perhaps are separated; the girl may undergo a false-death; eventually they are reunited.

3. In Chariton's *Chaereas and Callirhoe*, the earliest extant Greek novel, there is an abundance of historical detail that superficially classifies this novel as historical (cf. Hunter 1994). Since this late-blooming genre is written in prose, and since one of the major literary genres that employed prose was history (in addition to philosophy and letters), Chariton, with his numerous historical minutiae, could not but have relied substantially on historiographical structures and features. After Chariton, however, the historical began to change to the romantic or mythological.

4. Extended religious meanings, in particular whether the inclusion of a tale denotes

the author's belief in it, are outside the scope of this book, because the levels of religious beliefs of any of the ancient novelists are not ascertainable (cf. Veyne 1988).

5. For example, epic, New Comedy, Alexandrian erotic poetry, *periegesis*, and historiography. Amalgamations or syntheses of these genres could have led to the emergence of the novel, e.g., the Alexandrian erotic poetry and the travel story (*Reisefabulistik*) (Rohde 1960); this is not universally accepted, because not all the Greek novels include Eros, and moreover all other possible literary roots are excluded. The degeneration of literary forms may also be responsible: the novel is a Second Sophistic (Schwartz 1943, 154), unwanted by-product of the decay of Hellenistic historiography (Schwartz 1896, 1943; history's contribution to the novel was not a new idea [cf. Wilcken 1893, who speculates the novel as an offshoot of Hellenistic historiography]). This theory has Hellenistic historiography (similar to that of Duris) replacing the *Reisefabulistik* and joining it to erotic poetry, which appears to be the common literary ancestor (Giangrande 1962, 155). By Chariton's time the erotic gains primacy and begins the displacement of the historical and patriotic elements (Hadas 1952). Cf. Müller 1976, Holzberg 1995, 28–42, Ruiz-Montero 1996, 29–85.

Numerous other theoretical influences abound: rhetorical handbooks (Thiele 1890), legend and saga (Lavagnini 1921; 1950), adventure (Ludvivosky 1925), religion, and eastern cults (Kérenyi 1971). The religion and eastern cults ideas led to the *Mysterientexte* or romans à clef, which suggests that the novels were indoctrination manuals for cults. It is strange, however, that Chariton's novel is not considered a *Mysterientext* because Chariton, it is argued, was not aware that he was supposed to have composed a religious manual (Merkelbach 1962, 339–40). Any thesis that holds that novels are *Mysterientexte* seems vitiated by this, or any, admission that it does not apply to Chariton, the first novelist, who must have had appreciable influence on those who followed. Cf. Altheim 1948, who had noted the importance of religious elements on the novel.

The current focus on the development of the genre is on the reasons for its rise rather than the process: the Zeitgeist has discarded speculation on a biological development (Perry 1967). Historiography, New Comedy (Paduano 1980), and other literary species are now being studied as having influenced the development of the novel (cf. Reardon 1971, 312–33). For other reviews on the theories on the origins of the ancient novel see MacQueen 1990, 204–24, and Pervo 1987, 86–114.

6. On non-novel fiction see Pratt 1993.

7. The ancient novel is the least "defined," least "concentrated," and most "formless" of all the literary genres (Hägg 1983, 89). To whom did this chaotic genre appeal? Why would anyone be interested in reading a narrative that has a πάθος ἐρωτικόν as its main ingredient? The theorized readers are the middle class, who see in the novel "their own ideals and unfulfilled longings" (Scobie 1973, 96), the Hellenistic educated elite of the cities of Asia Minor (Edwards 1991, 200), scribes, women, youths (Hägg 1983, 90–91), and those poor in spirit (Perry 1967, 89f.). Wesserling (1987, 67–79) suggests that the audience of the novel probably was the intelligentsia and, like Perry (1967), also stresses that the primary function of the novel is entertainment, "satisfaction of emotional needs, wish fulfillment, escape, and, in addition, intellectual or aesthetic pleasure."

8. The audience of the ancient novel may therefore be identified in terms of the

authors of the genre. Since Chariton alone supplies autobiographical information, he may help in the identification of his readers. The frequent borrowing from earlier literary works (cf. chap. 1) shows that Chariton was not only literate but extremely well educated. He identifies himself as the ὑπογραφεύς of Athenagoras, an orator in Aphrodisias, who probably depended upon Chariton to maintain his written records; an orator would not employ someone who was not capable of writing down or composing a literary product. The author also mentions that his homeland is Aphrodisias in Asia Minor. Since this Carian part of the Mediterranean has a tradition of epic, historiography, and travel stories, it would not be too great a leap to suggest that Chariton wrote for an audience that valued its literary inheritance and was itself widely literate. If Chariton did not write for an audience that would be able to enjoy and, more importantly, understand the intertextual quality of his novel, why would he produce such a literary work? The answer can be that Chariton wrote for an audience that was at least educated enough to understand and appreciate his work (cf. Bowie 1994). J. R. Morgan notes that for the novel in general the genre "came to demand of its readers a degree of sophisticated self-awareness and reflexivity that would have restricted full appreciation to those with a high level of literary training" (1995, 143). See also for a possible audience Fusillo 1997, 222–23.

9. Fusillo (1988, 19) believes that in Chariton the historiographical elements ennoble the genre. For a thorough and superior analysis on history and its relationship to the novel see Fusillo 1991, 56–66.

10. Hägg 1988, 179. Scobie (1973, 19) remarks that it was "not altogether surprising that at a time of comparative peace and political stability Greek romance-writers were tempted if not by literary fashion, then by nostalgia to project much of the action of their romances back into the turbulent but free past before the emergence of Rome as the dominant political force in the Mediterranean where Greeks were still at war partly with themselves and partly with the Persians."

11. On Latin and its impact on the Greek world P. A. Brunt writes (1976, 163): "What was specifically Latin in the common civilization of the empire made little impact in the east. There Greek remained the language in which Rome communicated with her subjects, and Greeks rarely learned Latin, except for the few who entered the army or imperial administration; of its literary merits they were usually content to be ignorant. The form of the local institutions was rarely changed. Yet this phil-Hellenism, as well as the material benefits that Rome's protection assured, must surely have helped to win the political attachment of her Hellenic subjects, or at least of those who were politically conscious and articulate."

12. The dates of the Second Sophistic are usually given as end of the first century A.D. to the early third (Anderson 1993, 13). Bowie (1982, 30) identifies the sophists as men from the upper class, who declaim and "are among the political leaders of the Greek cities, their declamations train themselves and others for political activity; and where real political power is circumscribed by the dependence of the cities on Rome the fantasy world of declamatory themes allows a Greek aristocrat with a Roman name to play the role of Demosthenes" (45).

13. Bowersock 1965, 100–111, especially 108. Tim Whitmarsh (2001, 18) echoes this idea: "Greeks of the highest socio-economic ranks were, during this period, increasingly implicated in the structures of Roman power: even larger numbers of elite

Greeks acted as intermediaries between their cities and Rome, were awarded Roman citizenship, found their way into the Roman senate, and attained important offices."

14. Crawford 1978, 194: "Increased acceptance by the Greek world of Roman rule, indeed, did not lead to any decline in the value attached to traditional Greek institutions or to any reluctance to assert Greek cultural superiority"; there was limited influence of Roman elements on Greek culture.

15. On this reaction Reardon (1971, 17) writes: "Elle est une reaction aux grandes données de l'histoire contemporaine, et surtout à l'existence de l'empire romain; et cette réaction s'exprime sous la forme d'un manque d'intérêt pour ce qui est romain. . . . Sauf certaines exceptions, la littérature grecque de cette période ignore Rome. Non pas totalement, mais presque; le fait est significatif. Les Grecs se rendent pleinement compte du pouvoir de Rome, mais ils ne s'y intéressent pars. La matière littéraire de l'époque est en grande partie tirée de la tradition ancienne; c'est surtout cela qui va ressortir de toute cette enquête." García Gual (1972, 51) shares a similar view and sees this a general development in Greek culture: "1) la pérdida de interés en los asuntos públicos por los habitantes de esas ciudades de poblacíon mixta y de escasa autonomía política; 2) una descomposicíon moral y religiosa, producida por el choque de la cultura tradicional con nuevos elementos, en lo que se ha llamado sociedad abierta (culturalmente) frente a las cerradas de época anterior; y 3) una inestable situacíon social y económica, que se agrava a partir del s. II d. C., con crisis económicas que sacudieron periódicamente amplias regiones del imperio."

16. Why does the typical author of this period behave in such a fashion? Van Groningen (1965, 53–54) supplies a possible answer: "In the first place that he is contented with what has been achieved, with the heritage left by former generations. He wishes to keep, not to conquer. Why? Because, consciously or unconsciously, he realizes that he is unable to do what they did. He knows that he is inferior to them. This feeling of personal impotence, added to a sincere, but blind admiration for the great predecessors, induces him to look for help where this can be found, i.e., with these predecessors, in the past. It is possible that there is a certain connection with the general political situation. The Greek cultural world cannot hope any longer for further expansion. The Roman Empire defends its boundaries. Peace in prosperity is the idea. And in the numerous panegyrics of the emperors we notice the ease-loving gratitude which gladly leaves the decisions to them and shuns personal responsibility."

J. L. Lightfoot (2000, 244) concurs: "What underlay such backward-looking classicism? According to some, it had come about precisely because Greeks were now, effectively, politically impotent: it was a form of nostalgia for the days of the city-state. This needs nuancing: Greeks could rise to the highest positions of state albeit within the *Roman* administration, and the passion for classicism affected their political masters, the Romans, as well. In certain moods the Romans, no less than the Greeks, missed—or affected to miss—the cut and thrust of political rhetoric in the turbulent days when things were really happening, and expressed anxiety about their present state of well-fed inertia. Nevertheless the basic point remains: for Greeks the question underlying this whole, huge, period . . . is how does one respond to the realities of Roman rule?"

17. Gerald Sandy (1997) uses 323 B.C. as the cutoff date. The "pre-323 B.C. orientation" of the Second Sophistic is "notorious" (43), and it is a "cult of the past"

expressed through "linguistic artificiality" (atticism) (49). This interest in the past is also referred to as "linguistic retro-occupation" (51). See also Graham Anderson (1993), who comments that the sophists' view demanded Greek cultural "tradition and self-awareness" and a "look back to a period of Greek freedom and independence as if some of its most momentous events were still actually unfolding" (15). Sophists were concerned to preserve "a cultural whole[,] the world of classical Greece recreated through its literature" (69), and to restore that past time through its literature and language (87; see also 100). This was a literature in which Homer's *Odyssey* and Plato's *Phaedrus* were especially cherished (75–77).

18. Cf. Alcock (1993, 28): "Greek authors of the Principate, notably Plutarch and other members of the Second Sophistic, to some extent ignore contemporary and relatively recent history and personalities, preferring to engage with the more distant, more glowing past." On this topic Reardon (1991) observes that there is a "certain thematic unity" that "without exception" draws upon "Greek" and *classical* tradition"; in "enormous preponderance, the themes of these writers are taken from the fifth and fourth centuries, not even the Hellenistic age" (29). This harking back to a Roman-free world is "above all a manifestation of essentially political and civic sentiments of dissatisfaction with the subordinate political role that Greeks find themselves in, once the Roman Empire has established that it is there to stay" (39). This archaizing and exclusive use of pre-Alexandrian history is deliberate (Reardon 1991, 99).

19. Woolf (1994, 125–26) continues by stating that the "increasing insistence of the writers of the Second Sophistic that Greeks were special, and hence deserving of privileged treatment, masked and responded to their progressive incorporation into a world that was increasingly an artefact of Roman power."

20. The process that led to this Greek attitude is as follows: "Imperial Greek literature" (vis-à-vis Rome) has various stages: "first, assigning the Romans a place in a still Hellenocentric universe (some even claimed Latin as a dialect of Greek); then with various uneasy assertions of parity, or admissions of weakness which could be tempered by harking back to a glorious past. Yet, on the part of many, there was a publicly unproblematic identification with Rome, for Strabon already uses 'we' of Rome. And eventually Greeks, enfranchised as Roman citizens along with the rest of the Empire in 212 CE, became Romans, *Romaioi*" (Lightfoot 2000, 266). For the most recent work on the development of Greek literature and Greek cultural identity during Roman rule see Goldhill 2001.

21. E.g., Dionysius of Halicarnassus (Bowersock 1965, 131; see also 139 on the types of pro-Roman literature written by Greeks).

22. J. R. Morgan (1995) suggests that embracing of historical fact looks like a "deliberate strategy on the part of novelists at a particular juncture in the form's development" (133), and that the "historical nature of the early novels served to legitimize their very existence, a stratagem particularly effective in view of the fact that ancient historiography already acted on occasion as a receptacle for narrative which acknowledged the goal of pleasure above information. Historiography was being enlisted to provide fiction with the literary pedigree which, as a late arrival, it lacked" (134).

23. The suspension of disbelief is created by the inclusion of very few references to present history in the Greek novel; García Gual (1972) notes that this escapist

literature (60–61) arose as a literary form meant to be an "evasión de un tiempo sin ideales" (52).

24. The pre-sophistic novels are Chariton and Xenophon, and the sophistic novels are Longus, Achilles Tatius, and Heliodorus (Anderson 1993, 158). On the prominence of the historical in the earlier pre-sophistic novels see Pakcińska (1968), who writes that "the Greek novel at the beginning was above all historical in nature—especially Chariton" (598).

25. Cf. Morgan 1993, 208: "Chariton's stance as all-knowing, all-telling reporter is itself a fiction intended to win authority for the text: the authority of historical record."

26. Cf. Reardon 1991, 126: "Chariton sets his story in classical Greece because the antiquity of the setting adds a certain glamour to the actions of unexceptional people. . . . Historiography had little to do with the crucial matter of fictiveness. Historiographical form, prose narrative, was available, certainly, and surely suggested possibilities to the earliest romance writers." Gareth Schmeling (1998, 25) also notes that Chariton was quite adept at using historical texts and selecting, omitting, or adding details to suit his purposes.

27. Bowie (1999, 52) observes that in the case of Achilles Tatius the location of the novel "is no longer historical. The contemporary world of the East Mediterranean reader is envisaged and evoked with a fair measure of consistency and realism. Only the Byzantine's Thracian war invites the reader to imagine a particular date, less probably historical than intended."

28. Cf. Reardon 1991, 28: "Greek society had by now existed for centuries within the political framework of one large empire or another, Alexander's or his successors', or Rome's. While local life was assuredly busy, in the wider context of the cosmopolitan Greek world this was no longer the compact culture of Old Comedy, in which a man could aspire to having an effective voice in controlling his own social existence in his autonomous community; now there was a large-scale, open society, in which the individual cut a much smaller figure, was swallowed up and lost in the mass—as we may feel lost in today's large-scale open society. Chariton's story was written for those who lived in that world, and it reflects that world and its inhabitants, their situation, their anxieties, their aspirations."

29. Cf. García Gual 1972, 26: "Es la expression de un sentimiento vital muy distinto del clásico. Si el individuo de la «polis» griega gustaba de lo limitado y bien definido, e ciudadano de un imperio helenístico o del Imperio Romano, comunidad que no llegó a sentir ni comprender bien y en cuyo gobierno no participaba, se hallaba en un dominio político muy diferente donde la amplitud de relaciones en su mundo y la incertidumbre de los confines de su país era uno de los rasgos de su existencia. El «pathos» de la lejanía, de la distancia, es un reflejo de la desparicíon de las antiguas estructuras sociales."

30. On a similar phenomenon in the Jewish novels see Wills 1995.

31. See Swain 1996, 110–113, on the non-Roman historical elements and a Rome-free world. On this matter Konstan (1998, 15) remarks that "the mobile, deracinated world described in the novels resembles the world itself at a moment when the world might seem to transcend local particularisms. The Roman Empire had brought mul-

tiple cultures under its umbrella. The culture of the Roman Empire as a whole, however, was still relatively contentless, in the sense that there was no universal tradition constituted out of a generally accepted set of referents or paradigmatic narratives. The novel thus achieved a precarious autonomy from collective memory and heritage. Rather than addressing a defined and self-conscious cultural group, the novel constructed for itself a literary community of readers whose point of common reference was the novel itself. The implicit awareness on the part of writers and readers of the novel's referential independence is what constitutes the genre as fiction." See also Most 1989.

32. Cf. Walbank 1960, 222.

33. Morgan 1982, 248. Morgan's idea, however, may not be applicable to Chariton, who seems to include more historiographical elements in his novel than the other novelists.

34. Hägg 1983, 17. See also Philippides (1978, 18), who writes that the habit "of placing the plot within a specific period is only exhibited in the earliest romances that are extant, the *Ninus* romance, and Chariton's *Chaereas and Callirhoe.*" In the novels of Longus and Achilles Tatius there is, nevertheless, historical intent (79ff.).

35. This view is similar to the exoteric and esoteric readings of Plato.

36. See Reardon 1975, 87: "Once one begins to interpret things in a symbolizing, allegorical way, one very soon finds it impossible to turn around without stumbling on a symbol. Anything seems to be grist to the mill."

37. Fritz Graf 1993 supplies a thorough review of what myth can be: "traditional tales" (1), "implausible story," "the fabulous," "lies," "a thing widely believed false," "story," "transmitted from generation to generation" (2), "cultural relevance" (3). I prefer for this study "mythical narrative" (5; 119) or "traditional narrative" (e.g., a story found in Homer) (61) that dealt with the "gods and heroes" (143) and was "retold for the purpose of entertainment" (192). Cf. John Gould 1999, 107: "a traditional story, and by 'traditional' I mean (*a*) a story not thought of as the creation of some (potentially) nameable or datable individual; (*b*) the possession not of any individual or (solely) of any family but a collective possession shared by a whole community, where 'community' may cover anything from a single, city, town, or village to the entire Greek cultural world, from the Black Sea to the far West."

38. See also Veyne 1988, 17–26.

39. Cf. Lightfoot 1999, 231.

40. Reardon (1991, 11) writes that myth and "romance are close neighbors."

41. The source of these myths is of special importance. Chariton took the majority of his myths from the Homeric epics, and Xenophon seems to have imitated Chariton. Longus, Achilles Tatius, and Heliodorus, while showing Homeric influence on their selection of myths, employ myths that had been heavily reworked in the Hellenistic period by authors like Callimachus and Theocritus. Reardon (1971, 352) identifies the Hellenistic period as having been an important source for the myths used in the novels: "mythe hellénistique dans lequel nous avons cru voir le noyau du roman."

42. Consequently a few words on literary myth, and its relation to history, from the time of Homer to that of προγυμνάσματα (on προγυμνάσματα see Anderson 1993, 47–52) of the Second Sophistic, are in order. See appendix 1.

CHAPTER I

1. Hägg (1971a, 15 n. 1) lists and discusses the bibliography on the dating of Chariton and dates the novel to the first century B.C.

2. The papyri are Pap. Fayûm I, in *Fayûm Town and Their Papyri* (1900, 74–82); Pap. Oxyrhynchus no. 1019, in *Oxyrhynchus Papyri* vol. 8 (1910); Papyrus Michaelides I, in *Papyri Michaelidae* (1955).

3. "To Chariton: Do you think that the Greeks will remember your words when you're dead? If those who are nothing when alive, what can they be when dead?" All translations are my own unless cited otherwise.

4. Hägg 1987, 189; 1971a, 26. Ruiz-Montero (1989, 145) agrees with Hägg but stresses that Chariton also includes contemporary historical and social references.

5. On Chariton and the historians Zimmerman (1961, 329–30) comments that "Chariton war ein außerordentlich belesener Schriftsteller. Er kennt seinen Thukydides und von Xenophon besonders die Kyrupaideia sowie die Anabasis. Daß er jedoch auch historiche Werke von Autoren, die heute für uns verloren sind, ausgiebig herangezogen hat, steht außer allem Zweifel."

6. While scholars have examined Chariton's use of historical background, the importance of history in conjunction with myth in *Chaereas and Callirhoe* has not been adequately examined. Hetteger (1914–15) discusses only the roles of the gods and goddesses in the novel. Laplace (1980, 83) attempts to prove that "légendes définissent le schéma dramatique de la fiction de Chariton." These studies, however, focus on one function of myth and do not elucidate the overall use of myth in Chariton.

7. For an analysis of character development and delineation see Helms 1996. On the use of analogue as character delineation in the ancient Greek novel see Steiner 1969.

8. Schmeling (1974, 89) writes that it is "obvious from the frequency of comparison between Ariadne and Callirhoe that the reader was intended to see Callirhoe as a type of Ariadne, and that while Callirhoe was a somewhat unfamiliar character she was brought into focus, universalized, and delineated nicely by the simile."

9. Plutarch may not be the only source from which Chariton borrows for his attempt at a historical coating of a nonhistorical work. Hunter (1994) suggests that the novelist may have used Thucydides 6.30–31 in sections 3.5.2–3 of the novel and echoed the opening lines of Hecataeus, Herodotus, and Thucydides in the introduction to his novel. Hunter ends his argument by noting: "It was not modern scholars who first discovered the links which bind epic, historiography, and romance" (1084).

10. "There was, he says, a decree in force throughout Greece that no trireme should sail from any port carrying a crew of more than five men" (Scott-Kilvert 1960, 25). Shepard (1925, 16) suggests that the five men may be the (1) pilot, (2) the officer in charge at the bow (*proreus*); (3) the purser or supply officer (*pentecontarque*); . . . (4) the boatswain (*keleustes*), who commanded the oarsmen and regulated their movements in rowing," and (5) the trierarch. Casson (1991, 86) concurs with Shepard in the identification of these crew members.

11. "There are many different accounts of these events, and of the story of Ariadne, none of which agree in their details" (Scott-Kilvert 1960, 26).

12. Translation from Scott-Kilvert (1960, 26–27).

13. His speech is as follows: "Which of the gods is it, then, who has become my rival in love and carried off Callirhoe and is now keeping her with him—against her will, constrained by a more powerful destiny? That is why she died suddenly—so that she would not realize what was happening. That is how Dionysus took Ariadne from Theseus, how Zeus took Semele. It looks as if I had a goddess for a wife without knowing it, someone above my station. But she should not have left the world so quickly, even for such a reason. Thetis was a goddess, but she stayed with Peleus, and he had a son by her; I have been abandoned at the very height of my love. What is to happen to me? What is to become of me, poor wretch? Should I do away with myself? And who would share my grave? I did have this much to look forward to, in my misfortune—that if I could not continue to share Callirhoe's bed, I should come to share her grave. My lady! I offer my justification for living—you force me to live, because I shall look for you on land and sea, and in the very sky if I can reach there! This I beg of you, my dear—do not flee from me!" (3.3.4–7). Translation from Reardon (1989, 53–54).

14. Hesiod (*Theog.* 917), Diodorus Siculus (4.60.4), Ovid (*Fasti* 3.46off.), and Nonnos (47.27off.) relate that Ariadne was deserted by Theseus but immortalized in the heavens as a celestial crown. Homer (*Od.* 11.322), however, writes that she was killed by Artemis at a word from Dionysus.

15. ". . . but two ambassadors from the assembly and two from the council are enough; and Chaereas will sail with the group as leader" (Reardon 1989, 57).

16. ". . . bringing her forged letters, supposed to have been written by Theseus" (Scott-Kilvert 1960, 26).

17. The false pregnancy-and-birth component of the novel may also find a parallel in the Paeon account: ʾΕν δὲ τῇ θυσίᾳ, τοῦ Γορπιαίου μηνὸς ἱσταμένου δευτέρᾳ κατακλινόμενόν τινα τῶν νεανίσκων φθέγγεσθαι καὶ ποιεῖν ἅπερ ὠδίνουσαι γυναῖ- κες· ("at the sacrifice in her memory, which is held on the second day of the month of Gorpiaeus, one of the young men lies on the ground and imitates the cries and movements of a woman in labour" [Scott-Kilvert 1960, 27]). On this odd tradition of the *couvade* see Kouretas 1978; for further bibliography see Ampolo and Manfredini 1988, 226–27.

18. On the prototypical nature of the story Ampolo and Manfredini (1988, 226) write: "La storia da lui narrata ha uno scopo etiologico; mostra sopratutto i caratteri tardi di un romanzo ellenistico, come, p. es., nel particolare delle lettere false."

19. "My name is Chariton, of Aphrodisias, and I am clerk to the attorney Athenagoras. I am going to tell you the story of a love affair that took place in Syracuse" (Reardon, 1989, 21).

20. For a brief historical and archaeological study of Aphrodisias see Erim 1986.

21. Schmeling (1974, 21) notes that Aphrodite is the moving force in the novel's plot and that the work "is a tribute to her power and an aretalogy of her mystic power."

22. For example: *Il.* 21.114 in 1.1.14; *Il.* 18.22–24 in 1.4.6; *Od.* 17.485–87 in 2.3.7; *Il.* 23.66–67 in 2.9.6; *Il.* 10.540 and *Od.* 16.11 and 359 in 3.4.4; *Il.* 22.82–83 in 3.5.6; *Il.* 23.71 in 4.1.3; *Od.* 24.83 in 4.1.5; *Od.* 15.21 in 4.4.5; *Od.* 17.37 and 19.54 in 4.7.5; *Il.* 4.1 in 5.4.6; *Il.* 3.146 in 5.5.9; *Od.* 1.366 and 18.213 in 5.5.9; *Il.* 22.389–90 in 5.10.9; *Il.* 24.10–11 in 6.1.8; *Il.* 1.317 in 6.2.4; *Od.* 6.102–4 in 6.4.6; *Il.* 22.304–5

in 7.2.4; *Il.* 9.48–49 in 7.3.5; *Il.* 13.131 and 16.215 in 7.4.3; *Od.* 22.308 and 24.184 and *Il.* 10.483ff. in 7.4.6; *Od.* 23.296 in 8.1.17; *Il.* 19.302 in 8.5.2.

23. Schmeling (1974, 132) states that the "frequent quotations from Homer and various literary allusions and devices demand an audience acquainted with a respectably wide range of literature." Hägg (1971, 95) notes that the literal Homeric quotations "are a distinct and often-noticed feature of Chariton's narrative . . . only a few serve as similes . . . most of them are organic parts of the narration of this action. . . . The author simply substitutes for part of his own narration a well-known phrase from the epic—or, occasionally, from some classical prose author—and so gets a stylistic ornament, which, at the same time, has an associative value." The last part of Hägg's comment, the associative value of the Homeric phrase, is the second use of myth by Chariton: he employs the Homeric lines in order to lend structure to the plot. Cf. Pakcińska 1966.

24. 1.1.14. *Il.* 21.114 reads τοῦ instead of τῆς.

25. Wesserling (1987, 76) argues that Chariton, on account of his thorough "familiarity" with classical authors such as Homer, Herodotus, and Thucydides, perhaps planned to write for a category of people who could identify and understand his references.

26. "At these words a black cloud of grief covered him; / with both hands he took dark dust and poured it over his head, / defiling his lovely countenance" (Reardon 1989, 26).

27. Cf. Arist. *Pol.* 1305a17, 1316a36; Polyaen. 5.47, 5.1.1–2.

28. On the kick of death in ancient literature see: Diod. 3.112, 62.27; Diog. Laert. 1.94; Hdt. 3.32, 3.50; Nepos *Dion* 3; Suet. *Ner.* 35; Tac. *Ann.* 16. Cf. Ed. Frankel *RE* suppl. 6 625, 27–39.

29. "like to him in stature and fair looks and voice, and wearing just such clothes" (Reardon 1989, 47).

30. "Bury me so that I may pass through the gates of Hades as soon as possible" (Reardon 1989, 65).

31. "so that it may be seen by men far off, from the sea" (Reardon 1989, 65).

32. "Even if in Hades people forget the dead, even there I shall remember you, my dear" (Reardon 1989, 88).

33. "Lying now on his side, now on his back, now face down" (Reardon 1989, 90).

34. "Artemis the archer as she moves on the mountain, high Taygetus or Erymanthus, delighting in boars and swift deer" (Reardon 1989, 94).

35. "No, let me not die without effort, without glory, but after some great exploit that even our descendants will know about!" (Reardon 1989, 102).

36. "I and Polymarchus will fight, for it is at a god's behest that we have come" (Reardon 1989, 103). The Homeric text reads: Νῶι δ', ἐγὼ Σθένελός τε, μαχησόμεθ᾽εἰς ὅ τέκμωρ / Ἰλίου εὕρωμεν· σὺν γὰρ θεῷ εἰλήλουθμεν.

37. Cf. Hdt. 7.204–39; Diod. 11.3–11; and Plut. *Leonidas.*

38. Manuscript *L.* supplies Mithridates instead of Othyrades.

39. It can be argued that there was some sort of ring-composition in the use of these two lines. One instance refers to the Trojans going toward the Greek ships, and the second use shows the Trojans being repelled from the Greek ships. The ring-composition, if it does exist, exists in the Homeric text and not in the novel. The

action in the novel has not progressed, and in fact, the Homeric lines do not hint at anything but the battle formation.

40. Callirhoe did tell Chaereas that she had a son but that the father of the child was Dionysius.

41. Cyprus was a suitable island to arrive at since it is *the* island of Aphrodite. In Paeon's version of the Ariadne myth, Ariadne is left at Cyprus.

CHAPTER 2

1. Magie 1950, 647–48; 1514–15. See also Perry 1967, 345.

2. Papanikolaou (1973b) supplies a list of possible imitations of Chariton by Xenophon.

3. Heiserman 1977, 55. Schmeling (1980, 25) concurs on Xenophon's minimal use of myth: "Little use is made by Xenophon of myth to help him universalize his characters and stories. By comparison Xenophon's model, Chariton, uses graphic analogue from myth to compare Callirhoe to goddesses at least eight times." Hägg (1971b, 39) writes that most of the names of the characters in the *Ephesiaca* are found "in Greek literature as the names of mythical, historical or fictional characters." He further states (1971b, 58) that the "names of well-known mythological or historical figures, like Althaia, Apsyrtos and Kleisthenes, are given, as we have seen, to the characters of the romance without any discernible symbolic meaning, and this is true also when the names in question were uncommon in daily life, as seems to be the case especially with the first two."

4. Reardon 1991, 61. If this assumption is correct, it would be necessary to examine the historical elements of the *Ephesiaca*. Hägg (1971a, 49) has done so and writes: "The action in Xenophon's romance seems to have no connection with any known historical incident or person. The prefect of Egypt (ὁ ἄρχων τῆς Αἰγύπτου)—whose presence in the romance shows that it belongs to Roman imperial times—remains anonymous throughout the romance. All the action is of a private nature; no wars or other political events are mentioned, except the struggles of different officials against the pirates of Cilicia and Egypt respectively."

5. Hägg (1971b, 41) notes that Lycomedes is a Homeric "warrior who is characterized as κρατερός and ἀρηΐφιλος, who slays an enemy but who is not individualized beyond this (*Il.* 9.84; 12.366; 17.345–6; 19.240). In the *Ephesiaca* the name is applied to Habrokomes' father, an important man in Ephesus, who is characterized only by his behavior: he is worried about his son (1.5.5) and irresolute (1.7.1), he feels sorrow (1.10.7) and regret (5.6.3)—in short, there are no resemblances."

6. Leucon is a character in the *Ephesiaca*.

7. Although it may seem to be a very far stretch to connect Athamas's story with the plot of the *Ephesiaca*, I am attempting to show that Xenophon may have been familiar with myths other than those found in the Homeric epics.

8. For a discussion of the resemblance of Habrocomes' plight to those of Bellerophon and Joseph see Schmeling 1980, 42.

9. Hägg (1971b, 40–41) writes that the "name Ἱππόθοος is borne by two persons in the *Iliad*, by the leader of the Pelasgians who is killed by Ajax (2.840–43 and

17.288–318) and by one of Priam's sons who is mentioned only in an enumeration (24.251). In Xenophon, Hipothoos is the third character in importance, but his characteristics change from episode to episode: sometimes he is the ruthless robber who even tries to kill Antheia on two different occasions (2.13 and 4.6) and sometimes Habrokomes' best friend and helper (2.14–3.3; 3.9–10; 5.8–14); in his own story he is the ill-fated lover of a young boy (3.2). In none of these functions does he show any distinct similarities with his namesakes in the epos." Hippothous is also, according to Hyg. *Fab.* 187 and Paus. 1.5.1–2 and 1.39.3, the son of Poseidon and Alope, the daughter of Cercyon, the king of Eleusis. He was granted by Theseus the kingship of Eleusis.

10. "his good looks were phenomenal, and neither in Ionia nor anywhere else had there been anything like them. This Habrocomes grew more handsome every day; and his mental qualities developed along with his physical ones. For he acquired culture of all kinds and practiced a variety of arts; he trained in hunting, riding, and fighting under arms. Everyone in Ephesus sought his company, and in the rest of Asia as well; and they had great hopes that he would have a distinguished position in the city. They treated the boy like a god, and some even prostrated themselves and prayed at the sight of him. He had a high opinion of himself, taking pride in his attainments, and a great deal more in his appearance. Everything that was regarded as beautiful he despised as inferior, and nothing he saw or heard seemed up to his standard. And when he heard a boy or girl praised for their good looks, he laughed at the people making such claims for not knowing that only he was handsome. He did not even recognize Eros as a god; he rejected him totally and considered him of no importance, saying that no one would ever fall in love or submit to the god except of his own accord. And whenever he saw a temple or statue of Eros, he used to laugh and claimed that he was more handsome and powerful than any Eros. And that was the case: for wherever Habrocomes appeared, no one admired any statue or praised any picture" (Anderson 1989a, 128).

11. Schmeling (1980, 23) suggests that the Narcissus myth may be a possibility: "The subsequent overweening pride of Habrocomes drives him to consider himself beautiful and then, unfortunately, to disconnect this beauty from any erotic consideration. Because Xenophon develops nothing special out of this situation by way of graphic analogue with the Narcissus myth, we should be able to conclude that he had very little concern for such learned references and allusions, or for universalizing his story through the use of myth."

12. On the historical Habrocomes see Hägg 1971b, 41: "In Herodotus Ἀβροκόμης is a son of Darius, killed at Thermopylae (Hdt. 7.224; also mentioned in Isocrates 4.140). In Xenophon's Anabasis (I.3.20; 4.3–5; 7.12) another Ἀβροκόμας is the satrap of the Great King in Phoenicia at the time of Cyrus' expedition. Thus, both are Persians who fight against the Greeks; they do not play heroic parts in these sources, and there are no comments on their outward appearances or inner qualities. In the romance, Ἀβροκόμης is a Greek (from Ephesus), and he is described as beautiful, proud and persevering: it seems to be out of the question that Xenophon should have intended the name of his hero to allude directly to the colourless Persians, as they are depicted in Herodotus and Xenophon the historian." It is interesting that in Hdt.

7.224 it is mentioned that the brother of Habrocomes was Hyperanthes, another character in the *Ephesiaca*.

13. Hägg (1971b, 43–44) writes that the name Μεγαμήδης "recorded only for Xenophon, is now also to be found in a fragment, the so-called Chione romance, in which a man called Megamedes seems to be one of the principal characters. This has led to the interesting theory that Xenophon intentionally connected his romance with an earlier popular one by making his heroine, Antheia, the daughter of one of its characters with this unusual name." Μεγαμηδείδαο is also found in the *Homeric Hymn to Hermes* 100.

14. Euippe, according to Pausanias 9.34.5–9, was the daughter of Leucon and the granddaughter of Athamas, the husband of Themisto. Xenophon has definitely linked the mythological backgrounds of Themisto, the wife of Lycomedes, and Euippe, the wife of Megamedes.

15. "first the sacred objects, the torches, the baskets, and the incense; then horses, dogs, hunting equipment . . . some for war, most for peace" (Anderson 1989a, 129).

16. "Her hair was golden—a little of it plaited, but most hanging loose and blowing in the wind. Her eyes were quick; she had the bright glance of a young girl, and yet the austere look of a virgin. She wore a purple tunic down to the knee, fastened with a girdle and falling loose over her arms, with a fawnskin over it, a quiver attached, and arrows for weapons; she carried javelins and was followed by dogs" (Anderson 1989a, 129).

17. See the introduction to Dalymeda 1926; cf. Picard 1922, 185–89, 329–32. For an account of an actual procession of Artemis see Rogers 1991, 54, 68, 185. His account is based on the A.D. 104 foundation inscription of the Roman equestrian C. Vibrius Salutaris found in Ephesus.

18. For narrative and verbal similarities between Chariton and Xenophon see the Teubner text by Papanikolaou, who supplies a catalog of such incidents.

19. "At last they brought in diviners and priests to Anthia to find a remedy to her plight. They came and performed sacrifices, made libations of all sorts, pronounced foreign phrases, alleging that they were placating some demons or other, and pretended that her malady came from the underworld" (Anderson 1989a, 131).

20. For the superstitious climate of Ephesus see Picard 1922, 131–32.

21. "Why do you long to learn the end of a malady, and its beginning? / One disease has both in its grasp, and from that the remedy must be accomplished. / But for them I see terrible sufferings and toils that are endless; / Both will flee over the sea pursued by madness; / They will suffer chains at the hands of men who mingle with the waters; / And a tomb shall be the burial chamber for both, and fire the destroyer; And beside the waters of the river Nile, to Holy Isis / The savior you will afterwards offer rich gifts; / But still after their sufferings a better fate is in store" (Anderson 1989a, 132).

22. ". . . and touched at Colophon, to consult the oracle of the Clarian Apollo. There, it is not a woman, as at Delphi, but a priest chosen from certain families, generally from Miletus, who ascertains simply the number and the names of applicants. Then descending into a cave and drinking a draught from a secret spring, the man, who is commonly ignorant of letters and of poetry, utters a response in verse

answering to the thoughts conceived in the mind of the inquirer. It was said that he prophesied to Germanicus, in dark hints, as oracles usually do, an early doom" (Hadas 1942, 84).

23. The text of Aelius Aristides can be found in Behr 1968, 243.

24. The oracular response is found in Parke 1985, 142.

25. "Cupids were playing, some attending Aphrodite, who was also represented, some riding on Nabataean ostriches, some weaving garlands, other bringing flowers. These were on one half of the canopy; on the other was Ares, not in armor, but dressed in a cloak and wearing a garland, adorned for his lover Aphrodite. Eros was leading the way, with a lighted torch" (Anderson 1989a, 132–33).

26. Xenophon may also be foreshadowing the appearance of Ares in the *Ephesiaca*.

27. For a moderately detailed narrative of the plot see appendix 2.

28. Witt 1971; especially chapter 18, "Xenophon's Isiac Romance."

29. Witt (1971, 248) speculates: "At the very beginning we meet Antheia performing the duties of a priestess so admirably that she is honored by her associates as being herself godlike. Io is treated in the same manner as priestess of Hera. The father of Antheia consults the oracle of Apollo at Colophon concerning his daughter's future. Inachus goes to the Pythian Apollo at Delphi about Io. Io craves to be freed from her sufferings instead of lingering for death. So does Antheia. Io is promised the Nile with his hallowed sweet-tasting waters. Apollo's oracle makes clear to Antheia that she will have to make sacrifice to hallowed Isis on the banks of the Nile, when she has reached Egypt."

30. Schmeling (1980, 128), in dealing with the myth of Io, notes that Xenophon uses the Io myth but borrows "much of what he has from Chariton, and does not really care much whether it has a natural origin or basis." Witt (1971, 348–49), echoing Merkelbach, also sees Isis as playing a great role in the *Ephesiaca*. He partially based this idea on the use of the adjectives that are shared by Antheia and Isis, e.g., *lysikomos*, which in the novel described Antheia's hair and which is used by Philostratus (*Ep.* 16) to describe Isis's hair.

31. For studies on the possibility of abridgement see: Hägg 1966; Reardon 1971, 353; Rohde 1960, 429; Bürger 1892, 36ff.; most recently O'Sullivan 1995.

CHAPTER 3

1. "The book is so beautiful that, amid the bad circumstances in which we live, we cannot retain the impression we receive from it, but are astonished anew every time we read it. . . . It would need a whole book to estimate properly all the great merits of this poem; and it would be well to read it every year, to be instructed by it again and again, and to receive anew the impression of its great beauty." The translation is from Oxenford 1984, 323–34.

2. Longus scholarship overshadows research on the other Greek novels (cf. MacQueen 1990, 261–67).

3. Mittelstadt (1966) examines the artistic in the novel, rather than the mystical or religious.

4. MacQueen (1985, 122) writes, "Longus repeats certain groups of themes and

images in essentially chiastic order, so that a kind of frame is created around each μῦθος," and suggests that "Longus uses paired motifs and images to convert a linear, diachronic narrative into a synchronic frame" (129).

5. Δάφνις appears frequently in Theocritus. In *Id.* 1 Thyrsis asks a goatherd to his syrinx (one of the aitia of *D&C* concerns the syrinx), but the goatherd refuses because he does not want to anger Pan (an important god in *D&C*), since custom forbids him to play at noontime. The goatherd persuades Thyrsis to sing by offering a crafted cup, which has a woman standing between two men trying to win her love (cf. *D&C* 1.16). Not far off is an old fisherman (Philetas?) about to cast his net not far from a small boy (Eros?) standing near a vineyard (Philetas's garden?); the fisherman may be trying to catch the small boy. If this is true, this scene parallels *D&C* 2.3–7, where Philetas attempts to catch Eros. According to the goatherd the small boy is weaving a cage for grasshoppers (cf. *D&C* 1.26). There are other parallels in this idyll. One is Daphnis's resenting the he-goats whom he saw mounting the nannies (cf. *D&C* 3.14). In *Id.* 7 Xenea is the maiden for whom Daphnis yearned and wasted away like snow: χιὼν ὥς τις κατετάκετο μακρὸν ὑφ᾽ Αἷμον / ἢ Ἄθω ἢ Ῥοδόπαν ἢ Καύκασον ἐσχατόωντα (76–77). In *D&C* 3.10 Daphnis says that he will melt away before the winter snow that is keeping them separated: καὶ δέδοικα μὴ ἐγὼ πρὸ ταύτης τακῶ. Callimachus (*AP* 7.518) identifies Daphnis as the shepherd par excellence about whom poets sang before Astacides took his place. Zonas (*AP* 9.556) describes the beauty of Daphnis using Pan as his interlocutor. Parthenius writes that Daphnis was the son of Hermes, skilled in the syrinx, and beautiful, and that the nymph Echenais fell in love with him and told him never to associate with mortal women or else he would lose his sight. A Sicilian princess, however, got Daphnis drunk, and he, with his resolve weakened, slept with the princess. Consequently, Daphnis became blind. Aelian (*VH* 10.18) tells the same story as Parthenius.

6. Μυρτάλη is often depicted as a courtesan. Herondas (*Mimiamb* 1) groups her with Sime, a courtesan; and Horace (*Carm.* 1.33) writes that he was in love with the slave-born Myrtale. Λάμων dedicates rustic paraphernalia to Priapus in *AP* 6.102; he does not appear as a mythological character in any other extant ancient text.

7. Chloe (green) as a mythological character is not found in any extant ancient source, but the name Χλόη is found as being an epithet of Demeter (cf. Merkelbach 1988, 32 n. 8; Philippides 1978, 102–4).

8. Νάπη (wooded glen or vale) in Ovid (*Am.* 1.11) is Corinna's handmaiden, who is adept in gathering and placing in order the scattered locks of her mistress. She is also known for being useful in delivering love letters. In *Am.* 1.12 Nape is seen as portending doom when she tripped exiting Naso's abode. Strabo (9.4.5) writes ταύτην μὲν οὖν τὴν Βῆσσαν ἐν τοῖς δυσὶ γραπτέον σίγμα (ἀπὸ γὰρ τοῦ δρυμώδους ὠνόμασται ὁμωνύμως, ὥσπερ καὶ Νάπη ἐν τῷ Μηθύμνης πεδίῳ, ἣν Ἑλλάνικος ἀγνοῶν Λάπην ὀνομάζει. This passage caused Hunter (1983, 17) to write that "Longus wishes us to remember . . . that Νάπη was . . . the name of a place in the plain of Methymna, and this deepens the sense that we are reading a local μῦθος or aetiological tale."

9. Homer (*Il.* 1.263) calls Dryas (dry oak) a "ποιμένα λαῶν," which agrees, somewhat, with the profession Longus gives to Chloe's foster father. He is also the father of Lycurgus, and according to the *Homeric Hymn to Pan*, he is also identified as the grandfather of Pan (cf. Hunter 1983, 17).

10. Longus borrows the description of the grotto from Theoc. *Id.* 7.136–37.

11. Longus writes in 1.13: ἐδόκει δὲ τῇ Χλόῃ θεωμένῃ καλὸς ὁ Δάφνις, ὅτι <δὲ οὐ> πρότερον αὐτῇ καλὸς ἐδόκει, τὸ λουτρὸν ἐνόμιζε τοῦ κάλλους αἴτιον. This line recalls Sappho fr. 31 where she describes the effects she suffers upon seeing a man who seems to be as fortunate as the gods. More importantly, Longus may be pointing out the importance that the aitia have in his work when he mentions the transformation that Daphnis has undergone in Chloe's eyes, the cause of which was τὸ λουτρὸν or the αἴτιον of the transformation in beauty.

12. In this debate Daphnis states that he, like Zeus, was raised by a goat. He also stresses the fact that although he does associate with animals he does not smell bad, but like Pan, he is sweet-smelling company. As to his physical appearance Daphnis states that he is as beardless as Dionysus and that if he is black (tanned) in color, so is the hyacinth. By mentioning the hyacinth Longus is perhaps associating Daphnis with Hyacinthus, the son of Amyclas and the lover of Apollo. After all, the story of Hyacinthus is another tale of love and metamorphosis. In sum: Daphnis's rhetorical speech solidifies the notion that he and Chloe are analogues of mythical characters. In other words, Daphnis could have chosen historical persons with which to compare himself. Aition and its different forms appear in 1.8, 1.13, 2.26, 3.24, 3.26, 3.30, and 4.13.

13. The translation is from Thornley 1916.

14. This episode of Daphnis riding back to shore an oxen gives a new twist to the myth of Europa and the bull. Daphnis, while seeking escape from a kidnapping, rode on two oxen toward the shore, whereas Europa, while being kidnapped, rode on one bull away from shore.

15. Philetas is the innovator of the scholar-poet tradition and is the possible teacher of Theocritus. Hunter (1983) has included a very comprehensive and meticulous appendix on Philetas in his book *A Study of Daphnis and Chloe.*

16. The myth of Eros (2.5) by Eros recalls in the first part Hesiodic theogony and in the latter Plato's *Symposium,* particularly the flowery speech on love by Agathon.

17. He does not relate instructions until he has told his love story. The story of Amaryllis and Philetas is one of a love that never comes to fruition. Philetas wanted Amaryllis, but Amaryllis did not want Philetas or at least would not come to him. ᾿Αμαρυλλίς appears in Theoc. *Id.* 3 and 4. In *Id.* 3 she is the cave nymph whom an unnamed goatherd serenades. In *Id.* 4 she is a mortal maiden who had died, but when alive was loved by Aigon and Battos. Vergil includes an Amaryllis in *Ecl.* 1 where Meliboeus tells Tityrus (cf. Theoc. *Id.* 3) that he is teaching the woods to echo *formosam Amaryllida,* who, one may presume, is to have been loved by and been in love with Tityrus. Ovid also makes mention of Amaryllis in *Ars Am.* 2.267, where she is no longer a country shepherdess but rather a city lady.

18. "For there is no medicine for love, neither meat, nor drink, nor any charm, but only kissing and embracing and lying side by side" (Thornley 1916, 79). It should, of course, read "lying naked side by side."

19. Τίτυρος has already appeared in the discussion on Amaryllis. In Theoc. *Id.* 3 he is the shepherd to whom the anonymous goatherd entrusts his flock. Vergil also mentions him in connection with Amaryllis in *Ecl.* 1. Tityrus is also connected with sileni (cf. *Schol. Theoc.* 3.2) and may also be identified with he-goats (cf. *Schol. Theoc.*

1.c.). A τίτυρος may also be a musical instrument such as a pipe; if this is correct, the name would be very suitable for the son of Philetas, who in Longus's novel gives the panpipe to Philetas.

20. In Greek mythology, Apd. 2.7.7, Ἵπασσος was the son of Ceÿx, an ally of Heracles in his battle against the Eurytus, the king of Oechalia. In this battle Hipassus was killed. There seems to be no correlation between Longus's Hipassus and the Hippasus in Greek myth except for the fact that both men were warriors.

21. During this tranquil time the myth of Tereus and Itys is mentioned. Once again, this myth deals with metamorphosis. O'Connor (1987) suggests that Longus may have been using the literary version of this myth as found in Antoninus Liberalis's *Metamorphoseon Synagoge*.

22. On the name of Lycaenium see Lindsay 1948, 103; Scarcella 1972; Hunter 1983, 28, 60–61, and 68–69.

23. There is no mythological character by this name, except if Longus was thinking of the mythical Χρόμιος or Χρόμις found in Homer. In *Il.* 5.160 he is identified as one of the sons of Priam; in *Il.* 4.295 and in *Od.* 11.286 as the son of Neleus; in *Il.* 5.677 as a Lycian; in *Il.* 8.275 as a Trojan; in *Il.* 2.858 and 17.218, 494, and 534 as a chief of the Mysians. A χρόμις is also a sea-fish; Longus may have been pairing two different types of animals, a she-wolf with a fish, to show that the marriage between Chromis and Lycaenium was not normal, since it did not partake of the loyalty found in the other marriages of this novel. In addition, the name Χρόμις may be a joke on the part of Longus, who describes him, the man-with-the-fish-name, as being a γεωργὸς γῆς ἰδίας (3.15). The name Χρόμις also appears in Theoc. *Id.* 1.4, where he is a Lycian singer.

24. Διονυσοφάνης is an appropriate name for the father of Daphnis for two reasons. First of all, the novel seems to center around Dionysus as the main divinity in the novel, and secondly, the name can be interpreted in terms of a stage direction or foreshadowing device: Dionysus (Διονυσο-) will soon appear (-φάνης). This interpretation is possible since two of the parenting genres may be tragedy and comedy.

25. At the end of this book, Daphnis and Chloe see an apple tree that has had all its apples picked off except for one at the very top. Against the protests of Chloe, Daphnis climbs the tree and picks the lonely apple. He gives it to Chloe, but she, still angry with him, rejects the gift. He then reminds Chloe that Aphrodite took an apple as a prize for her beauty, and that Paris, a shepherd like Daphnis, gave the apple. It seems odd that Aphrodite is first mentioned at the end of book 3, since book 3 seems to finish the amorous and erotic quality of *D&C*. Book 4 is a somewhat tepid denouement to an otherwise steamy novel.

26. Λάμπις does not appear in any extant ancient literature as a mythological character. This name points to a trend in the last book, in which there is no actual metamorphosis (unless one considers Chloe's transformation from virgin to nonvirgin), except for the spring of Daphnis. The names have no connection to myth. This also applies to the names of Astylus, Dionysophanes' son; Gnathon, the parasite; Eudromus, a trusted slave; Sophrone, a slave of Dionysophanes; and Megacles, Chloe's biological father. Book 4 lacks the mythological/pastoral quality of the first three books and takes on aspects of New Comedy: kidnappings, anagnoriseis, a happy ending.

27. Upon discovering the ruined garden, Lamon laments to Dionysus, the one to whom the garden is dedicated, that he will be treated like Marsyas. Marsyas, of course, was the satyr who challenged Apollo to a music contest and who was flayed because he had done so. The allusion to this myth fits in perfectly with the musical (panpipes) quality of the novel.

28. "There was a spring, one that Daphnis first discovered, and that, although it was set apart for this purpose of watering the flowers, was nevertheless, in favour to him, always called Daphnis his fountain" (Thornley 1916, 193).

29. In keeping with the New Comedy atmosphere, Γνάθων is a suitable name for this character. Gnathon has the same name of that of the parasite in Terence's *Eunuchus*.

30. Cf. Hunter 1983, 115 n. 114. For further information on Pitys see Merkelbach 1988, 34–35.

31. For an excellent discussion of Pan and *D&C* see Philippides 1978, 241–72; for Eros, 177–80.

32. Ovid *Met.* I.689ff.; Achilles Tatius 8.6.7ff.

33. Hunter 1983, 53. The usual story is that Echo had incurred the wrath of Hera, who had cursed her with a speech impediment, which caused Echo to be able to repeat only the words of others; she was not able to start a conversation. She eventually fell in love with Narcissus, who was too busy being in love with himself, and consequently, out of grief over an unfulfilled love, she faded away. The only thing that remained of Echo was her voice. Cf. *Met.* 3.356–410.

34. This myth also appears in Achilles Tatius 5.5.

35. Hesiod's works do not include them nor do the *Homeric Hymn to Pan* 19, the *Homeric Hymn to Aphrodite* 5, or the *Orphic Hymn to the Nymphs* 51. For scholarly studies on nymphs see Hathorn (1977, especially 262–63); Roscher (reprint 1965, 499–567); De Harlez (1965); Otto (1955, chap. 1); Wilamowitz-Moellendorff (1931, 181–87).

36. "1. When I was hunting in Lesbos, I saw in the grove of the Nymphs a spectacle the most beauteous and pleasing of any that ever yet I cast my eyes upon. It was a painted picture, reporting a history of love. The grove indeed was very pleasant, thick set with trees and starred with flowers everywhere, and watered all from one fountain with divers meanders and rills. But that picture, as having in it not only an excellent and wonderful piece of art but also a tale of ancient love, was far more amiable. And therefore many, not only the people of the country but foreigner also, enchanted by the fame of it, came as much to see that, as in devotion to the Nymphs. There were figured in it young women, in the posture, some of teeming, others of swaddling, little children; babes exposed, and ewes giving them suck; shepherds taking up foundlings, young persons plighting their troth; an incursion of thieves, an inroad of armed men.

2. When I had seen with admiration these and many other things, but all belonging to the affairs of love, I had a mighty instigation to write something as to answer that picture. And therefore, when I had carefully sought and found an interpreter of the image, I drew up these four books, an oblation to Love and to Pan and to the Nymphs, and a delightful possession even for all men. For this will cure him that is sick, and rouse him that is in dumps; one that has loved, it will remember of it; one that has not, it will instruct. For there was never any yet that wholly could escape love, and never

shall there be any, never so long as beauty shall be, never so long as eyes can see. But help me that God to write the passions of others; and while I write, keep me in my own right wits" (Thornley 1916, 7–9).

37. Seiler 1843, 161; Valley 1926, 101–2; Chalk 1960; Turner 1960; McCulloh 1970, 31–32, 68, and 85; Scarcella 1972, 34; Hunter 1983, 4 n. 18, 85 n. 6, and 48–52; Pandiri 1985; Vieillefond 1987, cxviii–cxx; MacQueen 1990, 64, 140–41, 146–48, and 157–59.

38. The historical in *Daphnis and Chloe* has not gone unnoticed. Holzberg (1995) has shown that Longus in a historiographical manner "presents chronologically or relates the respective adventures of the separated protagonists in parallel accounts" (10) and argues that Longus purposely imitates historiographical methods (10). More recently, Ruiz-Montero (1996, in particular 42–48) writes that the earliest form of the novel, *Ninus*, uses history and historical figures as background, and because the historical can also be found in *Sesonchosis*, *Metiochus and Parthenope*, and *Chaereas and Callirhoe*, it has been theorized that "the novel was viewed as a deviation from historiography" (45). Ruiz-Montero is a bit more tempered in evaluating the role of history in the development of the novel: history played a "crucial part in the formation of the novels" (48). For a brief discussion on history and the novel see Holzberg 35–42, in particular 41–42. See also Morgan 1982. Hägg (1987) notes that the earlier novels are definitely historical in tone. On historiography and Chariton see Hunter 1994.

39. Valley (1926, 101) comments on the use of Thucydides in sections of the novel other than the prooemium: "'Daphnis und Chloe' ist ein bukolischer Roman. Seine hauptsächliche Aufgabe ist darum, das Idyllische zu schildern. Aber das Idyll lässt der Verfasser gegen den dunklen Hintergrund einiger störender Ereignisse hervortreten. . . . In der Schilderung der abenteuerlichen Szenen scheint Longus einige Ausdrücke von Thukydides, dem anerkannten Meister der Kriegsschilderung, benutzt zu haben." Vieillefond (1987, cxviii–cxix) also writes on the use of Thucydides in later episodes of the novel: "Quelques notations de détail, chez Longus, ont bien semblé provenir de Thucydide, mais c'est essentiellement dans la ressemblance des thèmes, c'est-à-dire des épisodes, que se découvre la dépendance du romancier par rapport à l'historien. Chez Longus, comme chez Thucydide, le conflit entre les deux villes se termine brusquement à l'amiable, après un discours pacificateur."

40. On the openings of the novels see Morgan 1993, 216.

41. Chariton, of course, has archetypes upon which to base this historical approach to opening a prose work, for example, Hecataeus of Miletus (*fr.* 1), Herodotus (1.1–5), and Thucydides (1.1).

42. "Among the most influential citizens of Ephesus was a man called Lycomedes. He and his wife, Themisto, who also belonged to the city, had a son named Habrocomes" (Anderson 1989a, 128).

43. The term ἱστορία can mean the written account of an investigation, e.g. Hdt. 7.96 and Arist. *Rhet.* 1.14.13. In the prooemium Longus's use of this term does not echo Thucydides, but rather Herodotus (1.1, 2.99, 2.118, 2.119). Philippides (1978, chap. 1) suggests that Longus is familiar with the elements that constitute a historical enquiry and knows that ὄψις and ἀκοή are therefore necessary. He includes these two elements in his preface in many different ways: εἶδον, ἰδόντα, ὀφθαλμοὶ βλέπωσιν. In addition, when Longus writes that his work is a ἱστορίαν ἔρωτος that νοσοῦντα

ἰάσεται, he is also categorizing the term ἱστορία, and consequently his work, as a searched-for and investigated cure for an erotic illness (cf. *Corpus Hippoc.*, *de Arte* 1.3 and *Praec.* 2.7, 8.5, 12.4, 13.9–13).

44. Although Pandiri (1985) examines the pastoral significance of the prooemium, she seems to be heading to this same conclusion (117): "Longus . . . slyly reverses his (Thucydides') values." This reversal of Thucydidean methodology is consistent with the experimental nature of *Daphnis and Chloe*. Longus deliberately adapts regular plot ingredients, such as the *Scheintod* of the heroine or voyages to distant places, into new forms. His uniqueness has caused some scholars to exclude him in their surveys of this genre: Todd (1940) does on the basis that this work "stands alone in ancient literature as a union of the Romance with the pastoral" (2); Hadas (1952, 258) views Longus as excessively contaminated by "the bucolic tradition"; Fusillo (1988, 17) isolates this novel because supposedly "it is a perfumed pastoral written by a sophisticated aristocrat for sophisticated aristocrats." *Daphnis and Chloe*, however, should be studied because it demonstrates that after Chariton and Xenophon of Ephesus, whether or not through the influence of the Second Sophistic, the novel genre begins to change from a historically detailed form to one that is more mythological in nature.

It can be said that the texts of Chariton and Xenophon, with their inclusion of the gods Venus, Eros, and Isis, are just as mythological as Longus. Longus's setting, however, is in a less obvious historical period. And although the war between Mytilene and Methymna may tie the narrative to the events of the fifth century B.C., Longus does not seem to want to make his narrative too realistic in nature because realism may spoil the idyllic milieu of the novel. Longus does supply some information on topography; for research done on this data see Mason 1979, Green 1982, and Bowie 1985. Although these scholars postulate that Longus knew the topography of Lesbos, this inclusion of topographical data tells us nothing about the novel's historical setting.

45. Wouters (1989–90) argues that the εἰκόνες in the last book of the novel form the painting mentioned in the prooemium (cf. 476). They are, according to Wouters, "the codification of Daphnis' and Chloe's experiences" (472).

46. Perhaps ἐξεπονησάμην may refer to Theoc. *Id.* 7.51 and not to Thucydides.

47. "Mytilene is a city in Lesbos, and by ancient titles of honour it is the great and fair Mytilene. For it is distinguished and divided (the sea flowing in) by a various euripus, and is adorned with bridges of white polished marble. You would not think you saw a city, but an island. From this Mytilene some two hundred furlongs there lay a manor of a certain rich lord, the most sweet and pleasant prospect under all the eyes of heaven" (Thornley 1916, 11).

48. The κτῆμα of 1.1.2 is reinforced by the κτήματα in 3.2.1, where the narrative dealing with the Mytilenean and Methymnaean skirmish comes to an end.

49. The following is a compilation of the passages as found in Valley and Vieillefond. Valley's contributions are marked with *'s, Vieillefond's with †'s, and mine with √'s.

50. κλυδώνιον is a *varia lectio* of Thuc. 2.84.3.

51. There are over sixty-five forms of ἐπιπλεῖν in the Thucydidean corpus (cf. von Essen 1887, 154).

52. For example: λαβέσθαι χωρίων √2.2.3, πολυχειρίας √2.2.4, ὑπέφευγε √2.4.2, προσκώπους *2.12.1, λίθου ἐς ἀνολκὴν *2.13.1, διαθέοντες √2.13.4, μετέωρον √2.14.1, ἐπεκαλεῖτο √2.14.4, κακουργεῖν √2.19.3, ἀπόβασιν

√ 2.20.2, ἀναλαβεῖν √ 2.25.1, αἰφνίδιον √ 2.25.3, κῶπαι καθιέντων √ 2.26.2, ἀπεσπάσατε √ 2.27.2, ἀποβάθρας √ 2.28.3, ὅπλα κινεῖν *3.1.1, οὐκ ἀνασχετὸν νομίσαντες *3.1.1, μετεγίνωσκον √ 3.2.2, ἀδεῶς ἐπιμίγνυσθαι καὶ κατὰ γῆν κατὰ θάλασσαν *3.2.3, ἐπεπήγει δὲ κρύσταλλος *3.3.2, αὐτοκράτωρ √ 3.2.4. All of these words and phrases can be found in the historian's text. This is not to say that Longus borrowed each and every instance from Thucydides, but these words give the novel narrative a distinctly Thucydidean flavor.

53. Hunter (1983, 85) has noted the use of Thucydidean phraseology for the purposes of coloring "the 'military' part of his narrative."

54. "It seemed very unlikely that, after having brought under their control the states who were fellow members with us, they would refrain from acting towards us, too, in the same way, if ever they felt strong enough to so do" (Warner 1954, 198).

55. "Therefore Hippasus dispatches away that herald to Mytilene, although he had bin created the general of war and so had power to sign as he listed; and pitching his camp about ten furlongs from the Methymna, there he attended mandates from the city. Two days after, the messenger returned, and brought a command that they should receive the plundered goods and all the captives, and march home without doing the least harm, because Methymna, when war or peace were offered to be chosen, found peace to be more profitable. And this quarrel betwixt Methymna and Mytilene, which was of an unexpected beginning and end, was thus taken up and composed" (Thornley 1916, 131).

56. Longus's use of Thucydides, it must be noted, is one of many instances of variation on earlier literature.

CHAPTER 4

1. Hägg (1971a, 63) writes that "the situation at the beginning of the romance . . . clearly gives the reader the impression that what is related is supposed to have happened in the author's own time, and there are actually details . . . which seem to reflect happenings in the second century A.D." On the subject of myth Hägg (1971a, 107 n.2) comments: "Similes from mythology are rare . . . but in their speeches the acting characters sometimes use such material (see I, 8, 1–9 and VI, 13,2)." Cf. Steiner 1969, 134.

2. *Leucippe and Clitophon* is the subject of four examinations that deal, in one way or another, with myth and its functions. Harlan (1965) examines the use of mythologically inspired *ekphraseis* and applies rhetorical and literary theories to them. Bartsch (1989) also explores the inclusion of myth and *ephkraseis*, but unlike Harlan, interprets the *ekphraseis* in terms of foreshadowing and prolepsis. Laplace (1983 and 1991) argues that Tatius uses literary sources to model Leucippe and Clitophon on mythological characters. Observing close similarities, she identifies Leucippe as Io: the same birthplace for the two women: the prominent figure of Argos in both stories; the madness that afflicts both women. The *Prometheus Bound* is probably the major source, according to Laplace, for the delineation of Leucippe. Helen can also be the mythological figure on which Tatius bases his Leucippe, and this correlation is partially supported by a comparison between Leucippe's counterpart, Calligone, and the Helen who went to

Egypt and her counterpart, the phantom Helen who went to Troy. Ovid, Aeschylus, Euripides, and other writers are the sources from which Tatius gathered his information. Adonis and Odysseus are suggested as prototypes for Clitophon. Cf. Wilhelm's article (1902), an excellent study of literary sources in *Leucippe and Clitophon*.

3. In book 1, e.g., Cadmus, Astarte, Europa, Zeus (as a bull), Erotes, Eros, Apollo, Daphne, Selene, the Sirens, Eriphyle, Philomela, Stheneboea, Aerope, Procne, Agamemnon, Chryseis, Achilles, Briseis, Helen, Penelope, Phaedra, Hippolytus, Clytemnestra, Aurora, Tereus, the peacock of Hera, Alpheus, and Arethusa.

4. Direct quotations, modified excerpts, parallels, and literary allusions to other authors are found in the following passages: *Il.* 21.257–59: 1.1.5; Ovid *Met.* 6.101ff.: 1.1.13; *Phdr.*: 1.2.3; Artem. 1.2: 1.3.3; *Il.* 4.141–42: 1.4.3; Musaeus 92–98: 1.4.4; Dem. *De Cor.* 296: 1.6.1; Hes. *Op.* 57–58: 1.8.2; Ovid *Ars Am.* 2.373ff., Juv. 6.634ff., *Anth. Pal.* 9.166, Ath. 13.8ff., Stob. 67ff.: 1.8.4; *Il.* 2.478: 1.8.7; Pl. *Symp.* 203, Xen. *Cyr.* 6.1.14: 1.10.1; Soph. *El.* 723ff., Eur. *Hipp.* 1173ff.: 1.12–13; *Anth. Pal.* 8.815 and 8.712: 1.13; Ael. *N A* 4.21, Lucian *Dom.* 11, Philostr. *VS* 2.27 and *Imag.* 2.21: 1.16; Philostr. *Imag.* 2.6.1; Pliny *NH* 31.5: 1.18.1–2; Ael. *NH* 1.50 and 9.66, Oppian *Hal.* 1.554, Pliny *NH* 9.76 and 32.14: 1.18.3; *Il.* 16.823–26:2.1.1; Hes. *Op.* 587, Theoc. 14.15, *Od.* 9.197, Ath. *Dipnosoph.* 11.484: 2.2.2; Hdt. 1.25: 2.3.1; Apollod. 2.6.3: 2.6.2–3; Lucian *D. deorum* 5.2: 2.9.2; Hdt. 2.45, Chariton 7.2: 2.14; *Il.* 10.435ff.: 2.15.3; Hdt. 4.195, Ktesias *Indika* 4: 2.14.9; *Il.* 10.435, Aen. 12.84: 2.15.4–5; Pliny *NH* 10.21: 2.21.2; *Od.* 9: 2.23.2; *Il.* 9.302: 2.34.7; Pl. *Symp.* 180D–182A: 2.36.2–3; *Il.* 20.234: 2.36.3; Xen. *Symp.* 8.29: 2.36.4; *Il.* 21.385: 3.2.3; Strab. 16.760: 3.6.1; Pliny *NH* 10.2, Hdt. 2.73: 3.25; Ovid *Met.* 2.235: 4.5.1; Eur. *Hec.* 570: 4.9.2; Hdt. 2.60: 4.18.3; Hyg. *Fab.* 2: 5.5.2; Theoc. 2.10, Hor. *Sat.* 1.8.21: 5.26.12; Thuc. 2.87.4: 7.10.4; Macrob. *Sat.* 5.19: 8.12.9. Although this is not an exhaustive list of such occurrences, there is nevertheless a noticeable decrease of them as the novel progresses. I am including references only to pagan classical authors; Tatius includes numerous references to Christian authors (cf. Vilborg 1955).

5. "Sidon is a city beside the sea. The sea is the Assyrian; the city is the metropolis of Phoenicia; its people are the forefathers of Thebes" (Winkler 1989, 175).

6. "the picture was of Europa; the sea was Phoenicia's; the land was Sidon. On the land were represented a meadow and a chorus of maidens, on the sea swam a bull, and on his back was seated a beautiful maiden, sailing on the bull towards Crete" (Winkler 1989, 176). The description of the meadow recalls the details of *Il.* 21.257–59. On the description of Europa being carried away see Ovid *Met.* 6.101ff.

7. For other works that have narratives based on paintings compare Cebes, *Pinax* 1–4, Petronius, 81–88, Lucian, *Toxaris* 5–8, Ps.-Lucian, *Erotes* 6–7, and Longus's preface.

8. For an interesting approach to the function of Eros and the unique construct of love in the ancient Greek novels, with the exception of Xenophon Ephesius, see Konstan 1994.

9. Tatius echoes *Phaedrus* 229f. and its discussion on love in 1.2.3 and in 2.35–38, where there is a debate on whether homosexuality or heterosexuality is better.

10. "I shall give them in payment of fire an evil which all shall / take to their hearts with delight, an evil to love and embrace" (Frazer 1983, 98).

11. Cf., on Sirens and other winged females, Pollard 1977, 188–91. See also Hyg. *Fab.* 125; Apollod. 1.7.10; and *Argon.* 4.893ff.

12. *Phaedrus* 229f. in 1.2.3.

13. On the influence of the *Phaedrus* on the second-century A.D. literature see Trapp 1990.

14. Anderson (1988) suggests that the character of Satyrus may be Tatius's attempt at writing satire. He also notes that Pan plays a very important role in the novel: "The plot is run by Satyrus, and taken over by Pan. The former is the confidant of two dubious love-affairs; he has his fair share of education; he has charge of the money-bag; he pulls off a pastoral trick with a sheep's stomach; and all begins in an erotic garden" (191–92).

15. "And then there is the transoceanic wedding of waters: the lover is a river from Elis, the mistress a spring in Sicily. This lover flows across the sea as he would across a plain, and the sea does not absorb the lover's sweet waters in her briny waves but parts herself for him to flow along her surface: this crack in the sea is the river's bed. And so she escorts Alpheios the bridegroom to Arethousa the bride. When the games at Olympia are celebrated, many toss gifts into the streams of this river, and he carries them to his mistress, love tokens from a suitor" (Winkler 1989, 188).

16. "This time, Leukippe, you are without doubt dead twice over, divided in death between land and sea. I hold a headless relic; I've lost the real you. Oh, what an unfair division between land and sea: I have been left the smaller part of you in the guise of the greater, whereas the sea, in a small part of you, possesses all of you. Yet now, since Fortune denies me the kisses of your lips, come then, let me kiss your butchered neck" (Winkler 1989, 236–37).

17. "It was the feast of Dionysos of the Harvest. Since the myth of Kadmos is a living part of Tyrian tradition, they regard Dionysos as one of their own gods, and this is the myth they tell about the origins of the feast.

No wine ever existed among men before the Tyrians had it—not 'the *noir* of fine bouquet,' not 'the vine of Biblia,' not 'the Thracian vintage of Maron,' not 'the Chian froma Lakonina cup,' not 'the island wine of Ikaros.' All of these are colonies sent out by Tyrian wines, where the mother of all vintages first grew" (Winkler 1989, 192).

18. *Deipnosophistae* 1.26b, 1.28e–f, 1.29a and e, 1.31a, 1.32f, 1.33c, 4.167e, 11.473a, 11.484f, et al.

19. Cf. Hyg. *Fab.* 130 and *Poetica Astronomica* 2.4.

20. "He lusted after your wife, and used his pharmaceutical genius to concoct an aphrodisiac which he then persuaded your Egyptian valet to mingle in Leukippe's cup. But by mistake he administered it full strength and the undiluted dose brought insanity" (Winkler 1989, 230).

21. The text of the lemma is from Dübner 1872.

22. πόλις is included in Garnaud's text based on an emendation by Jacobs.

23. "In a dream I saw my sister's body and mine grown together into a single body from the navel down and separating into two above. Over me there hovered a huge, fearsome woman who glowered at me savagely: eyes shot with blood, rough cheeks, snakes for hair, a sickle in her right hand, a torch in her left. In a wild attack she aimed her sickle at our groin where the two bodies joined, and severed the girl from me.

Waking up from sheer fright, I decided to tell no one but brooded over my troubles privately" (Winkler 1989, 178).

24. "His strategy was dictated by a Byzantine law, to the effect that if a man kidnapped a maiden and made her his wife before he was caught, his only penalty was to stay married to her" (Winkler 1989, 195).

25. Harlan (1965, 94–95) sees the description of Europa and the bull as having only "symbolic significance"; Bartsch (1989) notes that the garden in the painting of Europa and the garden of Clitophon help to equate Europa with Leucippe (50) and goes as far as to make Europa synonymous with Calligone (63).

26. For a thorough listing of ancient authors who have written on this myth see *Apollodorus: The Library*, Loeb Classical Library, vol. 2, 89 n. 1.

27. See, for example, fragment 2 of Davies 1988, 141.

28. On the sexual nature of Hephaestus see Caldwell 1978, 43–59.

29. "She was being disturbed by a dream, in which she saw a bandit with a naked sword seize her daughter, drag her away, throw her down on her back, and slice her in two all the way up from her stomach, making his first insertion at her modest spot" (Winkler 1989, 201).

30. "'I bet you, by all the gods—ours and anyone else's, get me out of my mother's sight, anywhere you like. If you go and leave me behind, I will hang myself" (Winkler 1989, 203).

31. Toward the end of the second book Tatius tacks on references to the myths of Patroclos, Tantalus, Ganymede, Alcmene, Danae, Semele, Hebe, Europa, Antiope, and Perseus.

32. There is no known painter in the ancient world called Evanthes. In myth Evanthes is the son of Oenopion and the father of Maron the Ismarian priest. Cf. Diod. 5.79.2, Paus. 7.4.8, Hes. *Catalogues of Women* 86, and *Od.* 9.197.

33. "Her arms were spread against the rock, bound above her head by a manacle bolted in the stone. Her hands hung loose at the wrist like clusters of grapes" (Winkler 1989, 212).

34. Her stance is compared to that of Marsyas when he was flayed.

35. Clitophon says that when he saw Leucippe disemboweled he felt like Niobe when she saw her children slaughtered by Apollo and Artemis.

36. "He next raised a sword and plunged it into her heart and then sawed all the way down to her abdomen" (Winkler 1989, 216).

37. Cf. Elsom (1992, 216–17) on the reversal of genders through myth in this scene.

38. When revived, Leucippe is thought by Clitophon to be Hecate.

39. On the humorous aspects of the Phoenix story cf. Anderson 1982, 28. See also Durham 1938.

40. Can this be the god Asclepius, who is invoked in 4.17 in order that Leucippe may recover from an epileptic sort of madness?

41. "War doesn't allow a man leisure to postpone desires. How can a soldier with a war on his hands have any idea of how long he will live? There are so many ways to die. Ask Fortune to grant me a safe-conduct, and I will wait. I am about to battle against the Rangers, but another battle is being waged in my soul. The enemy within is besieging me with his bow, harassing me with arrows: I have lost the fight; I am

bristling with his shafts. Call the doctor, sir, and quickly; my wounds demand immediate attention. True, I fight mortal enemies with fire, but Eros hurls his own burning brands at me" (Winkler 1989, 225).

42. The epileptic fit is analyzed by MacLeod (1969) in view of Erasistratus's treatment and diagnosis of this disease.

43. The use of the word *Satrap* is not an attempt by Tatius to place the action of the story in historic times. Rather, either he prefers to use pre-Roman terminology for the different offices, or it is another piece of Herodotean romanticism. Cf. Mason 1970.

44. For an analysis of the rape motif in Greek myths see Zeitlin 1986.

45. Most manuscripts of 1.4.3 read Σελήνην (β reads Εὐρώπην), and since this is so, Tatius perhaps has correlated Leucippe with Selene from the very start of his novel.

46. Cf. Lucan *Pharsalia* 6.58 and Seneca *Heracles on Mount Oeta* 449–72.

47. "She told me she would spend the night in the fields fathering herbs so she might pluck them by moonlight" (Winkler 1989, 249).

48. Tatius supplies a variation of the myth of Syrinx as found in Ovid *Met.* 1.691ff. Rattenbury (1926, 67) notes that "the differences [between the myth in Tatius and in Ovid] are enough to make it likely that Achilles Tatius did not copy it from Ovid, but that the two authors used different versions of one popular legend."

49. Pine is the favorite tree of Pan; cf. Nonnus 2.118 and 42.259.

50. "This is why when someone is accused in affairs of Aphrodite, she enters the spring to bathe. The fountain is a small one, reaching only to the mid-calf. The ordeal is this: she writes the oath on a tablet and ties it around her neck with a string. If she has not been false to her oath, the spring remains in place. Is she is lying, the water seethes and rises to her neck and covers the tablet" (Winkler, 1989, 280).

51. Cf. Segal 1984.

CHAPTER 5

1. Sandy 1982, 1–5. Perry (1967, 349) dates the novel to the mid-third century, while Reardon (1971, 334) states that the probable date of composition is somewhere in the third or fourth century A.D.; Hägg (1971a, 15 n. 1) agrees with Reardon.

2. For example: Eur. *Med.* 1317: 1.8.7; Soph. *Aj.* 293 and Eur. *Heracl.* 476: 1.21.3; Eur. *Hec.* 612: 2.4.3; Eur. *Or.* 1625: 2.18.4; Aesch. *Pers.* 599 and Soph. *OT* 1527: 3.15.3; Eur. *Phoen.* 625: 4.6.7; Soph. *OT* 1409; 4.10.2; Eur. *Hipp.* 439: 4.10.5; Eur. *Ion* 927ff.: 5.20.1; Eur. *Alc.* 301: 5.25.3; Aesch. *Cho.* 64: 5.27.3; Soph. *Aj.* 131f.: 7.5.2; Eur. *Hipp.* 802: 8.15.2.

3. For useful basic material on the function of analogue in the ancient Greek novel see Steiner 1969.

4. The large number of lines from tragedy has inspired much scholarly work, beginning with Walden 1894. See also Feuillatre 1966, Rocca 1976, Anderson 1982, Paulsen 1992.

5. Keyes 1922. Reardon (1971, 320) likewise writes: "Homère est le père non seulement des sophistes mais aussi des romanciers, surtout d'Héliodore—ni Hérodote, ni Euripide, ni Ménandre et la Nouvelle Comédie."

6. Morgan 1989b, 320. In a later article Morgan (1991) concentrates on the reader-response of the fictional and true audiences of the *Aethiopica* and concludes by proposing that Heliodorus expected the reader of the novel to share the experiences of the true-to-life, though fictional, literary audiences of the novel. On the structure and narratological patterns of the *Aethiopica* also cf. Szepessy 1957, Mazal 1958, Feuillatre 1966, Weinrich 1962.

7. Heliodorus quotes Demosthenes (*Against Meidias* 21.138) in 1.7 and then refers to the Upper Council of the Aeriopagos (1.9), the Panathenaia (1.10), the phratria (1.13), and the barathron (1.13). Morgan (1982, 248) demonstrates that the "story-patterning" of an incident in Heliodorus is "sometimes modeled closely on the shape of an event in history." He proceeds to suggest that this historical quality does not mean that Heliodorus's primary aim in writing the *Aethiopica* is to write history but rather that he wants to lend some authenticity to his work.

8. Rougemont (1992) appraises the information that Heliodorus supplies about Delphi and compares the novelistic data with known fact, while Cauderlier (1992) examine the specificity and technical aspects of Heliodorus's language when he writes about Egypt. Cf. Pinheiro 1989.

9. For example: Hdt. 5.16: 1.5.2; Dem. *Meid.* 21.138: 1.6.2; Hdt. 2.134–5: 2.25.1; Hdt. 1.65: 2.27.1; Hdt. 2.19: 2.28.5; Philostr. *Heroikos* 19.5: 2.35,1; Plut. *Mor.* 680c–83b: 3.7.3; Plut. *Mor.* 681a: 3.7.5; Plut. *Mor.* 3.10.5; Dem. *De Cor.* 248: 5.29.6; Dem. *De Cor.* 97: 6.4; Thuc. 1.2.2: 6.10.2; Hdt. 4.183: 8.16.4; Hdt. 3.23: 9.1.5; Philon of Alexandria *Life of Moses* 2.195: 9.9.3; Strab. 17.1.48: 9.22.4; Hdt. 3.18: 10.1.3; Hdt. 1.216: 10.6.5.

10. For example: *Il.* 1.46–47: 1.2.5; *Il.* 6.202: 1.14.5; *Il.* 4.450f. and 8.65: 1.22.5; *Il.* 6.312ff.: 1.27.3; *Il.* 6.490–93: 1.28.1; *Il.* 4.45 and 8.65: 1.30.3; *Od.* 17.222: 2.19.1; *Il.* 11.474ff.: 2.19.5; *Il.* 16.799 and *Od.* 9.58: 2.19.6; *Il.* 11.241: 2.20.2; *Il.* 2.311ff.: 2.22.4; *Od.* 17.287 and *Il.* 19.155ff., 19.216ff: 2.22.5; *Il.* 18.437: 2.33.3; *Il.* 9.59 and *Od.* 3.154: 3.2.1; *Od.* 11.613–14: 3.4.2; *Od.* 7.137f.: 3.5.1; *Od.* 19.547: 3.12.1; *Il.* 13.71f.: 3.12.2; *Il.* 1.199f: 3.13.3; *Il.* 9.381ff.: 3.14.2; *Il.* 18.571f.: 4.3.3; *Il.* 13.636f.: 4.3.3; *Il.* 16.21: 4.7.4; *Il.* 17.103f.: 4.19.3; *Od.* 19.392ff: 5.5.2; *Od.* 6.180: 5.11.3; *Il.* 3.65: 5.15.2; *Od.* 8.499ff.: 5.16.5; *Od.* 18.74, 13.332, *Il.* 19.47ff.: 5.22.1; *Il.* 5.79ff.: 5.32.6; *Il.* 1.106f.: 6.5.3; *Il.* 8.491: 6.13.6; *Od.* 11.24ff.: 6.14.3; *Il.* 22.136ff: 7.6.3; *Il.* 24.3ff.: 7.9.3; *Il.* 6.234ff.: 7.10.5; *Il.* 6.234ff.: 9.2.1; *Od.* 1.22ff.: 9.6.2; *Il.* 11.678f.: 9.23.1; *Il.* 4.141: 10.15.2; *Od.* 19.209ff.: 10.15.2; *Il.* 9.612: 10.17.9.

11. Aratus *Phaen.* 96–136 or Hes. *Op.* 197f.: 1.14.4; Pl. *Phd.* 99c: 1.15.8; *Hymn. Hom. Hermes* 289: 2.20.2; Moschos *Megara* 21ff.: 2.22.4; Pl. *Grg.* 447a: 3.10.1; Hes. *Theog.* 984f.: 4.8.3; Lucian *Salt.* 18:9.19.3.

12. Much ink has been spilled over the use of tragedy in the *Aethiopica*. The interest in the dramatic stems not only from the generous borrowing of lines and passages from tragedy but also from the stage terms used in the novel and from the very fact that Heliodorus at different times in the narrative calls or designates his narrative as tragedy. Cf. Walden 1894; Rocca 1976; Anderson 1982, 33–40.

13. "In that small space the deity had contrived an infinitely varied spectacle, defiling wine with blood and unleashing war at the party, combining winning and dying, pouring drink and spilling of blood, and staging this tragic show for the Egyptian bandits" (Morgan 1989a, 354).

14. For a very thorough analysis of the theatrical imagery and terminology in Heliodorus see Paulsen, in particular 21–41. See also Bühler 1976 for a cinematic interpretation.

15. Haight (1950) examines the novel genre in terms of the modern detective story. She does not, however, examine the stage trappings of the novel but opts to analyze the religious component.

16. Frye (1976, 73) writes: "Throughout the ten books of her adventures, which are spent mainly with pirates, soldiers, and other nonvirginal types, Chariclea pursues, unremittingly, three objectives. The first is to marry Theagenes; the second is to solve the mystery of her origin and find out who she is; the third is to defend her virginity from everyone, including Theagenes, until after the mystery is dispelled."

17. "But now that you have had a taste of love, and Theagenes has captured your heart at first sight—this was revealed to me by a voice from heaven—you must realize that you are not the first or the only woman ever to have experienced this pain; it has been felt by many noble ladies and many maidens who were otherwise paragons of virtue" (Morgan 1989a, 435).

18. On the Hippolytus myth in relation to the novel see the very important works by Braun 1934 and 1938.

19. Heliodorus clearly wants, for the time being, to depict Cnemon as Hippolytus when he has Demainete address Cnemon as ὁ νέος Ἱππόλυτος (1.10.2).

20. The Hippolytus-Phaedra paradigm upon which Heliodorus bases the Demainete-Cnemon episode is a bit quirky. One would expect that Demainete would accuse Cnemon of having attempted sexual violence upon her, but instead she accuses him of having kicked her in the stomach, thereby causing her to miscarry (1.10).

21. Once again the letter motif to the Phaedra-Hippolytus paradigm is employed (8.3 and 8.13)! In this episode, however, the letter causes the death of the woman and not of the man.

22. "So huge, so primordially titanic, was he that even as he knelt to kiss the king's knee he was almost as tall as those seated on elevated thrones" (Morgan 1989a, 576).

23. "Theagenes, who was a lifelong devotee of the gymnasium and athletic endeavor and a past master in the art of combat whose patron god is Hermes" (Morgan 1989a, 581).

24. For example, Feuillatre (1966, 116) sees Theagenes as the Sophoclean Haemon.

25. See Steiner (1969, 126–27) on Achilles as the analogue of Theagenes.

26. I would also like to mention two other incidents in the novel that may further establish the mythical analogue of Theagenes as being Hippolytus. The first incident occurs when Calasiris recounts a strange comment made by Theagenes: ἀεὶ γὰρ διαπτύσαι πάσας καὶ γάμον αὐτὸν καὶ ἔρωτας εἴ τινος ἀκούσειεν (3.17.4) ("he had never felt anything but contempt for their whole sex, he said, and even for married love, if it was ever mentioned to him" [Morgan 1989a, 422]). This comment is very much in keeping with the Hippolytus analogue because Theseus's son is known for not associating with women, on account of his hatred for them. Secondly, in the sixth book, Charicleia, instead of celebrating the wedding of Cnemon and Nausicleia, he says and does something quite unusual: Ἀλλ᾽ ὦ Θεάγενες, ὦ μόνη μοι γλυκεῖα φροντίς, εἰ μὲν τέθνηκας καὶ τοῦτο πεισθείην ὃ μήποτε γνοίην, τότε μέν σοι συνεῖναι ὑπερθήσομαι· τὸ παρὸν δέ σοι τάσδε ἐπιφέρω χοάς, καὶ ἅμα ἔτιλλε τὰς

τρίχας καὶ ἐπὶ κλίνην ἐπέβαλλε, καὶ τάσδε ἀποχέω τὰς σπονδὰς ἐκ τῶν σοι φίλων ὀφθαλμῶν (6.8.6) ("'Theagenes, the thought of whom is the one thought that brings me any joy, if you are dead, if I am brought to believe the news that I pray never to hear, I shall not hesitate to join you in death. For the present I make you this offering'—as she spoke, she tore her hair and laid the tresses on the bed—'and I pour you this libation from the eyes that love you" [Morgan 1989a, 480]). This ritual of Charicleia, which takes place immediately after the marriage of Nausicleia resembles, in my opinion, the wedding ritual that the Troezen maidens performed before marrying: they cut their hair and offered it to the god Virbius, who is Hippolytus brought back to life. Charicleia's actions become all the more understandable, therefore, when she states that she does these things because she believes Theagenes to be dead.

CONCLUSION

1. Morgan (1994) examines several passages in the novel that must be interpreted. These passages are in the form of riddles, whose solutions are found in the narrative.

APPENDIX 1

1. "And with regard to my factual reporting of the events of the war I have made it a principle not to write down the first story that came my way, and not even to be guided by my own general impressions; either I was present myself at the events which I have described or else I heard of them from eye-witnesses whose reports I have checked with as much thoroughness as possible" (Warner 1954, 48).

2. See Pembroke 1981, 301–3; Reardon 1991, 46–76; Gill 1993, 38–87; Vernant 1988, 203–60; Brilliante 1990, 91–140; Dowden 1992, 39–53.

3. "not to tell what happened but the kind of things that *can* happen, i.e., the kind of events that are possible according to probability or necessity" (Else 1967, 301).

4. "So one should not try to hang on at all costs to the traditional stories, around which our tragedies center. And in fact it is absurd to strive for this, since even the familiar names are familiar to few, but all enjoy them for essentially the <same> reason" (Else 1967, 315).

5. "Again, if a myth comes along you must tell it but not believe it entirely; no, make it known for your audience to make of it what they will—you run no risk and lean to neither side" (Kilburn 1959, 71).

APPENDIX 2

1. On Apsyrtus see Hägg 1971b, 43: "Ἄψυρτος, Medea's brother . . . was murdered during her and Jason's flight from Colchis. With this child or youth (according to different versions of the myth) the chief pirate in the romance has obviously no point of contact (1.14–2.12)."

2. Hägg (1971b, 41–42) writes that Hyperanthes is "another son of Darius who is

killed at Thermopylae (Hdt. 7.224)." Xenophon must have been using Hdt. 7.224, since Habrocomes is also mentioned in the same passage as being a son of Darius. Hyperanthes may also be the character foil of Antheia: Habrocomes loves Antheia, blossom, while Hippothous loved Hyperanthes, one who blossoms exceedingly.

3. "Hippothous fashioned this tomb for far-famed Hyperanthes, / a tomb unworthy of the death of a sacred citizen, / the famous flower some evil spirit once snatched from the land into the deep, / on the ocean he snatched him as a great storm wind blew" (Anderson 1989a, 148). The narrative of the drowning of Hyperanthes parallels the almost-fatal voyage that Antheia had on the Cilician ship. Xenophon is drawing attention to the similar experiences that have made Habrocomes and Hippothous so compatible.

4. A reflection of Xenophon's time?

5. For other instances of fires being miraculously quenched see Schmeling 1980, 166 n. 38.

6. For the myth of Androkles and the founding of Ephesus see Rogers 1991, 2, 103, 144.

7. On the subject of necrophilia see Schmeling 1980, 166 n. 40. Euripides also uses this motif in his *Alcestis*.

Bibliography

Achille Tatius d'Alexandrie. *Le roman de Leucippé et Clitophon*. 1991. Ed. J.-P. Garnaud. Paris.

Achilles Tatius. 1955. *Achilles Tatius: Leucippe and Clitophon*. Ed. Ebbe Vilborg. Stockholm.

Achilles Tatius. 1969; 1917. Trans. S. Gaselee. Cambridge.

Alcock, Susan E. 1993. *Graecia Capta: The Landscapes of Roman Greece*. Cambridge.

Altheim, F. 1948. *Literatur und Gesellschaft im ausgehenden Altertum*. Vol. 1. Halle.

Ampolo, Carmine, and Mario Manfredini. 1988. *Le vite di Teseo e di Romolo*. Milan.

Anderson, Graham. 1979. "The Mystic Pomegranate and the Vine of Sodom: Achilles Tatius 3.6." *AJP* 100: 516–18.

———. 1982. *Eros Sophistes: Ancient Novelist at Play*. Chico.

———. 1984. *Ancient Fiction: The Novel in the Graeco-Roman World*. London and Sydney.

———. 1988. "Achilles Tatius: A New Interpretation." *The Greek Novel AD1–1985*. Ed. Roderick Beaton. London and New York. 190–93.

———. 1989a. *An Ephesian Tale. Collected Ancient Greek Novels*. Ed. B. P. Reardon. Berkeley and Los Angeles. 125–69.

———. 1989b. "The *pepaideumenos* in Action: Sophists and Their Outlook in the Early Roman Empire." *ANRW* 2.33.1:79–208.

———. 1993. *The Second Sophistic: A Cultural Phenomenon in the Roman Empire*. London and New York.

Aristotle. 1968. *Poetics*. Ed. D. W. Lucas. Oxford.

Bartsch, Shadi. 1989. *Decoding the Ancient Novel*. Princeton.

Behr, C. A. 1968. *Aelius Aristides and* The Sacred Tales. Chicago.

Billault, A. 1977. "Le mythe de Persée et les *Ethiopiques* d'Héliodore: legendes, représentations et fiction littéraire." *REG* 90:56–68.

Bonnard, André. 1961. *Greek Civilization: From Euripides to Alexandria.* New York.

Borgeaud, Philippe. 1988. *The Cult of Pan in Ancient Greece.* Trans. Kathleen Atlass and James Redfield. Chicago.

Bowersock, G. W. 1965. *Augustus and the Greek World.* Oxford.

———. 1969. *Greek Sophists in the Roman Empire.* Oxford.

———. 1994. *Fiction as History.* Berkeley, Los Angeles, and London.

Bowie, E. L. 1974. "Greeks and Their Past in the Second Sophistic." *Studies in Ancient Society.* Ed. M. I. Finley. 166–209.

———. 1982. "The importance of Sophists." *Yale Classical Studies* 27:29–59.

———. 1985. "Theocritus' Seventh Idyll, Philetas and Longus." *CQ* 35:67–91.

———. and S. J. Harrison. 1993. "The Romance of the Novel." *JRS* 83:159–78.

———. 1994. "The Readership of Greek Novels in the Ancient World." *The Search for the Ancient Novel.* Ed. James Tatum. Baltimore. 435–59.

———. 1999. "The Greek Novel." *Oxford Readings in the Greek Novel.* Ed. Simon Swain. 39–59. Originally published in P. E. Easterling and B. M. W. Knox (eds.), *The Cambridge History of Classical Literature,* 1. *Greek Literature* (Cambridge, 1985). 683–99.

Braun, Martin. 1934. *Griechischer Roman und hellenistiche Geschichtschreibung.* Tubingen.

———. 1938. *History and Romance in Graeco-Oriental Religion.* Oxford.

Bremmer, Jan. 1986. "What Is Greek Myth?" *Interpretations of Greek Mythology.* Ed. Jan Bremmer. Totowa. 1–9.

Brillante, Carlo. 1990. "Myth and History." *Approaches to Greek Myth.* Ed. Lowell Edmunds. 91–138.

Brunt, P. A. 1976. "The Romantization of the Local Ruling Classes in the Roman Empire." *Assimilation et résistance à la culture Gréco-Romaine dans le monde ancien.* Paris. 161–73.

Bühler, W. 1976. "Das Element des Visuellen in der Eingangsszene von Heliodors Aithiopika." *WS* 10:177–85.

Bürger, K. 1892. "Zu Xenophon of Ephesos." *Hermes* 27:36–67.

Burkert, W. 1985. *Greek Religion.* Trans. J. Raffan. Cambridge.

Buxton, Richard. 1999. *From Myth to Reason? Studies in the Development of Greek Thought.* Ed. Richard Buxton. Oxford.

Caldwell, R. 1978. "Haephaestus: A Psychological Study." *Helios* 6:43–49.

Casson, Lionel. 1991. *The Ancient Mariners.* Princeton.

Cauderlier, Patrice. 1992. "Réalités égyptiennes chez Héliodore." *Le monde grec: Actes du colloque international tenu à l'École Normal Supérieure (Paris 17–19 décembre 1987.* Paris. 221–31.

Chalk, H. H. O. 1960. "Eros and the Lesbian Pastorals of Longos." *JHS* 80:32–51.

Chariton. 1979. *Le roman de Chairéas et Callirhoé.* Trans. Georges Molinié. Paris.

Conradie, P. J. 1977. "The Literary Nature of Greek Myths." *AClass* 20:49–58.

Crawford, M. H. 1978. "Greek Intellectuals and the Roman Aristocracy in the First

Century B.C." *Imperialism in the Ancient World*. Ed. P. D. A. Garnsey and C. R. Whittaker. Cambridge. 193–207.

De Harlez, C. 1956. "Les nymphes des sources en Grèce." *Le Muséon* 69:187–94.

Deligiorgis, Stavros. 1974. "Longus' Art in Brief Lives." *PhQ* 53:1–9.

Dihle, Albrecht. 1994; 1989. *Griechische Literaturgeschichte*. Trans. Manfred Malzahn. London and New York.

Dowden, Ken. 1992. *The Uses of Greek Mythology*. London.

Durham, Donald Blythe. 1938. "Parody in Achilles Tatius." *CP* 33:1–19.

Eckermann, Johann Peter. 1945. "Sonntag, den 20. März 1831." *Eckermanns Gespräche mit Goethe in den letzten Jahren seines Leben*. Basel.

Edwards, Douglas E. 1991. "Surviving the Web of Roman Power: Religion and Politics in the Acts of the Apostles, Josephus, and Chariton's *Chaereas and Callirhoe*." *Images of Empire*. Ed. Loveday Alexander. Sheffield.

———. 1994. "Defining the Web of Power in Asia Minor: The Novelist Chariton and His City Aphrodisias." *Journal of the American Academy of Religion* 62.3: 699–718.

Else, Gerald F. 1967. *Aristotle's Poetics: The Argument*. Cambridge.

Elsom, Helen E. 1992. "Callirhoe: Displaying the Phallic Woman." *Pornography and Representation in Greece and Rome*. Ed. Amy Richlin. Oxford. 212–30.

Epicorum Graecorum Fragmenta. 1988. Ed. M. Davies. Göttingen.

Epigrammatum Anthologia Palatina cum Planudeis et Appendice Nova. 1864. Ed. Fred. Dübner. Paris.

Erim, Kenan T. 1986. *Aphrodisias: City of Venus Aphrodite*. New York.

Euripides. 1981. *Fabulae*. Ed. J. Diggle. Oxford.

Fayûm Town and Their Papyri. 1900. London.

Festugière, André-Jean. 1954. *Personal Religion among the Greeks*. Berkeley.

Feuillatre, E. 1966. *Études sur les Éthiopiques d'Héliodore: contribution à la connaisance du roman grec*. Paris.

Finley, M. I. 1965. "Myth, Memory, and History." *History and Theory* 4:281–302.

Frazer, R. M. 1983. *The Poems of Hesiod*. Norman and London.

Frost, Frank J. 1984. "Plutarch and Theseus." *CB* 60:65–73.

Frye, Northrop. 1976. *The Secular Scripture: A Study of the Structure of Romance*. Cambridge.

Fusillo, Massimo. 1988. "Textual Patterns and Narrative Situations in the Greek Novel." *Groningen Colloquia on the Novel* 1. 17–31.

———. 1991; 1989. *Il romanzo Greco. Polifonia ed Eros*. Translated into French by Marielle Abrioux. Paris.

———. 1997. "How Novels End: Some Patterns of Closure in Ancient Narrative." *Classical Closure: Reading the End in Greek and Latin Literature*. Ed. Deborah H. Roberts, Francis M. Dunn, and Din Fowler. Princeton. 209–27.

García Gual, C. 1972. *Los orígenes de la novela*. Madrid.

Garson, R. W. 1975. "Notes on Some Homeric Echoes in Heliodorus' *Aithiopika*." *AClass* 18: 137–40.

Giangrande, G. 1962. "On the Origins of Greek Romance." *Eranos* 60:132–59.

Gill, Christopher. 1993. "Plato on Falsehood—Not Fiction." *Lies and Fiction in the Ancient World*. Ed. Christopher Gill and T. P. Wiseman. Austin. 38–87.

Goldhill, Simon (ed.). 2001. *Being Greek under Rome. Cultural Identity, the Second Sophistic and the Development of Empire*. Cambridge.

Gould, John. 1999. "Myth, Memory, and the Chorus: 'Tragic Rationality.'" *From Myth to Reason? Studies in the Development of Greek Thought*. Ed. Richard Buxton. Oxford. 107–18.

Graf, Fritz. 1993; 1987. *Griechische Mythologie*. Trans. Thomas Marier. Baltimore and London.

Green, P. 1982. "Longus, Antiphon, and the Topography of Lesbos." *JHS* 102: 210–14.

Hadas, Moses. 1942. *Complete Works of Tacitus*. New York.

———. 1952. "Cultural Survival and the Origins of Fiction." *South Atlantic Quarterly* 51:253–60.

———. 1953. *Three Greek Romances*. Indianapolis.

———. 1972. *Hellenistic Culture*. New York.

Hägg, Tomas. 1966. "Die Ephesiaka des Xenophon Ephesios—Original oder Epitome?" *C&M* 27:118–61.

———. 1971a. "The Naming of the Characters in the Romance of Xenophon Ephesius." *Eranos* 69:25–59.

———. 1971b. *Narrative Technique in Ancient Greek Romances*. Stockholm.

———. 1983. *The Novel in Antiquity*. Berkeley.

———. 1987. "Callirhoe and Parthenope: The Beginnings of the Historical Novel." *CIAnt* 6:184–204.

———. 1988. "The Beginnings of the Historical Novel." *The Greek Novel AD1–1985*. Ed. Roderick Beaton. London. 169–81.

Haight, Elizabeth. 1950. "Ancient Greek Romances and Modern Mystery Stories." *CJ* 46:5–10.

Harlan, E. C. 1965. "The Description of Paintings as a Literary Device and Its Application in Achilles Tatius." Ph.D. dissertation. Columbia University.

Hathorn, Richmond Y. 1977. *Greek Mythology*. American University of Beirut.

Heehs, Peter. 1994. "Myth, History, and Theory." *History and Theory* 33:1–19.

Heiserman, Arthur. 1977. *The Novel before the Novel: Essays and Discussions about the Beginnings of Prose Fiction in the West*. Chicago.

Helms, Johannes. 1966. *Character Portrayal in the Romance of Chariton*. The Hague.

Herodotus. 1954. *Historiae*. Ed. Carol Hude. Oxford.

Hesiod. 1958. *Carmina*. Ed. A. Rzach. Stuttgart.

Hetteger, G. 1914–15. "Über des Mythologie bei Chariton." I° Teil 42. *Jahresberichte des Staatsgymnasium Krumau*. 1–14.

Holzberg, N. 1955; 1986. *The Ancient Novel: An Introduction*. London.

Homer. 1952. *Opera*. Ed. Thomas W. Allen. Oxford.

Hunter, R. L. 1983. *A Study of Daphnis & Chloe*. Cambridge.

———. 1994. "History and Historicity in the Romance of Chariton." *ANRW* 2,34,2:1055–86.

Jacobs, F. 1821. *Achillis Tatii Alexandrini de Leucippes et Clitophontis amoribus libri octo*. Leipzig.

Jacoby, F. 1923. *Fragmente der griechischen Historiker*. Berlin and Leiden.

Jones, A. H. M. 1963. "The Greeks under the Roman Empire." *Dumbarton Oaks Papers* 17:3–19.

Jones, C. P. 1992. "Hellenistic History in Chariton of Aphrodisias." *Chiron* 22: 91–102.

Juvenal. 1983. *Satires*. Trans. and ed. Pierre de Labriolle and François Villeneuve. Paris.

Kerényi, K. 1927. *Die griechisch-orientalische Romanliteratur in religionsgeschichtlicher Beleuchtung*. Tübingen.

————. 1971. *Der Antike Roman*. Darmstadt.

Kestner, Joseph. 1974. "Ekphrasis as Frame in Longus' *Daphnis and Chloe*." *CW* 67: 166–71.

Keyes, Clinton Walker. 1922. "The Structure of Heliodorus' *Aethiopika*." *SPh* 19: 42–51.

Kilburn, K. 1959. *Lucian*. Cambridge.

Konstan, David. 1994. *Sexual Symmetry: Love in the Ancient Novel and Related Genres*. Princeton.

————. 1998. "The Invention of Fiction." *Ancient Fiction and Early Christian Narrative*. Ed. Ronald F. Hock, J. Bradley Chance, and Judith Perkins. Atlanta. 3–17.

Kouretas, D. 1978. "Δυο επεισοδια απο την ζωην Θησεως." *Platon* 30:128–33.

Kristeva, Julia. 1970. *Le Texte du roman*. Paris.

————. 1984. *Revolution in Poetic Language*. Trans. Margaret Waller. New York.

Laplace, M. 1980. "Les légendes troyennes dans le 'roman' de Chariton *Chairéas et Callirhoe*." *REG* 93:83–125.

————. 1983. "Légende et fiction chez Achille Tatius: les personages de Leucippé et de Iô." *BAGB* 311–18.

————. 1991. "Achille Tatius, 'Leucippé et Clitophon': des fables au roman de formation." *GCN* 4:35–56.

Lavagnini, B. 1950; 1921. *Studi sul romanzo Greco*. Messina and Florence.

Leach, Edmund. 1982. "Critical Introduction." *M. I. Steblin-Kamenskij's* Myth. Trans. Mary P. Coote. Ann Arbor.

Letters of Alciphron, Aelian, and Philostratus. 1948. Trans. Allen Rogers Benner and Francis H. Fobes. Cambridge.

Lightfoot, C. S. 1988. "Fact and Fiction—The Third Siege of Nisbis (A.D. 350)." *Historia* 38:107–25.

————. 1999. *Parthenius of Nicaea: The Poetical Fragments and the Ἐρωτικὰ Παθήματα*. Oxford.

————. 2000. "Romanized Greeks and Hellenized Romans: Later Greek Literature." *Literature in the Greek World*. Ed. Oliver Taplin. Oxford. 239–67.

Lindsay, J. 1948. *Daphnis & Chloe*. London.

Longus. 1916; 1657. *Daphnis and Chloe*. Ed. J. M. Edmonds; revised by George Thornley. London.

————. 1987. *Longus: Pastorales*. Trans. and ed. Jean-René Viellefond. Paris.

Lucian. 1966. Ed. Carol Jacobitz. Hildesheim.

Ludvivosky, J. 1925. *Recky Roman Dobrodruzny, le roman grec d'aventures: étude sur sa nature et son origine*. Prague.

MacLeod, A. M. G. 1969. "Physiology and Medicine in a Greek Novel: Achilles Tatius' *Leucippe and Clitophon.*" *JHS* 89:97–105.

MacQueen, Bruce D. 1985. "Longus and the Myth of Chloe." *ICS* 10:119–34.

——. 1990. *Myth, Rhetoric, and Fiction.* Lincoln.

Magie, David. 1950. *Roman Rule in Asia Minor.* Princeton.

Maróth, M. 1979. "Le siège de Nisbe en 350 ap. J.-C. d'après des sources syriennes." *AAntHung* 17:239–43.

Martial. 1990. *Epigrammata.* Ed. D. R. Shackleton Bailey. Stuttgart.

Mason, H. J. 1970. "The Roman Government in Greek Sources." *Phoenix* 24:150–59.

——. 1979. "Longus and the Topography of Lesbos." *TAPA* 109:149–63.

Mazal, O. 1958. "Die Satzstruktur in den Aithiopika des Heliodor von Emesa." *WS* 71:116–31.

McCulloh, William E. 1970. *Longus.* New York.

Merkelbach, R. 1960. "Daphnis und Chloe: Roman und Mysterium." *Antaios* 1:47–60.

——. 1962. *Roman und Mysterium.* Munich and Berlin.

——. 1988. *Die Hirten des Dionysos. Die Dionysos-Mysterien der römischen Kaiserzeit und der bukolische Roman des Longus.* Stuttgart.

Millar, Fergus. 1969. "P. Herennius Dexippus: The Greek World and the Third-Century Invasions." *Journal of Roman Studies* 59:12–29.

——. 1981. "The World of the *Golden Ass.*" *Journal of Roman Studies* 71:63–75.

Mittelstadt, Michael C. 1966. "Longus: *Daphnis and Chloe* and the Pastoral Tradition." *C&M* 27:162–177.

——. 1967. "Longus, *Daphnis and Chloe,* and Roman Narrative Painting." *Latomus* 26:752–61.

Morgan, J. R. 1982. "History, Romance, and Realism in the *Aithiopika.*" *ClAnt* 1: 221–65.

——. 1989a. *An Ethiopian Story. Collected Ancient Greek Novels.* Ed. B. P. Reardon. Berkeley and Los Angeles. 349–588.

——. 1989b. "The Sense of an Ending: The Conclusion of Heliodoros' *Aithiopika.*" *TAPA* 119:299–320.

——. 1991. "Reader and Audience in the 'Aithiopika' of Heliodoros." *GCN* 4: 85–103.

——. 1993. "Make-Believe and Make Believe: The Fictionality of the Greek Novels." *Lies and Fiction in the Ancient World.* Ed. Christopher Gill and T. P. Wiseman. Austin.

——. 1994. "The *Aithiopika* of Heliodoros: Narrative as Riddle." *Greek Fiction: The Greek Novel in Context.* Ed. J. R. Morgan and Richard Stoneman. New York. 97–113.

——. 1995. "The Greek Novel: Towards a Sociology of Production and Reception." *The Greek World.* Ed. Anton Powell. 130–52.

Most, Glenn W. 1989. "The Stranger's Stratagem: Self-Disclosure and Self-Sufficiency in Greek Culture." *JHS* 109:114–33.

——. 1999. "From Logos to Mythos." *From Myth to Reason? Studies in the Development of Greek Thought.* Ed. Richard Buxton. Oxford. 25–50.

Müller, C. W. 1976. "Chariton von Aphrodisias und die Theorie des Romans in der Antike." *A&A* 22:115–36.

Munz, Peter. 1956. "History and Myth." *Philosophical Quarterly* 6:1–16.

Nagy, Gregory. 1990. *Pindar's Homer: The Lyric Possession of the Past*. Baltimore and London.

O'Connor, Eugene. 1987. "A Note on the Nightingale's Itys Song in Longus' *Daphnis and Chloe*." *CB* 63:82–84.

O'Sullivan, J. N. 1995. *Xenophon of Ephesus: His Compositional Technique and the Birth of the Novel*. Berlin.

Otto, Walter F. 1955. *Die Musen*. Tübingen.

Ovid. 1875. *Metamorphoses*. Ed. Rudolph Merkel. Leipzig.

Oxenford, John. 1984. J. W. *Goethe: Conversations with Eckermann {1823–1832}*. San Francisco.

Oxyrhynchus Papyri, vol. 8. 1910. London.

Paduano, G. 1980. "Uno dei tanti: l'eroe comico di Menandro." *Introduzione à Menandro, Commedie, a cura di G.P.* Milan.

Pakcińska, Maria. 1966. "Motywy Homerowe w romansie Charitona." *Meander* 21: 149–57.

———. 1968. "Chariton, représentant le plus eminent de la première phase du roman grec." *Acta Conventus XI "Eirene."* Warsaw. 597–603.

Pandiri, T. 1985. "*Daphnis and Chloe*: The Art of Pastoral Play." *Ramus* 14:116–41.

Papanikolaou, A. D. 1973a. *Chariton-Studien: Untersuchungen zur Sprache und Chronologie der griechischen Romane*. Göttingen.

———. 1973b. *Xenophon Ephesius: Ephesiacorum Libri V*. Leipzig.

Papyri Michaelidae. 1955. Aberdeen.

Parke, H. W. 1967. *Greek Oracles*. London.

———. 1985. *The Oracles of Apollo in Asia Minor*. London.

Pastoralia Graeca ad optimorum librorum fidem emendavit, adnotationes priorum editorum selectas ineditas R. Fr. Ph. Brunckii, God. Henr. Schaeferi, Franc. Boissonadii et suas adiecit Ernst Eduard Seiler. 1843. Ed. E. E. Seiler. Leipzig.

Paulsen, T. 1992. *Inszenierung des Schicksals*. Trier.

Pembroke, S. G. 1981. "Myth." *The Legacy of Greece*. Ed. M. I. Finley. Oxford. 301–24.

Perry, B. E. 1967. *The Ancient Romances: A Literary Historical Account of Their Origins*. Berkeley.

Pervo, Richard I. 1987. *Profit with Delight*. Philadelphia.

Philippides, Marios. 1978. "Longus: Antiquity's Innovative Novelist." Ph.D. dissertation State University of New York at Buffalo.

———. 1981. "The 'Digressive' *Aitia* in Longus." *CW* 74:193–99.

Picard, C. 1922. *Éphèse et Claros*. Paris.

Pinheiro, Futre Márilia. 1989. "Aspects de la problématique sociale et économique dans le roman d'Héliodore." *Piccolo mondo antico: le donne, gli amori, i costumi, il mondo reale nel romanzo greco*. Ed. P. Liviabella Furiani and A. M. Scarcella. Perugia. 15–42.

———. 1991. "Calasiris' Story and Its Narrative Significance in Heliodorus' 'Aethiopika.'" *GCN* 4:69–83.

Plato. 1992; 1902. *Platonis opera*, vol. 4. Ed. John Burnet. Oxford.

Plutarch. 1964. *Vies*. Trans. and ed. Robert Flacelière, Émile Chambry, and Marcel Juneaux. Paris.

Pollard, John. 1977. *Birds in Greek Life and Myth.* London.

Pratt, Louise H. 1993. *Lying and Poetry from Homer to Pindar: Falsehood and Deception in Archaic Greek Poetics.* Ann Arbor.

Rattenbury, R. M. 1926. "Chastity and Chastity Ordeals in the Ancient Greek Romances." *Proceedings of the Leeds Philosophical & Literary Society, Literary and Historical Section* 1:59–71.

Reardon, B. P. 1971. *Courants littéraires grecs des IIe et IIIe siècles après J.-C.* Paris.

———. 1975. "Novels and Novelties, or Mysteriouser and Mysteriouser." *The Mediterranean World: Papers Presented to Gilbert Bagnani.* Peterborough. 79–100.

———. 1984. "The Second Sophistic." *Renaissances before the Renaissance: Cultural Revivals of Late Antiquity and the Middle Ages.* Ed. Warren Treadgold. 23–41.

———. 1989. *Collected Ancient Greek Novels.* Berkeley and Los Angeles.

———. 1991. *The Form of Greek Romance.* Princeton.

Reeve, Michael D. 1982. *Longus: Daphnis et Chloe.* Leipzig.

———. 1989. "Conceptions." *PCPhS* 215:81–112.

Rhetores Graeci. 1883–6. Ed. Leonard Spengel. Leipzig.

Rhetorique a Herrenius. 1989. Trans. and ed. Guy Achard. Paris.

Robertson, N. 1985. "The Origin of the Panathenaea." *RhM* 127:231–95.

Rocca, Rosanna. 1976. "Eliodoro e i due « Ippoliti» euripidei." *Materiali e contributi per la storia della narrativa greco-latina 1.* Perugia. 25–31.

Rogers, Guy MacLean. 1991. *The Sacred Identity of Ephesos: Foundation of Myths of a Roman City.* London.

Rohde, E. 1960; 1876. *Der griechische Roman und seine Vorläufer.* Hildesheim.

Rohde, Georg. 1937. "Longus und die Bukolik." *RhM* 86:23–49.

Roscher, Wilhelm R. 1965, reprint. *Ausfuhrliches Lexikon der griechischen und romischen Mythologie.* Leipzig.

Rougemont, Georges. 1992. "Delphes chez Héliodore." *Le monde grec: Actes du colloque international tenu à l'École Normal Supérieure (Paris 17–19 décembre 1987).* Paris. 93–100.

Ruiz-Montero, Conseulo. 1980. "Una observacion para la cronologia de Caritón de Afrodisias." *EClás* 24:63–69.

———. 1981. "The Structural Pattern of the Ancient Greek Romance and the Morphology of the Folk Talk of V. Propp." *Fabula* 22:228–38.

———. 1989. "Caritón de Afrodisias y el mundo real." *Piccolo mondo antico: le donne, gli amori, i costumi, il mondo reale nel romanzo antico.* Perugia. 107–50.

———. 1996. "The Rise of the Greek Novel." *The Novel in the Ancient World.* Ed. Gareth Schmeling. Leiden. 29–85.

Sandy, Gerald N. 1982. *Heliodorus.* Boston.

———. 1997. *The Greek World of Apuleius: Apuleius and the Second Sophistic.* Leiden.

Scarcella, A. M. 1972. "La donna nel romanzo di Longo Sofista." *GIF* n.s. 3:63–94.

Schmeling, Gareth. 1974. *Chariton.* New York.

———. 1980. *Xenophon of Ephesus.* Boston.

———. 1998. "The Spectrum of Narrative: Authority of the Author." *Ancient Fiction and Early Christian Narrative.* Ed. Ronald F. Hock, J. Bradley Chance, and Judith Perkins. Atlanta. 19–29.

Schönberger, Otto. 1960. *Hirtengeschichten von Daphnis und Chloe.* Berlin.

Schwartz, E. 1943; 1896. *Fünf Vorträge über den griechischen Roman*. Berlin.

Schwyzer, E. 1923. *Dialectorum Graecarum Exempla epigraphica potiora*. Leipzig.

Scobie, Alexander. 1969. *Aspects of the Ancient Romance and Its Heritage*. Meisenheim am Glan.

———. 1973. *More Essays on the Ancient Romance and Its Heritage*. Meisenheim am Glan.

Scott-Kilvert, Ian. 1960. *The Rise and Fall of Athens: Nine Greek Lives by Plutarch*. Harmondsworth.

Seel, Otto. 1942. "Paion." *RE* 18:2401–03.

Segal, Charles. 1984. "The Trials at the End of Achilles Tatius' *Clitophon and Leucippe*: Doublets and Complementaries." *SIFC* 3d ser. 2:82–91.

Shepard, Arthur. 1925. *Sea Power in Ancient History: The Story of the Navies of Classic Greece and Rome*. London.

Sinko, T. 1940–46. "De ordine quo erotici scriptores Gracei sibi successisse videantur." *Eos* 41:113–58.

Sophocles. 1955. *Fabulae*. Ed. A. C. Pearson. Oxford.

Stadter, Philip A. 1965. *Plutarch's Historical Methods*. Cambridge.

Steiner, G. 1969. "The Graphic Analogue from Myth in Greek Romance." *Classical Studies Presented to B. E. Perry*. Urbana. 123–37.

Stephens, Susan A. 1994. "Who Read Ancient Novels?" *The Search for the Ancient Novel*. Ed. James Tatum. Baltimore. 405–18.

——— and J. Winkler. 1995. *Ancient Greek Novels: The Fragments*. Princeton.

Swain, Simon. 1996. *Hellenism and Empire: Language, Classicism, and Power in the Greek World AD 50–250*. Oxford.

Syme, Ronald. 1979. "The Greeks under Roman Rule." *Roman Papers II*. Ed. E. Badian. 566–81. Originally published in *Proceedings of the Massachusetts Historical Society* 73 (1963):3–20.

Szepessy, T. 1957. "Die Aithiopika des Heliodorus und der griechische sophistiche Liebesroman." *AAntHung* 4:241–59.

———. 1976. "Le siège de Nisbe et la chronologie d'Héliodore." *AAntHung* 24: 247–76.

Thiele, G. 1890. "Zum griechischen Roman." *Aus der Anomia*. Ed. C. Robert. Berlin. 124–33.

Thucydides. 1953. *Historiae*. Ed. Henry Stuart Jones. Oxford.

Todd, F. A. 1940. *Some Ancient Novels*. Freeport.

Trapp, M. B. 1990. "Plato's *Phaedrus* in Second-Century Greek Literature." *Antonine Literature*. Ed. D. A. Russell. Oxford. 141–74.

Turcan, R. 1963. "Le roman "initiatique."" *RHR* 163:149–99.

Turner, Paul. 1960. "*Daphnis and Chloe*: An Interpretation." *G&R* 7:117–23.

Valley, Gunnar. 1926. *Über den Sprachgebrauch des Longus*. Uppsala.

Van Groningen, B. A. 1965. "General Literary Tendencies in the Second Century A.D." *Mnemosyne* 18:41–56.

Van Seters, John. 1986. "Myth and History: The Problem of Origins." *Historie et conscience historique dans les civilisations du Proche-Orient ancien*. Leuven. 49–61.

Vergil. 1983; 1969. *Opera*. Ed. R. A. B. Mynors. Oxford.

Vernant, Jean-Pierre. 1988. *Myth and Society in Ancient Greece*. New York.

Veyne, Paul. 1988; 1983. *Les Grecs ont-ils cru à leurs mythes?* Trans. Paula Wessling. Chicago and London.

Viellefond, Jean-René. 1987. *Pastorales (Daphnis et Chloé)*. Paris.

Vogliano, A. 1938. "Un papiro di Achille Tazio." *SIFC* 15:121–30.

Von Essen, M. H. N. 1887. *Index Thucydideus*. Berol.

Walbank, F. W. 1960. "History and Tragedy." *Historia* 9:216–34.

Walden, J. W. H. 1894. "Stage-Terms in Heliodorus' *Aethiopica*." *HSCP* 5:1–44.

Walton, Kendall L. 1983. "Fiction, Fiction-Making, and Styles of Fictionality." *Philosophy and Literature* 7:78–88.

Wardman, A. E. 1960. "Myth in Greek Historiography." *Historia* 9:403–13.

Warner, Rex. 1954. *Thucydides: History of the Peloponnesian War*. Middlesex.

Weinrich, O. 1962. "Heliodor und sein Werk." *Der griechische Liebesroman*. Zurich. 32–55.

Wesserling, Berber. 1987. "The Audience of the Ancient Novels." *GCN* 1:67–79.

Whitmarsh, Tim. 2001. *Greek Literature and the Roman Empire: The Politics of Imitation*. Oxford.

Wilamowitz-Moellendorff, Ulrich. 1931. *Der Glaube der Hellenen*. Berlin.

Wilcken, U. 1893. "Ein neuer greichischer Roman." *Hermes* 28:161–93.

Wilhelm, F. 1902. "Zu Achilles Tatius." *RhM* 57:55–75.

Williamson, Margaret. 1986. "The Greek Romance." *The Progress of Romance*. Ed. Jean Radford. London and New York. 23–45.

Wills, Lawrence M. 1995. *The Jewish Novel in the Ancient World*. Ithaca and London.

Winkler, John J. 1982. "The Mendacity of Kalarisis and the Narrative Structure of Heliodorus' *Aithiopika*." *YCS* 27:93–158.

———. 1989. *Leucippe and Clitophon*. *Collected Ancient Greek Novels*. Ed. B. P. Reardon. Berkeley and Los Angeles. 170–284.

Witt, R. E. 1971. *Isis in the Graeco-Roman World*. New York.

Woolf, Greg. 1994. "Becoming Roman, Staying Greek: Culture, Identity and the Civilizing Process in the Roman East." *Proceedings of the Cambridge Philological Society* 40:116–43.

Wouters, A. 1989–90. "The *Eikones* in Longus' Daphnis and Chloe IV 39,2: 'Beglaubigungsapparat'?" *Sacris Erudiri. Jaarboek voor Godsdienstwetenschappen* 31:465–79.

Xenophon. 1926. *Xénophon d'Éphèse. Les Éphésiaques ou Le roman d'Habrocomès et d'Anthia*. Trans. Georges Dalymeda. Paris.

Zeitlin, Froma. 1986. "Configurations of Rape in Greek Myth." *Rape*. Ed. Sylvana Tomaselli and Roy Porter. Oxford. 122–51.

Ziegler, Konrat. 1951. "Plutarchos." *RE* 21.1:947–49.

Zimmerman, F. 1961. "Chariton und die Geschichte." *Sozialökonomische Verhältnisse in alten Orient und klassischen Altertum, Tagung der Sektion Alte Geschichte der Deutscher Historiker Gesellschaft 12–17 Okt. 1959*. Berlin. 329–45.

Index